D1061458

DATE DUE

Tales of Adventurous Enterprise

TALES OF ADVENTUROUS ENTERPRISE

Washington Irving and the Poetics of Western Expansion

PETER ANTELYES

Columbia University Press New York

Columbia University Press
New York   Oxford
Copyright © 1990 Columbia University Press
All rights reserved

Library of Congress Cataloging-in-Publication Data

Antelyes, Peter.
Tales of adventurous enterprise : Washington Irving and the
poetics of Western expansion / Peter Antelyes.
p.   cm.
Includes bibliographical references.
ISBN 0-231-06860-3 (alk. paper)
  1. Irving, Washington, 1783–1859—Knowledge—West (U.S.)
  2. Adventure stories, American—History and criticism.
  3. Frontier and pioneer life in literature.
  4. Western stories—History and criticism.
  5. United States—Territorial expansion—Historiography.
  6. West (U.S.)—History—To 1848—Historiography.
  7. West (U.S.) in literature.
  I. Title.
PS2092.W48A58   1990
818'.209—dc20
                                        89-28086
                                           CIP

Casebound editions of Columbia University Press books are Smyth-sewn
and printed on permanent and durable acid-free paper

Printed in the United States of America

c 10 9 8 7 6 5 4 3 2 1

for Leslie

Contents

Preface

"Adventurous enterprise," a phrase that first appeared in an 1834 guide-book to the American West, points to a merger of literature and the marketplace that helped shape many Americans' perceptions of west-ward expansion throughout the nineteenth century. Western adventure tales, with their heroes and villains, their motifs of exploit and exploi-tation, became so popular a form for the expression of the contempo-rary ideals of American economic enterprise that they acquired the cultural centrality of a genre, the "tale of adventurous enterprise."

Such interplay between the popular forms of adventure and the forms of economic expansion had long been a commonplace in world literature. One critic has located its origins as far back as the courtly romances of the twelfth century, with the knightly adventures repre-senting tensions between the feudal order and the emerging bourgeoi-sie. Certainly the "ideology of adventure," as Michael Nerlich has characterized it (1987), was already a prominent feature of the European colonial literature of the sixteenth and seventeenth centuries. One finds the presence of prevailing economic practices and beliefs in the narrative patterns, characterizations, and figurative language of ex-plorer reports, guidebooks, promotional pamphlets, plays, and poems. These works greatly influenced the development of the American tale of adventurous enterprise, but it wasn't until the early nineteenth century that the confluence of an emerging national marketplace, West-ern expansion, and Western adventure tale brought the first uniquely American examples before an eager reading public.

The first proliferation of these works was in the Jacksonian period. The business beliefs and practices that had begun to transform the American West into a marketplace of economic expansion had also begun to transform the national literature into a marketplace of specu-lation, with the subject of the West as one of its first arenas of success. In the Western writings of Washington Irving and his contemporaries, one finds the emergence of a narrative form that embodied both the ideals of, and tensions created by, the expansion of American market capitalism. However varied the ostensible subjects of these books, from exploring to Indian fighting to beaver trapping, and however varied the characters, from explorers to mountain men to Indians and traders, the adventures defined and promoted the ideals of the marketplace, and cast a warning against its dangers. They enacted the enterprise of "making it" in an expanding America.

It is no surprise, of course, that many Americans conceived of the Western movement as an economic venture, and that their writings evaluated many of the events of the migration in economic terms. But literary form was not thereby reduced to a simple calculus of profit and loss. What is remarkable about these tales is the extent to which those economic evaluations had become part of the texture of the literary imagination. When events were transformed into "adventures," they captured not only the concrete consequences but also the ideological "spirit" of American economic enterprise; and they did so not only in the selection of incidents, but also in such diverse elements as the configuration of character, the mapping of the landscape, and the construction of language itself. Ultimately, these were accounts of Western economic expansion in more ways than one.

That "spirit" of enterprise is not so easily isolated, however. On the most general level, I use the term "adventurous enterprise" to refer to the embodiment in literary form (adventure) of certain forms of mar-

ketplace expansion (enterprise). But the process of embodiment includes a large range of connections: adventurous enterprise is also a
prescription for conduct in the marketplace, and an ideological template for textual production. At the same time, this process is itself
affected by the different forms of marketplace expansion, which include
not only the conditions of production and the underlying modes of
exchange, but also the economic ideologies associated with them. During the period under consideration in this study, for instance, the marketplace was in transition from merchant to industrial capitalism, and
this transition affected the shape of the Western adventure tale. The
wide range of contexts in which the terms "adventurous enterprise"
and "marketplace expansion" appear thus reflects the many connections
between literary and economic form during this volatile period.

In articulating these connections, one should not reduce the adventure tale to a simple enumeration or unequivocal endorsement of the
interests of any one class or group. As recent debates about economic
ideology in Jacksonian America suggest, opinions about the marketplace were as varied as the conditions themselves. Hierarchy and privilege continued to exist alongside the new forms of social mobility,
indeed became an integral impetus to that mobility. While some Americans criticized the rise of commerce as a threat to social order, others
celebrated it as a liberation from social rigidity, and still others endorsed the tenets of both positions in uneasy equilibrium. The literature of enterprise represented this diversity of views, as well as the
conflicts among them.

But the tales were also more than vehicles of pluralistic expression.
In their formal patterns, one finds competing economic views organized so as to isolate and identify particular ideals of the marketplace
and accommodate the tensions of economic expansion. This context of
conflict and resolution marks an early stage in that process whereby the
marketplace became an integral part of American imaginative expression; in time, the culture itself would become commercialized. Where
early in the century, hierarchy and social mobility were perceived as
antithetical forms of social order by critics and advocates alike, by mid-
century they stood together as foundations of the marketplace, equally
endorsed by the rhetoric of economic idealism. Where the marketplace
had once occupied a marginal position in American cultural life, it was
now a central arena in which the terms of social order, of success and
failure, self-interest and the common good, were defined; the debate

over the value of the marketplace had become a debate over market-place values.

It was during this period that both the West and the Western adventure tale entered the debate. The West was itself transformed into a marketplace, a "debatable land" of resources and claims, while an emerging marketplace of national literature provided a vehicle for that debate. In part the evolution of the tale chronicles the development of an indigenously democratic fiction, one that acknowledged and ex-pressed a variety of competing views in the open marketplace. But this was, specifically, an American democracy and an American market-place, defined by hierarchical distinctions based on race, class, and gender. Such distinctions were evident in the condemnation or ideali-zation of Indians, and in the elaboration of class differences between white characters and "half-breeds," or among the white characters alone. The higher the class the more lofty the lineage, the more noble the "natural" abilities, the more precise the traits of refinement and restraint, and the greater the mastery of the language. Even the land-scape itself was inscribed with metaphors of hierarchy and privilege: it could be "composed" and "sublime" or "savage" and "dreary."

These differentiations were also evident in what was excluded from the tales. Certainly not all attitudes present in the culture toward economic mobility were given equal representation in this democratic form: just as there were other stories to tell of Western expansion, such as settlement and monotony and poverty and discrimination, so there were other characters to consider, such as women and Blacks and Chinese, stories that had little to do with Western adventure as a commercial venture. For instance, most of the writers I consider are men, and the economic ideology with which they are concerned was essentially defined by their interests. With notable exceptions, the ad-ventures in most women's Western writings from this period were confined to the "economy" of the household with its particular tasks of settlement and cultivation.

This is not to say, of course, that women did not face or write about many of the same experiences—the confrontations with Indians, the crossings of difficult terrain, the daily deprivations—only that the narrative formulations they used were not confined, as were the men's, to the arena of free market expansion.[1] The emigrant and writer Mary Bailey noted even at the time the cultural tendency to divide the Western experience according to gender, restricting the attributes of adventurous enterprise—bravery, individuality, shrewdness—to the men: "Forded the Green River. Had to raise our wagons but did not get into the water although we were somewhat frightened. Do not know as there was much danger, but the men say the women must always be frightened" (Myres 73). In fact, it is difficult to find significant female characters in these early tales of adventurous enterprise, not because they were absent from the westering experience, but because they were excluded from the male vision of that experience as an extension of the marketplace. Their appearance in works later in the century was largely limited to roles that confirmed the men's perspective.

One must be cautious, then, when assigning to any literary form or set of ideals the status of dominant cultural practice or belief; cautious, too, when designating any particular writer or work the "representative" of that culture as a whole. I have chosen this genre, and the works of Washington Irving in particular, precisely because of the range of contemporary ideals, conflicts, and prejudices that are expressed in them. Irving himself played a pivotal role in the social and economic developments of the period. He was one of many writers to embrace, albeit tentatively, the Jacksonian "persuasion" in his public writings; one of the first American writers of any stature and renown to attempt an American literature, and to do so through an American literary marketplace; one of the first American writers to practice his craft as a profession, thus identifying its purposes and forms with his nation's cultural and economic ideals; one of the first professional writers to travel in the Western territories, and one of the first to write about the fur trade, which was among the first large-scale businesses to emerge on the continent. In addition, Irving's works are, for the most part, incisive about just these issues. When examined in relation to equally popular, if lesser, works of the period, they help articulate these connections between economic and literary forms during this crucial stage in the histories of both the marketplace and American letters. In his Western works, he saw not only an opportunity to profit as an American writer in the new marketplace of American literature, but also a vehicle through which to define the role of the American imagination in the Western venture and, more generally, in the new marketplace of America.

One would have to look hard, though, to find an assessment of Irving as businessman and writer that acknowledges his divided relation to the marketplace. Generally he emerges in the criticism either as an "escape artist" fleeing from the complexities of the world of business to the complacencies of class and privilege, or as a mercenary of the marketplace exploiting a trusting readership: a failed writer or an unscrupulous businessman. Henry Pochmann (xi-xcii), for instance, argued that Irving's writings were limited by an essentially Federalist perspective, an adherence to those conservative values associated with hierarchy and the preservation of an already propertied aristocracy. Vernon Louis Parrington (2:203–212), on the other hand, singled Irving's works out as especially troubling examples of the distortions of greedy Jacksonianism; his Irving was eager to manipulate his readers and sacrifice his art to achieve financial success. Henry Seidel Canby (67–96) concurred with Parrington by identifying greed as a dominant feature of the writer and his works, but found it aligned with the Federalist pursuit of classed privilege described by Pochmann. As recently as Jeffrey Rubin-Dorsky's excellent book on Irving's earlier work, *Adrift in the Old World* (1988), we find the writer's literary career characterized by an increasing distance from the conflicts and burdens of American independence, culminating in a retreat into the treasures of the imagination in *The Alhambra*.

Behind these criticisms lies the premise that the marketplace was as hostile to the cultivation of art as art was to the marketplace. Irving himself, however, was deeply divided on the subject; in William Hedges's words, he was "an American torn between bourgeois attitudes, between romantic and classical attitudes, uncertain of the role and function of the writer in a commercial society" (Myers 1972, 34). If he wanted to turn the writer into a businessman and his works into articles of commerce, he also wanted to turn the marketplace into an arena of culture, to inform commerce with the values of his art. Hence his interest in the stance of "professionalism" in his Western works, a stance which, in his view, combined the perspectives of both art and the marketplace, and thereby maintained the decorum of hierarchy and privilege even while it participated in the drives of self-interest and mobility.

By insisting that such a merger is by its very nature either destructive to the art or an evasion of economic realities, these critics not only diminish the intricacies of many of Irving's works forged along these lines, but also deny the importance of the works themselves. Usually, for instance, critical accounts of his oeuvre consider most carefully those works written before his return to America from Europe in 1832 and his subsequent engagement with Jacksonian culture.[2] The works written later, foremost among them the Western writings, are presented as a mediocrity resulting from his immersion in the marketplace. What modern readers often fail to recognize is that Irving's tales of adventurous enterprise were constructed precisely out of these concerns and conflicts, and illustrate not only many of the predominant contemporary attitudes toward expansionism, but also the literary strategies by which those attitudes were "entertained" in the culture. In the end, Irving hoped to establish a literary form by which he could reproduce, and readers recognize, the experience of the marketplace, and, at the same time, to provide, specifically, a national imaginative form by which both he and his reader could enlist self-interest in the communal interest of American expansionism. Here was a form in which many divergent views might find expression, yet one in which that expression might itself become a mode of reconciliation. The literature would represent the tensions and ideals of the expanding marketplace by itself becoming part of the marketplace.

In the first of his Western works, *A Tour on the Prairies*, (1835), an account of his travels in the Oklahoma territory, Irving took the already popular forms of the Indian adventure tale and tourist account and tested them against the values of professional conduct; the result was a revised adventure tale form that endorsed expansionism while noting the dangers posed to American society by that expansion. The reader was led to distinguish between the adventurings, and adventure tale formulations, that were leading the country into excessive self-interest, and those that could provide for the measured expression of economic expansion.

In his next two books, *Astoria, or Anecdotes of an Enterprize Beyond the Rocky Mountains* (1836) and *The Adventures of Captain Bonneville* (1837), he applied the terms of his revised adventure tale to the forms of the romantic history, explorer report, and trapper journal, in an effort to construct the history of the American fur trade, and by extension, to reconstruct the history of America itself. The professionalism of America's adventurous enterprise in the West was identified with the origins and founding principles of America itself: heroic confrontations establish the enterprise as the proper course of American history. In the first of these books, Irving broadly celebrates that enterprise, while in the latter he criticizes its excesses, warning against its divergence from those original principles. Irving thus reinvested America's adventuring imagination with the principles of market expansion.

The purpose of this book, then, is twofold: to examine the tale of adventurous enterprise as an American literary form, and to identify Irving's role in the development of the tale. In the first chapter I establish the tradition of adventurous enterprise from its antecedents in European and American colonial literature to its formative development in the Jacksonian period. Chapter 2 then places Irving at this juncture of the emerging marketplace with the emerging national literature, particularly Western literature. I focus on the circumstances of his Western tour, his response to the growing relation between the marketplace and the literature, and his efforts to formulate a genial meeting-ground in literary terms. The next two chapters focus on the Western books themselves, as they illustrate the range of responses Irving identified as possible ways of applying the "work" of the imagination to the "work" of economic expansion. Finally, in an afterword I offer some notes on the further developments of this genre as it accommodated itself to changing conditions of expansion.

Historians have long noted how the West was "inscribed" by explorers and settlers, the territories parsed and mapped, the actual landscape scrawled with names and dates. In the case of this Western adventure tale, the inscription involved more than a pattern of capitalist possession: it involved the emergence of capitalist expansion as a narrative in itself, a narrative of American progress in the West. Its power and allure resided in its ability to seem at once an accurate representation of America's experience in the West and a prescription for the conduct of American expansionism. As always, Americans had shaped their adventures in the image of their enterprising imaginations, and had turned both into the tale of America itself.

Acknowledgments

I have many people to thank for many kinds of help and support. Without the timely, thoughtful, and conscientious guidance of my readers, this book would have been much diminished. Sacvan Bercovitch and Ann Douglas, my advisors on the first phase of this study, were superb teachers. Their influence can be felt not only in ideas and approaches, but in my engagement with the pleasures of criticism. I am also indebted to the members of the Pickwick Club study group—Mark Schenker, Jennifer Wicke, and Greg Myers—for their unceasing interest and good fellowship. Greg's detailed comments, in particular, led me to reconsider virtually everything I had written, and influenced everything I went on to write. Frank Bergon deserves a special thanks. He provided precise and valuable suggestions at every stage of composition, from the original idea to the construction of the argument to the refinement of the prose. He also provided, in his own work and in his friendship, examples that I hope I have followed with some care.

My editor at Columbia University Press, Jennifer Crewe, was a model of patience and tact; I benefitted, too, from Leslie Bialler's expert assistance. And a number of institutions have been generous in their support: the staff at the Huntington Library was very helpful during an early stage of research; the Bancroft Committee at Columbia University not only supported my efforts but gave me the confidence to continue the work; and the Committee on Research at Vassar College provided me with assistance in preparing the manuscript. My parents aided and encouraged me in so many ways throughout the process that it would be impossible to thank them enough. Finally, I am indebted to my wife, Leslie Dunn, who offered me all the kinds of help and support I received from everyone else, and more. To her I dedicate this book.

A Note on Abbreviations and Editions Cited

For Irving's texts I have generally used the volumes included in *The Complete Works of Washington Irving* (Madison: The University of Wisconsin Press and Boston: Twayne, 1969–19—). In two cases, though—*A History of New York* and *The Alhambra*—my discussion required earlier editions than those used as text copies for *The Complete Works*. While Irving's revisions were numerous, especially in the Author's Revised Edition of 1848–51, they were mostly minor: alterations or corrections in phrasing, punctuation, capitalization, spelling, and the like. In those two works, the changes were major enough to require use of the earlier editions.

Abbreviations used in citations are given below. Wherever possible, I have included only page numbers, but where required, I have also indicated author, title, year, or volume number. Complete bibliographical information can be found in "Works Consulted."

From *The Complete Works of Washington Irving*:

    A *The Alhambra*
   Ast *Astoria*
    B *The Adventures of Captain Bonneville*
   BH *Bracebridge Hall*
    J *Journals and Notebooks* (5 vols.)
    L *Letters* (4 vols.)
 MW *Miscellaneous Writings* (2 vols.)
  SB *The Sketch Book*
    T *A Tour on the Prairies* (included in *The Crayon Miscellany*)
 WR *Wolfert's Roost*

Other editions of Irving's works:

    Al *The Alhambra* (1832 edition)
 HNY *A History of New York, from the Beginning of the World to the End of the Dutch Dynasty* (1809 edition)

Tales of Adventurous Enterprise

1
The Tale of Adventurous Enterprise

And what *is* adventure, when it comes to that, and by what sign is the listening pupil to recognize it?

—Henry James, "The Art of Fiction"

In 1813 the writer Daniel Bryan published an epic poem on the American West entitled *The Mountain Muse*. His subject, the exploits of the "adventurous woodsman" Daniel Boone in "the glorious enterprise" of Western expansion (1.719, 900), had recently become a popular one for American writers, as had his choice of genre, a Miltonic epic designed to secure for the expansion of the new nation a legitimate place in the panorama of sacred universal history. What was striking, though, was his representation of the poem itself as an expression of the enterprise. In the poem, Daniel Boone does not so much choose to go West as is chosen, charged, and guided by the "Spirit of Enterprise" (1.794); and his mandate is not so much a personal as a national and spiritual imperative: the "enterprising Angel" (1.895) instills his imagination with "the prospect of discovery, usefulness, and fame" (Book 2, Argument), and directs him to perform

A thousand valorous, soul-ennobling feats
Attendant on the patriot enterprise,
Grandly preparing, an expanded sphere
For commerce, Wealth, and all the brilliant Arts,
Where they before had never cast a beam[.]
                              (2.86–90)

Boone's adventures thus become the adventures of enterprise, and the poem of those adventures, a literature of enterprise. A new muse of enterprise had been introduced into the literature of the American West.[1]

Within a few decades, this connection between the spirit of enterprise and the adventures of Western expansion would become an essential aspect of the literature. The terms of the connection, though, would become more particularized, as the enterprise became more specifically associated with the marketplace, and the adventures with the expansion of the marketplace. In his 1834 guidebook to the American West, for instance, Robert Baird distinguished Westerners by their *"spirit of adventurous enterprise*: a willingness to go through any hardship or danger to accomplish an object" (102). Westerners are not only adventurers, individuals characteristically encountering "hardship or danger"; nor are they only enterprising opportunists, the "object" of their adventures being settlement and cultivation leading to profitable trade. They are both of these. The enterprise is firmly embodied in the adventure, and together they constitute the "spirit" of Western economic expansion.[2]

The literary origins of this American narrative form predate the colonial settlement of the continent, and can be located as far back as the beginnings of "adventure" itself. The adventure tale is one of the oldest literary forms. Formally speaking, it is a supergenre whose constitutive elements can be found operating in a variety of works from epics to courtly romances to Westerns and detective stories. Central to the form is the narrative of the hero's journey through alien or hostile territory to accomplish some goal. Along the way he or she encounters a number of dangers and obstacles that are usually exterior, such as villains, beasts, or a treacherous landscape, but they can be interior as well, a matter of character or conscience. In either case, it is the adventures, and not the goal per se, that determine the nature of the heroism and villainy, and indicate the social, political, psychological, or economic conditions that have brought them into conflict.[3]

This emphasis on the adventures reveals one of the form's ideological premises: its commitment to expansionism as a model of human conduct. From the first appearance of adventure as a separate and distinct literary formula in the *avanture* of courtly romance, the adventure tale concerned the task of conquering, of expanding and exploiting. By the fifteenth century, and the first record of the word "adventure" in English, that task had become explicitly associated with economic activity. English craftsmen and traders formed what were called "merchant adventurer" societies to extend foreign commerce. In this case, the term "adventurer" specifically referred to the financial risks such individuals took in this movement of goods across the seas. Thereafter, one the meanings of "adventure" was to remain "a commercial enterprise" (*OED*), a use that survives today in the word "venture."

Such a view of adventure as economic risk seems to run counter to the traditional reading of the adventure tale as a form of "low" culture escapism, designed to "remove us radically from ourselves," and take us " 'out of this world,' if this world is taken to mean the circle of relationships and responsibilities that we know" (Zweig 4). According to this reading, the adventures are either unrelated to that "circle of relationships and responsibilities," or function only as wish-fulfillment fantasies enabling the reader to forget, if only momentarily, the frustrations associated with everyday life. The form may endorse economic expansionism, but it does so by denying or diminishing the risks involved, by alleviating the anxieties the reader might associate with the normative economic practices of the culture.

As Georg Simmel has pointed out, however, the very experience of adventure as a "dropping out of the continuity of life" (187) may indicate how closely related the tale is to the life. The adventure tale is like a dream: existing outside of the continuity of experience, its form becomes the emblematic expression if its "inner sense" (188–189). And insofar as this dream is also shared by a larger public, the form of the tale represents not only the inner sense of personal responses but particular beliefs and conditions prevalent at the time. In the sixteenth and seventeenth centuries, for instance, certain forms of the adventure tale emerged as vehicles for the expression of beliefs, and examination of conditions, associated with colonialist expansionism.

Certainly not all of these tales were explicitly concerned with the marketplace. But what was absent from direct commentary was expressed in the indirect discourse of the form itself, as in Simmel's "dream": in the narrative formulations of goals, conflicts, challenges, and confrontations; in the traits associated with the heroes and villains; in the language associated with each. Through this discourse, the writings of the early colonists—the promotional pamphlets, explorer reports, histories, and religious tracts—represented the exploration and colonization of the New World as adventures of economic expansion. In the harshness of the sea voyages, the savagery of the Indians, the bravery of the explorers, the eloquence of the leaders, one finds the emergence of adventurous enterprise.

But if the form itself provided an implicit endorsement of economic expansionism, the tales were more than simple fantasies of economic idealism. In these adventures one also finds the presence of the anxieties and tensions that were part of that expansionism: the conditions and critiques and contentions of the marketplace. A representative figure in this tradition is the Daniel Boone who appeared in Timothy Flint's enormously popular 1833 biography. In contrast to Bryan's and Baird's adventurers, Flint's Boone appears deaf to the calling of the muse of enterprise. He flees deeper and deeper into the American wilderness, burdened by the fear that "go where he would, American enterprize seemed doomed to follow him, and to thwart all his schemes of backwoods retirement" (246). This Boone's adventures thus represent a criticism of certain elements of marketplace expansion, such as an invasive opportunism and a leveling conformity. In the end, however, they remain the adventures of enterprise. While Flint's Boone shuns the actual presence of industry in the wilderness, he shares with Bryan's Boone an implicit belief in the guiding principles of the marketplace. For instance, the "schemes" he embraces hardly amount to a rejection of American business: his attributes as a character, such as industriousness and shrewdness, and the nature of his challenges in the wilderness, such as a struggle for unhindered mobility, precisely represent those values promoted by the culture of the marketplace. The muse of enterprise had thus not only come to shape the adventures of Western expansion, but to suspend the contradictions between these two Daniel Boones, and the different views of the marketplace they represented.[4]

While adventurous enterprise can be traced back to the earliest colonial writings, it first appeared as a distinctive, recognizable and consistent literary form in the Jacksonian period. The economic expansion that had permeated the East and drawn the nation Westward had also permeated the newly emergent marketplace of the national literature. When Washington Irving returned to America in 1832 after seventeen years in Europe, he found an already well developed market in Western literature, and an already well developed form of Western writing. Writers such as Flint, James Paulding, Charles Fenno Hoffman, and others, had been producing novels, histories, travel books, and essays that shared both basic formal structures and implicit, as well as explicit, economic concerns. In charting the emergence of this tale, then, we can discover that relation between contemporary American business practices, economic rhetoric, and the modes of imaginative production during this formative period in the development of a national marketplace.

Literary Antecedents

It was a commonplace since the first European explorations of discovery to the "New World" to identify the "adventure" of the journey with the "enterprise" to extend the boundaries of empire; and, within that adventurous enterprise, to identify the sacred with the secular motivations of that expansion. The enterprise was perceived as sacred because those boundaries were represented as the division between the redemptive forces of civilization and the unredeemed forces of savagery, and secular because those same boundaries were also associated with the national and personal goals of power and economic profit. In the context of colonialism, then, "sacred" and "secular" were not so much discrete categories as mutually defining constructs in a rhetoric of justification.

Providing a form for the the expression of these expansionist ideals, the "adventure" also supplied the terms by which the sacred "enterprise" would be associated with the secular "commodity." In the accounts of the New World voyages, the terms "adventure," "enterprise," and "commodities" often predominate. Naturally, the particular definitions applied to those terms differed from culture to culture and period to period, as did the underlying attitudes toward race, class, and gender with which they were associated. But these changing definitions and attitudes also derived from certain shared suppositions about the

relation between adventure and enterprise. Through a close look at
these texts, one can discern the basic narrative form as it evolved
toward its nineteenth-century American manifestation.

One of the first of such accounts was Álvar Núñez Cabeza de Vaca's
Adventures in the Unknown Interior of America, a book about the Span-
iard's disastrous experiences in crossing the North American continent
in the early sixteenth century. In 1527 Cabeza de Vaca, a military man,
was assigned to be treasurer of an expedition under Pámfilo de Narváez
to conquer Florida. During the early portions of the voyage, a rivalry
quickly developed between the two men. Cabeza de Vaca offers his
side of the story by characterizing Narváez as greedy, cruel and incompetent. This last quality is given the most emphasis as the source for
the final confrontation between them, Cabeza de Vaca's refusal to
follow Narváez's order to lead the ships on an expedition up the coast.
Narváez took what men remained loyal to him and sailed off, leaving
Cabeza de Vaca and three hundred others to fend for themselves. In
an apparent attempt to continue with their mission, these men then
began an extraordinary inland journey that was to last eight years and
take them from Florida to northern Mexico, all the while diminishing
the number of the party. At the end, only four remained. The majority
of Cabeza de Vaca's account concerns these years of hardship, deprivation and longing, and offers a glimpse into the ideological resources
which the author drew upon to explain his adventure, his passage
through the savage "unknown" in the name of God and the interests
of Spain.

In the book's opening dedication to the "Sacred Caesarian Catholic
Majesty," Charles V, Cabeza de Vaca places his travels in the context
of both sacred and secular fortunes: "Although everyone wants what
advantage may be gained from ambition and action, we see everywhere
great inequalities of fortune, brought about not by conduct but by
accident, and not through anybody's fault but as the will of God" (25).
First, then, as might be expected, the search for profit and power is
subordinated to God's will, a precept amply supported by Cabeza de
Vaca's insistent reiteration of his many misfortunes. At the same time,
however, the search for profit and power is also equated with God's
will. Where the secular goals of the expedition are achieved, so too is
the divine mission, however transitory that secular success, or subordinate to a greater judgment. Cabeza de Vaca defines this all-encompass-
ing context of mission in these terms: "to subdue those countries and

bring them to a knowledge of the true faith and true Lord and bring them under the imperial dominion" (26), the latter conquest to be measured as much in gold as in faith. And it is the presence, the "assurance of plentiful gold" that preoccupies Cabeza de Vaca throughout his trials, that eases his "pain and fatigue" (38). It is not surprising that Cabeza de Vaca was the treasurer of the expedition, nor that he chose to rely on Indian trading as a means of survival: "This occupation suited me; I could travel where I wished, was not obliged to work, and was not a slave. Wherever I went, the Indians treated me honorably and gave me food, because they liked my commodities" (67).

I do not mean to suggest that Cabeza de Vaca was merely a mercenary interested in spoils. Indeed he was especially sensitive to the relationship of this search for profit with the expansion of Christianity to these regions, and particularly with the frequent injustices that, as he witnessed in the case of his own commander, seemed to threaten that expansion. He was most concerned with those injustices produced in the name of Christianity, by the authority of church and state and civilization. And while these concerns do not significantly alter the basic narrative endorsement of the Christian mission, they do highlight the dramatic tensions—between civilization and savagery, economic expansion and the consolidation of the empire—upon which that endorsement rests.

The company's interactions with Indians provided the focus of his concern. Despite his acceptance of the view that the Indians must be brought to abandon their savage ways and adopt Christianity, he was nonetheless remarkably curious about, and even respectful of, their culture. Thus he moves quickly from a scene in which he praises God for his release from Indian captivity into the hands of fellow Christians, to a scene in which he excoriates these same Christians as cruel abusers of the Indians and betrayers of their own claims to goodness. Most interestingly, he puts the criticism in the mouths of the Indians, and does so carefully in the cadences of Indian oratory. Disputing Cabeza de Vaca's claims that he belongs with the Christians, the Indians explain to him how he and his men differ from these "Christians": "We [Cabeza de Vaca's party] had come from the sunrise, they [the Christians] from the sunset; we healed the sick, they killed the sound; we came naked and barefoot, they clothed, horsed, and lanced; we coveted nothing but gave whatever we were given, while they robbed whomever they found and bestowed nothing on anyone" (128). Cabeza de

Vaca does prefer in the end to remain with these Christians, but his sympathies are decidedly with the Indians, however savage and unregenerate, however needful of "subduing."

Indians were, of course, principal characters in both the religious and secular concerns of this narrative of expansion: as vehicles for, or impediments to, the dissemination of God's word, as well as obstacles to the acquisition of land and gold and trade. And they would remain so from the sixteenth to the nineteenth centuries, from the wilderness of Spanish colonialism to the American "Indian wilderness." The connections we find in Cabeza de Vaca's account among Indian adventure, commodity discovery, and sacred mission, provided the informing narrative structure in many of the travel and exploration writings that appeared over the next century.

The full title of another chronicle of Florida exploration, written by the Frenchman Jean Ribault and published about twenty years after Cabeza De Vaca's book appeared, indicates how common these connections were at the time: *The whole and true discouerye of Terra Florida, (englished the Florishing lande) Conteyning aswell the wonderfull straunge natures and maners of the people, with the merueylous commodities and treasures of the country: As also the plesaunt Ports, and Hauens and ways therevnto. Neuer founde out before the last yere 1562. Written in Frenche by Captaine Ribauld, the fyrst that wholly discouered the same.*[5] Once again we see the association of Indian adventure with commodities; in this case, the commodities themselves seem to promise their own adventurous "marvels" commensurate with the "wonders" of Indian life. The sacred context does receive less emphasis, to be sure; and while that context is addressed in the book itself, it is not so urgently integrated. Ribault's approach does not eliminate or deny the divine imperative, but rather embodies it in the material itself. In this sense, the book does represent an important change in the development of the narrative form of adventurous enterprise, the emergence of the promotional pamphlet.

From the middle of the sixteenth century to the end of the seventeenth, the promotion of exploration, investment and settlement in the New World as a source of profit came to predominate as the organizing principle for the information offered in the accounts. The perspective of sacred duty was not abandoned altogether; most often it was relegated to the frame—usually the dedication—and to an occasional zealous exhortation, and so provided only a larger context of mission within which the secular motives of national and personal profit could be more justifiably situated.

In this context, it is not surprising that Ribault's book was first published in English, for the English held especially fervent interests in the colonization of America. The earliest and most influential works by the English themselves attest to the strength of these interests, and to the strength of the narrative form of adventurous enterprise. Foremost among these was Thomas Harriot's work on the first Virginia expeditions. As with Ribault's book, the title of Harriot's reveals much about the narrative structure employed throughout: *A briefe and true report of the new found land of Virginia, of the commodities and of the nature and manners of the naturall inhabitants. Discovered by the English Colony there seated by Sir Richard Greinvile Knights In the yeere 1585. Which Remained under the governement of twelve monethes, At the special charge and direction of the Honourable SIR WALTER RALEIGH Knight lord Warden of the Stanneries Who therein hath beene favoured and authorised by her MAJESTIE and her letters patents: This fore booke Is made in English BY Thomas Hariot servant to the abovenamed Sir WALTER, a member of the Colony, and there imployed in discovering.* Again we find commodities and Indians combined as the two primary focuses of the account, though as the order suggests, it is the former that is accorded precedence as the chief subject of the work. This subordination of the Indian adventure finds its dramatic justification in Harriot's promotional stance: he reassures potential settlers and investors that "in respect of troubling our inhabiting and planting," the Indians "are not to be feared; but. . .they shall have cause both to feare and love us, that shall inhabite with them" (24).

Accordingly, most of the book enumerates what Harriot describes as the three forms of commodity readily available in Virginia: commodities for trade and profit, for sustenance, and for utility, such as building materials. (Significantly, Harriot includes his examination of Indian life as part of this last section, thus identifying Indians themselves as commodities to be "used.") It is to the first of these that the book is designed to speak, as the author indicates by directly addressing his readers as "the enterprisers in general" (6), and everyone involved in the project as "the adventurers, favorers, and welwillers of the enterprise for the inhabitting and planting in Virginia" (5). By "inhabitting and planting," Harriot is not referring to simple subsistence farming but to active trading: he tells the reader to use his book to "consider how your dealing therein if it proceede, may returne you profit and gaine; bee it either by inhabitting & planting or otherwise in furthering thereof" (5).

In the end, of course, this "enterprise" is not just economic exploitation but the combination of economic, imperial and sacred elements found in the other books in this lineage. The frame of the book, the dedication to Sir Walter Raleigh, sets the tone for what is to follow. Harriot praises Raleigh for overseeing the creation of a "Collonye. . .established to your great honnor and prayse, and noe lesser proffit unto the common·welth" (2–3). In a later invocation of Raleigh at the end of the book, Harriot reminds the reader that this notion of a commonwealth founded upon "common welth" is the assumption behind that praise. Raleigh is presented as providing the initial land grants that will enable the settlers to profit by their adventure into the New World: "The least that he hath granted," Harriot points out, "hath beene five hundred acres to a man only for the adventure of his person" (32). By "adventure" Harriot means investment, a common use of the term at the time. Thus the settlers are transformed into investors, and investors into adventurers in the enterprise of gaining profit for themselves, for their nation, and for their God.

The persuasive power of such promotional pamphlets depended as much on this narrative formulation as it did on the image of the paradisiacal array of available resources. In some cases, the adventure tale alone conveyed the promotion, especially when the hardships and dangers, so conspicuously absent from Harriot's account, were seen as hampering the promise of success. Perhaps the most prominent writer of such pamphlets was John Smith, whose numerous histories, autobiographies, "descriptions," and advertisements depicted America as a vast arena of economic exploitation that could be conquered and cultivated only by the most adventurous and hardy of individuals.[6]

In general terms, Smith's books were much like the others. He ends his *True Relation* (1608) with the assurance that

> we doubt not but by Gods gracious assistance, and the adventurers willing minds and speedie furtherance to so honorable an action in after times, to see our Nation to enjoy a Country, not onely exceeding pleasant for habitation, but also very profitable for comerce in generall, no doubt pleasing to almightie God, honourable to our gracious Soveraigne, and commodious generally to the whole Kingdome. (*Complete Works* 1:97)

By "adventurers," Smith, unlike Harriot, is distinguishing the investors from the actual settlers, though this does not suggest a gap between the adventure and the enterprise. In the context of the narrative form shared by Smith's *True Relation* and Harriot's *A Briefe and True Report*, the "adventure" of investing was enacted in the enterprise of settling. Similarly, in both works, the "business" interests are given priority. Virginia itself, he wrote in *A Map of Virginia* (1612), was "a nurse for souldiers, a practise for marriners, a trade for marchants, a reward for the good, and that which is most of all, a businesse (most acceptable to God) to bring such poore infidels to the true knowledge of God and his Holy Gospell" (1:159). In this intermixing of business and religion, the causes of both become strengthened, but it is the economic motivations which Smith's rhetoric deems as primary among his readers, or at least as providing the appropriate terms with which to speak of both. As Smith bluntly put it: "For, I am not so simple, to thinke, that ever any other motive than wealth, will ever erect there a Commonweale" (1:346).

Of course, Smith never abandons his belief in the sacred mission. While he identifies self-promotion as the central source of dramatic motivation in that book's narrative shape, he still periodically reintroduces the sacred context through typological allusion or simple exclamation. For instance, after acknowledging the importance of the motivation for profit, he subtly enhances the actual conditions of profit by embellishing them with religious overtones. Fish, he points out, are to be the staple commodity of the colony, and are almost infinitely plentiful; what cannot be eaten can be sold or traded, an indication of the potential riches of American life: "Thus, though all men be not fishers: yet all men, whatsoever, may in other matters doe as well" (1:347). A reader of the time would be likely to recognize the reference to Christ as the fisherman, and thus come to see Virginia as the promised land of opportunity.

Still, like Harriot, Smith placed profit as the primary motive for investment and emigration, and as such the primary route for the furthering of both God and the empire. But unlike Harriot, Smith did not promise that success was so easily acquired. In fact, he promoted the colony through the opposite strategy of underscoring the certainty of hardship and danger, of "adventure." His Virginia is filled with as many unfriendly as friendly Indians, and has a terrain as inhospitable and fickle as it is full of promise. Within the framework of adventurous enterprise, however, these are not finally depicted as impediments but rather as incentives, an enticement to the "adventure" of the enterprise as the measure of achievement. For Smith, the enterprise was embodied wholly in the adventure. Even when employing the religious perspective, he still emphasized the presence of hardship and danger: "Adam and Eve did first beginne this innocent worke," he notes in *A Description of New England* (1616), "To plant the earth to remaine to posteritie; but not without labour, trouble and industrie. Noe, and his family, beganne againe the second plantation; and their seed as it still increased hath still planted new Countries. . . . But not without much hazard, travell, discontents, and many disasters" (1:360). The passage serves a double function: first, it supplies a typological justification for the settlers' own "labour" of economic expansion, identifying that expansion as the proper work of the "fortunate fall"; and second, it transforms that "trouble" of expansion into an incentive to further "industrie." Adventure thus became a medium for the expression of a sanctified economic expansion, and the promotion of adventurousness became the promotion of expansion.

As Edwin Rozwenc has pointed out (11–21), Smith merged the literary conventions of the chivalric romance with the values of economic opportunism: the heroic knight became the self-made man, and his quest to rescue the fair maiden became a quest to succeed on the field of economic advancement. The dragons of the scheme were the Indians and the landscape, and they were dangerous precisely insofar as they threatened to prevent that advancement. Yet they were also integral parts of the story, the animating challenges without which the adventure would cease to have a viable form, a shape for validating, by valorizing, economic expansion.[7]

The economic imperatives thus embodied in the form were finally invoked not, as one might expect, by the resolution of a simple and complete victory of self-made man over economic impediment, but rather by the reassertion of that danger and hardship; such reassertion would, in turn, assure the continued exercise of economic expansion. As he put it in *The General Historie of Virginia* (1624), "every thing of worth is found full of difficulties, [and] nothing so difficult as to establish a Common-wealth so farre remote from men and meanes" (2:144). In other words, the promotion of the mission of expansion depended upon an expansion of the adventure form: the adventure must be maintained if the enterprise is to succeed. The implicit assumption is that with the brave and continuing conquest over these villains, and the ardent application of heroism to the actual "work" of settlement and cultivation, a social order would evolve that would profit the individual, the local community, the commonwealth of England, the advancement of civilization, and the divine mission that subsumed them all.

The narrative features we find in this scheme, and in many of these early accounts of the New World—the reduction of dramatic field to the pursuit of commodity, the emergence of the Indian and the wilderness adventures as paradigms of that pursuit, the framing of the adventure within the interrelated contexts of the expansion of empire, civilization, and Christianity—would soon take a special shape in the literature written by the later settlers themselves, the Americans. John Smith's chivalric enterpriser would develop into the economic adventurer Henry Clay canonized on the floor of the Senate in 1832 as the "self-made man." What did remain fairly constant, though, was the translation of economic realities and ideals into narrative form, the enterprise into the adventure.

The American Tale of Adventurous Enterprise

The early British colonial writings followed many of the same principles established in the European tradition. William Bradford, often considered the first American historian, was also the first to describe the origins of the American settlement as an enterprise with bravery at its center: "all great and honorable actions," he wrote in *Of Plymouth Plantation* (1651), "are accompanied with great difficulties and must be both enterprised and overcome with answerable courages" (27). The Puritans were quick to define those "great and honorable actions" in terms both sacred and secular. If the rhetoric placed God as the axis of authority, it also praised economic advancement as a righteous honor: in the daily exercise of journal-writing, an accounting of one's money was as necessary a task as an accounting of one's sins, for both spoke to the glory of God. This glory also relegated Indians to their customary place in the drama, as impediments to, or implements for, the advancement of the colonists' sacred and secular mission. Even among those writers outside the Puritan community, such as the Virginia merchants, New England pilgrims, and Spanish and French settlers, a similar rhetoric of mission and mobility underlay the narrative vision of the movement to and through the American wilderness.

But from the beginning, certain of these literary elements were shaped by distinctly American cultural perceptions of the nature of adventure and the aims and conditions of Western economic expansion. For the early settlers, that translation of enterprise into adventure was part of a larger framework of literary typology that was refined early in the nation's development. From the first colonial writings, the progress of American history was represented as a manifestation of the "Word," and America was itself designated a literary form. In such works as explorer reports, captivity narratives, and sermons, the early Americans represented their movement West across the seas to the "American Strand" as a re-writing of their fate as the chosen people, a manifest destiny preordained in scripture, ascribed to the historical present, and recounted into the future. With each further movement West into the continent, this story was repeated and retold. Soon Western expansion became a typological narrative of all American history, a model of indigenous literary tradition which continued into the exploration and settlement of the Far West in the nineteenth century. From the first settlements, all America was the West, the "Indian wilderness," the proving ground for the enterprise of the New Israel.

As the enterprise merged with the adventure, so too did history merge with myth. The historical West was represented in the accounts of expansion by the movement of expansion, and the mythic West, by the narrative form of the ideology of expansion, specifically the ideology of enterprise drawn into the storied realm of adventure. This mythic perspective has been familiar in American historical thought since the end of the nineteenth century, when Frederick Jackson Turner delivered his influential paper on "The Significance of the Frontier in American History" at the World's Columbian Exposition in Chicago. "Since the days when the fleet of Columbus sailed into the waters of the New World, America has been another name for opportunity," Turner wrote, and each successive frontier of Western expansion, he added, was another "new field of opportunity" out of which America evolved (37–38). Hence America began before the first migration and was reborn with each subsequent movement West: "American social development has been continually beginning over again on the frontier" (2). According to William Cronon, it was Turner's thesis that "set American space in motion and gave it a plot" (1987, 166). But, in fact, that plot had existed as early as the first migrations. Turner's paper may have legitimized it, and American history itself, as a respectable object for "scientific" study, but its rapid acceptance suggests that Turner was summarizing rather than departing from the rhetorical tradition and poetics of American historical thought. So when Owen Wister introduced his novel *The Virginian* to his readers a few years after Turner's article appeared, he declared it not a new form of Western literature for the twentieth century, but "a colonial romance": "For Wyoming between 1874 and 1890 was a colony as wild as was Virginia one hundred years earlier. As wild, with a scantier population, and the same primitive joys and dangers. There were, to be sure, not so many Chippendale settees" (vii). On the typological level, Wister's "one hundred years" is really two hundred, and his nineteenth-century Wyoming is really one of the "original" colonies. His "colonial romance," then, returns the reader to America's wild and rugged birthplace, to the origins of America itself.

The version of American history that emerges from this thesis is of a repeated exercise in regression and mastery, a drama presented as dynamic and progressive but founded on ideological principles that remain static and repetitive. For instance, while Turner attributed the "perennial rebirth" (2) of America to the overpowering forces of the Western experience—"The wilderness masters the colonist" (4) was his formulation—his rhetoric represented the colonist mastering the wilderness. The process thus recapitulates the national imperative of expansion as the narrative of American history. He opens the essay by characterizing the process of frontier expansion as "winning a wilderness" (2). In the end, his narrative model followed the mission as outlined in scripture: "The United States lies like a huge page in the history of society. Line by line as we read this continental page from West to East we find the record of social evolution" (11). Turner thus "reads" a "written" America, and reads it backwards (the last settlements become the first), as if he were reading the testament of the chosen people as they moved toward the promised land. His history is a form of literary criticism, literary insofar as it is exegetical and poetic, and critical insofar as it calls for a revived historical vision of the importance of the West in the origin and evolution of America. Ultimately, that vision was both historical and prophetic, reproducing the narrative of America as a search for origins and a "recommencement" of the mission, a sacred history within the secular realm of expansion.

This odd mixture of nostalgia and prophecy, which has character-ized much of American historical thought, also informed the Western adventure tale.[8] Within this narrative, certain conventions emerged to represent the progress of the nation's expansion. The frontier, in partic-ular, became the characteristic setting, and the boundary line became the dramatic axis around which the terms of the adventure were speci-fied. At the boundary line, for instance, one might find the forces of savagery distinguished from the powers of civilization, or the condi-tions that bring poverty from those that bring success, and by these lines one was to "read" the narrative of American economic, national, and spiritual expansion.

As the central image in this context, the "frontier" identified the entire West as a threshold, the boundary line of the American mission. Just as all America was seen as a tale of Western expansion, so too was the West seen as a tale of frontier adventure. By designating at once the West as a whole, and the demarcation between the settled and unsettled territories, the "frontier" came to represent the West as a place in constant movement, development, expansion; that is, as a narrative form in itself. The figure of the boundary line provided not only the locus of dramatic movement of the narrative, but the set of images which instilled that drama with the imperatives of the American mission. In the same way that the markings, crossings, and remarkings of boundaries established by Cabeza de Vaca's confrontations with Indians and Christians, or John Smith's with Indians and merchants, represented their respective national ideals of expansionism, so too the characters, pivotal moments, and crucial movements of the American drama. The mountain man and pioneer, the rescue from Indian captiv-ity and the showdown, represented the particular religious, social, and economic boundaries by which the progress of that enterprise was measured—boundaries between the wilderness and the settlements, savagery and civilization, degeneration and regeneration, success and failure. The crossing of those boundaries, and the ensuing adventures, prolonged the anxiety associated with that progress, impelling the reader to determine the boundaries' proper location and meaning.[9]

The meanings of those boundaries were not always the same, of course. They changed as the conditions of expansion and the notions of the "enterprise" itself changed. During the nineteenth century, as

John Juricek pointed out, "frontier" was defined by a variety of terms and meanings: the word "border" referred to the "outer edge or tract of land that runs along a country"; "boundary," to "that which bounds or limits"; and "frontier," to a "military line"; all of which terms stipulated different attitudes toward American expansionism (12). But a close look at the currency of these terms throughout the century also reveals a basic continuity which has great implications for the way in which these images took shape in a national literary form.

At first expansion was measured by the location of the fixed border between the nation of American whites and the Indian nations, and the tales that arose focused on the discovery, exploration, claiming and cultivation of a prescribed territory in the New World. Later, expansion had become characterized as the movement, and even crossing, of the boundaries between the nations, and so the tales focused on the plight of brave Americans in a lawless and alien land, a territory destined to become part of America but as yet a "debatable ground" of conflicting claims and interests. Finally expansion had itself expanded to transform this movement through a borderland into a passage between sections of an all-white and all-American continent. These tales now focused on the struggles between Americans in showdowns on the streets of already established American towns.

While this progression represents changes in the nature of Western expansion, it also represents a continuity in the nature of Western adventure. At each stage one finds a recapitulation of one of the fundamental prescriptions of American narrative thought: as Myra Jehlen puts it, "the very being of America. . .is entwined with 'horizon' and 'frontier,' and is therefore affronted by borders" (235). With each crossing of the boundary comes a new reading, or rereading, of the American mission according to the conditions and interests of the period. With the emergence of the marketplace, for instance, the frontier adventure was shaped by the new modes of exchange, new types of risks, new virtues and vices associated with economic expansion; in particular, the crossing of the frontier became a model for the mobility of Americans in the marketplace. Yet both sides of the boundary line were thus still part of America and the American marketplace. Each new reading, that is, also re-established the claims of the adventure itself to transform the West into all America, the history into the story.

America was thus designated a literary form, and American literature, the vehicle by which its boundaries were discovered, explored, expanded. From the early colonial sermons defining the plight of a spiritual quest bounded by the wilderness to the eighteenth-century sermons attempting to recapture the faith in the face of a society drawn deeper into the wilderness as the boundary advanced, from William Bradford's *Of Plymouth Plantation, 1620–1647* to William Byrd's *History of the Dividing Line Betwixt Virginia and North Carolina* (1728), the literature both reflected and reflected upon the boundaries of the American experience. When Turner chose to open his essay by quoting the announcement of the Superintendent of the 1890 census that the frontier was now closed, that "at present. . .there can hardly be said to be a frontier line" (1), he was voicing a preoccupation with boundary and expansion long implicit in this literary formulation of the frontier. Throughout the century every reference to the "boundless continent" was accompanied by an anxious call to possession, a demarcation of land into territories, homesteads, ranches, a society settling by deeds and distinctions. These seemingly opposite rhetorical perspectives were expressions of a culture that demanded both expansion and new guidelines for that expansion. As boundaries were disrupted during the westward movement, the narrative of adventurous enterprise reasserted and redefined those boundaries so as to preserve the society in its course of expansion. Individualism would reassert itself in the face of outlawry, and opportunity would triumph over a villainous opportunism.

At the beginning of the nineteenth century, when the first explorations of the Far West, and the books about those explorations, were germinated in the East, the adventures associated with the boundary had become specifically identified with the expansion of the marketplace. Among the early forms of this literature by American writers were the accounts of direct observation published early in the century: the explorer reports, trapper journals, travel books, and settlement and captivity narratives. One of the first was Zebulon Montgomery Pike's *An Account of Expeditions to the Sources of the Mississippi and Through the Western Parts of Louisiana,* published in 1810. Pike was an army officer in charge of a number of expeditions sent into the newly purchased Louisiana territory to note the conditions for expansion and trade. His most celebrated observation was his description of the Great Plains as a great American desert. Pike saw in this seemingly arid land not an insurmountable obstacle to expansion, but a boundary line providing that expansion with a renewed sense of its limitations and ends:

> But from these immense prairies may arise one great advantage to the United States, viz: The restriction of our population to some certain limits, and thereby a continuation of the Union. Our citizens being so prone to rambling and extending themselves, on the frontiers, will, through necessity, be constrained to limit their extent on the west, to the borders of the Missouri and Mississippi, while they leave the prairies incapable of cultivation to the wandering and uncivilized aborigines of the country. (Part 2, Appendix, 8)

The comments may seem anti-expansionist, but they engage the narrative assumptions that support expansion: the border between civilization and savagery, and the challenge to extend that border while preserving the distinction it represents. Pike's desert is much like the Puritans' "Indian wilderness"; the task, or embodied narrative, conveyed through both images is the conquering of an inhospitable terrain, for within the wilderness, or the desert, lay the Garden—"the Gardens of the Desert," as William Cullen Bryant put it in his poem "The Prairies" (1834, line 1). The very boundary that Pike perceives as an impasse to expansion inspires Bryant's vision of "unshorn fields, boundless and beautiful" (line 2). Josiah Gregg was more explicit a few years later when, in his *Commerce of the Prairies* (1844), he celebrated the ability, and thus the imperative, of civilization not only to transform this great American desert into a fertile possession, but also to enlist nature itself in the process:

> The high plains seem too dry and lifeless to produce timber; yet might not the vicissitudes of nature operate a change likewise upon the seasons? Why may we not suppose that the genial influences of civilization —that extensive cultivation of the earth—might contribute to the multiplication of showers, as it certainly does of fountains? Or that the shady groves, as they advance upon the prairies, may have some effect upon the seasons? At least, many old settlers maintain that the droughts are becoming less oppressive in the West. . . . Then may we not hope that these sterile regions might yet be thus revived and fertilized, and their surface covered one day by flourishing settlements to the Rocky Mountains? (2:202–203)[10]

As with the earlier promotional pamphlets, reports such as Pike's and Gregg's provided Americans with information they needed in order to assess as well as undertake the prospects of an expansion to the West. In their form as well as their commentary, the reports contextualized this information within the rationale of economic expansion. The conditions noted were resources to be mined, the natives described were savages to be conquered. The "discovery" of the Far West became another discovery of America, and the narratives of exploration settled into a familiar perspective of boundary and mission, the sacred quest and the quest for commodity.

This perspective is evident in the original guidelines drawn up for the exploration by Thomas Jefferson. The acquisition of scientific knowledge was deemed paramount, and yet, as Henry Nash Smith has pointed out, "a responsible statesman was not likely to forget that geographical knowledge was a necessary preliminary to economic penetration and eventual political domination. Scientific knowledge was to be sought for the sake of the fur trade" (16). But the fur trade was only part of Jefferson's larger design for the commercial development of the West. "The object of your mission," he wrote to Meriwether Lewis, was to locate "the most direct & practicable water communication across this continent, for the purposes of commerce" (Bergon 1989, xxiv). When this vision of Western expansion became endorsed later in the century by the narrative logic of Manifest Destiny, the "purposes of commerce" had become seemingly inscribed on the geography itself, an inextricable part of the narrative of the Western movement. Forty-three years later, on the floor of the Senate, Thomas Hart Benton praised the expedition in just these Jeffersonian terms: "Lewis and Clarke were sent out to discover a commercial route to the Pacific Ocean; and so judiciously was their enterprise conducted that their return route must become, and forever remain, the route of commerce" (Smith 30).[11]

Jefferson himself recognized this conjunction of commercial progress and the narrative of Western expansion. In earlier support of the expedition, he offered Congress a line of reasoning founded upon the narrative premises of American expansionism:

> While other civilized nations have encountered great expense to enlarge the boundaries of knowledge by undertaking voyages of discovery, and for other literary purposes, in various parts or directions, our nation seems to owe to the same object, as well as to its own interests, to explore [the Missouri River], the only line of easy communication across the continent, and so directly traversing our own part of it. (8:202)[12]

This "line of communication" is more than a tool for prospective commerce. It is a connection between those "interests of commerce" and the "literary purposes" of scientific and geographic knowledge. The literary purpose, that is, encompasses an understanding, or proper "reading," of the meaning of those boundaries and the "interests" they contain, a meaning that is itself literary: it is the written narrative of expansion into the New World, now the New World of the Far West.

While this translation of economic interests into literary form provided the basis of that narrative, the particular economic meanings associated with the enterprise differed from period to period. Like the image of the frontier, the concept of enterprise had always been tied to the aims and conditions of expansion and emigration. Since the first stages of colonization, the term was commonly used in American rhetoric to designate the American mission, the settlement and cultivation of a spiritual and material empire. But its particular stipulations about that mission, the focus of its insistence, differed from period to period. In the colonial period, it referred to the communal religious experiment, the "Citty upon a Hill," under the rubric of which were included economic, social and political programs. Over the following two centuries, the explicitly religious denotation diminished, and by the nineteenth century, enterprise was particularly tied to the terms provided by the marketplace, such as the individual dream of economic success, the control of market forces, and an industriousness and a shrewdness in business practice. As Francis Bowen described it in his *Principles of Political Economy* (1856), enterprise was essentially "industrious, and adventurous habits" (Neufeldt 237).

But this "cultural bearing of business enterprise," to use Thorstein Veblen's phrase (1904, vi), was not without a larger frame of reference. The rhetorical sanctification of economic programs had remained a constant since the colonial period; consequently, even as an economic term, "enterprise" invoked the "mission" of America.[13] Richard Hofstadter, for instance, described the Jacksonian enterpriser in just these terms: "The typical American was an expectant capitalist, a hard-working, ambitious person for whom enterprise was a kind of religion, and everywhere he found conditions that encouraged him to extend himself" (1977, 55–56). The advent of romanticism had transformed the community of souls into a democracy of selves; the growth of laissez-faire capitalism had translated the religious experiment into an economic endeavor. "Enterprise" had primarily come to refer to the endeavors and spirit of the marketplace, and to the gestures of self-interest and mobility upon which the destiny of America was now deemed to rest.

But even with so precise a frame of reference, there remained much latitude in the meanings ascribed to the term, and the attitudes evoked by it. It was used to refer to both the national mission, a "free enterprise," and a quality of individual character, a "private enterprise." It was generally used in a positive manner, to describe the attendant impulses of progress, though it sometimes also appeared as a criticism, to characterize a restlessness or greed. Significantly, the word "adventure" had a similar history in this economic context, shifting from the positive "adventure" of investment to the negative "adventuring" of exploitation.

To understand these variations, one must go to the marketplace itself. During this period the marketplace went through many changes, and these changes affected not only the conditions of expansion but the attitudes toward expansion as well, the way that it was "figured" in the national imagination. A close look at the rhetoric of economic enterprise, and particularly at the conflicts between Jacksonians and Federalists, will help us identify the way these changes and their accompanying social tensions were translated into the literary form of the adventure tale.

Often designated, as Edward Pessen has explained, the "prefatory age, or what economic historians have called the age of merchant capitalism" (22), the Jacksonian period was also a period of early industrialization. By 1812, according to Thomas Cochran, those social changes associated with "what is generally called the Industrial Revolution" had arrived in both England and America (1979, 1). Two of these changes are particularly relevant to our discussion here: first, the emergence of new forms of nationally accepted currency and modes of exchange, such as paper money, credit, and speculation, which placed an increasing emphasis on fluid over fixed wealth, and mobility over given social station; and second, the emergence of new forms and routes of transportation, which facilitated a broadened scope of settlement, cultivation of resources, and distribution of goods. As a result, the local marketplace was in the process of becoming national, and this national marketplace, of becoming a model of American social life. Self-interest was introduced as a viable social motivation, and mobility as a viable social norm. These developments had a special impact on the West, where a new market in land and resources provided an arena for the expansion of this new national marketplace, and fostered the development of new social structures and economic ideologies. Like America itself, the West was being transformed into a marketplace, and expansion into an adventure of economic mobility.

Not everyone favored these changes. The gradual replacement of the fixed social bonds of class or family with the fluid relations of the marketplace as the constitutive elements of social stability troubled even many of those who endorsed the change. "High mobility, both geographic and social, [had] weakened family ties," Cochran tells us, and money, "or 'economic rationality,' " had become the "common measuring rod of the society" (1981, 12–13), as well as the "major social bond" (Vernon 20). But that bond was itself challenged by its necessary incentive to self-interest and mobility. While some people at the time perceived the expansion of the marketplace as an expansion of economic and social opportunity, others saw it only as a threat to American stability and unity.

Generally this debate has been represented as a conflict between the Federalists and the Jacksonians, or more particularly, between the Whigs and the Democrats; and the central issue of that debate, as the role that self-interest and mobility should play in the American social order. According to this formulation, the Federalists favored republican values and saw in the self-interest of the marketplace an abandoning of public virtue; they also preferred the preservation of the given hierarchical relations of class, land, and lineage, and saw in mobility an undermining of social order and cultural achievement. The Jacksonians, on the other hand, valued self-interest as a republican virtue in itself, and mobility as a means to a new, more equitable, and more successful, social order.

In support of these positions, both groups called upon that narrative model of American history described earlier: expansion as the unit of measurement by which to recognize and evaluate changes in the cultural life. History was reduced to a succession of transitional states, a movement across the boundary between periods of expansion and consolidation. So one finds the proponents of Jacksonianism defining their cause as the antidote to Federalism, the ideological stance of the previous "period": the "common man" was to be liberated from the rigidly bound social and economic systems of his predecessors. The critics, in turn, positioned themselves in opposition to this mobility. And both sides offered much evidence to support their positions: the proponents, a seeming increase in economic opportunities, most vividly illustrated in the emergence of a class of newly wealthy and powerful men such as John Jacob Astor and Jackson himself; the critics, a deterioration of social and financial stability, as evidenced by a series of scandals and bankruptcies. Both claimed victory in the year of Jackson's retirement, 1837, when Jackson declared in his farewell address that "nothing can impede [our] march to the highest point of national prosperity" (Blau 2), while at the same moment the nation was plunged into its first major financial depression.

This formulation of the conflict, at any rate, was the model upon which the opponents represented their differences to themselves and each other, and it was well in keeping with the traditional modes of American political debate. One finds the same terms of opposition recapitulated in the conflicts between North and South before the Civil War, in which the North became identified with the "world of business and. . .the kind of man—the style of life—which this world seemed to be generating," and the South with "the vestiges of an old-world aristocracy, a promise of stability and an assurance that gentility—a high sense of honor, a belief in public service and a maintenance of domestic decorum—could be preserved under republican institutions" (William R. Taylor 18). The terms appear again at the end of the nineteenth century in the debates between agrarian populists and urban moneyed interests, with the division established between a conservative pastoral tradition and a progressive industrialism.

While this model provides a useful enough version of the Federalist-Jacksonian debates in general terms, it fails to recognize the views of American history and expansion the two sides shared. While they disagreed about the aims of economic expansion, and the ends and limits of the marketplace, they agreed upon the underlying premise that the progress of the American mission lay in harnessing the tension between self-interest and the common good, mobility and stability. As it would be for the Southerners and Northerners that were to come after them, the Federalists were no more against self-interest than the Jacksonians were against hierarchy. As Richard Slotkin has pointed out, the

> republican political economy of careers (and resources) "open to talents" was not restricted to the agrarian-yeoman sphere, but included manufac-

turing as well, and even a certain kind of banking or small-scale money-lending. It followed that the "Jacksonian" ideology, equating democracy with the chance to rise and accumulate property, was not the exclusive program of Jackson and his party. Rather, it was part of a broad consensus, shared by Whigs and Democrats (and later by Republicans and Free Soilers)—a consensus in which there might be different visions of the ultimate economic felicity (the planter on his acres, the farmer in his field, the ironworker in his mill, the merchant or banker at his desk), but in which the form and direction for pursuing happiness were parallel. (1985, 114)

The basis for that consensus was not just an eager acquisitiveness, the "possessive individualism" that C. B. Macpherson (1962) identified as the central feature of the economic thought of the age; nor was it just an avid defense of power and privilege, the hierarchical order that stood as both obstacle and incentive to that acquisitive individual. Rather, it was the combination of these views that lent coherence to the "form and direction" of American economic idealism. If the Federalists presented themselves as guardians of a social structure in which inherited wealth was the apt measure of social status, they also sanctioned the pursuit of profit and the accumulation of wealth as measures of personal success; if the Jacksonians presented themselves as "simple" agrarians struggling against the monopolied moneyed interests, they also supported political programs that would bring them more power in the marketplace. Their attack on the Bank, for instance, was "in no sense a blow at capitalism or property or the 'money power.' " As Bray Hammond has explained, "It was a blow at an older set of capitalists by a newer, more numerous set" (Benson 333). Their cause was the "sophisticated one of enterpriser against capitalist, of banker against regulation, and of Wall Street against Chestnut" (333).

My argument here makes use of the current debate among historians about which economic ideology was dominant in the Jacksonian period. J. G. A. Pocock, for instance, has argued that an hostility toward the marketplace based on the Machiavellian principles of classical republicanism was more central to eighteenth and early nineteenth-century American economic thought than has been previously considered, while Joyce Appleby and John Diggins have claimed that the Lockean embrace of the marketplace was the more common ideology of the period.[14] My own position is that both views were dominant, and both shared by the two parties, regardless of the differences articulated in

the rhetoric. What Pocock has called "a bitter, conscious, and ambiva-
lent dialogue" about the marketplace (1985, 71) in fact took place in the
shared context of the marketplace. While significant differences did
indeed exist between the views held by Federalists and Jacksonians,
and while class conflict did indeed play a significant role in determining
these views, the ideals held by the two parties derived from a shared
belief in the union of mobility and hierarchy as the foundation of
American prosperity. And these principles, in turn, derived from the
shared narrative principle that the story of America was the story of its
expansion, that the essence of that expansion was economic, and that
the dramatic principle of economic expansion was anxiety. The persis-
tence of this story, and its ability to absorb variant views, attests to the
power of the ideology of enterprise in the American cultural imagination.

While there was much debate about the forms that enterprise might
take in the West, there was little debate about the efficacy of enterprise
itself as an ideal of American progress. Americans, in fact, had long
developed a peculiar cultural language in which contradictory views
might be expressed, so as to contain individual differences within a
paradigm of democracy and national mission. As we have seen, "enterprise" was one of the key words in that language. Within its purview
was a variety of images and symbols which were grouped together in
such a way as to provide a consensus of rhetoric for competing views,
a system of shared beliefs and guidelines for belief and action. I am
here using Abner Cohen's definition of symbols as "objects, acts, con-
cepts, or linguistic formations that stand ambiguously for a multiplicity
of disparate meanings" (preface, n. pag.). In the case of enterprise, the
symbols included the West itself and its attendant conditions and
characters, and the meanings of these symbols included just those
economic principles we have been discussing, such as mobility, hierarchy, self-interest, and the common good.

In the context of expansion, for instance, the West had come to be
represented by a number of opposing images in the popular imagination: the Wild West and the domesticated West, the land of the primitive and the land of progress, the Great American Desert and the
Garden of the World. Oppositions such as these were hardly neat; even
single images contained oppositions within them. The Garden image,
for example, included both the agricultural Garden (the domesticated
community of subsistence farmers) and the industrial Garden (the

farming community designed for trade), both the green of nature and the green of money. Jefferson himself neatly suspended both views, embracing the West as an agrarian utopia of self-sufficient farmers and a foundation for the expansion of American commerce. Yet with all the possibilities for confusion, contradiction, and misinterpretation, these oppositions were suspended in the single collating image of "the West." Hence while Western expansion might be characterized as a dangerous or liberating expression of market forces, as an "enterprise" it becomes an expression of the American mission, and a description of American historical development. With each call to the Western enterprise came the simultaneous calls to mobility and hierarchy, self-interest and the common good.

The ideology of enterprise thus both contained and promoted the dramatic anxiety of expansion by invoking the basic tension between self-interest and the common good that was of such concern to the Federalists and Jacksonians in the context of expansion at the time. The profit motive was leading more and more people into the West, dispersing the population across the continent, and thus threatening to weaken the ties which unified the nation. At the same time, commerce was providing the means of exchange, and the ideological consensus, that might, in Henry Nash Smith's words, "bind the parts of the nation together" (158). Appropriately, the ideology of enterprise supplied many of the terms by which the boundaries of expansion were set.

But the ideology was not independent from the narrative form in which the symbols and images were embedded; its dissemination was effected in part through Western adventure tales, and through the "story" of Western expansion in general. As the designated arena for the exercise of enterprise, the Western movement provided the underlying narrative principles and superficial dramatic forms, the "adventure" of the enterprise. The dualistic images of the West, for instance, came to seem mutually confirming elements of the same ideal because they were dramatized as such in the tale. As we have seen, the form of the adventure tale was uniquely suited to the subject of expansion. The Western adventure tale that emerged during this period functioned both as a vehicle for the expression of those ideals and concerns associated with the marketplace, and as a literary strategy for representing Western economic expansion. Through its adventure form, the tale posited expansion as the foundation of American progress, and through its selection of adventures, its configuration of character, its mapping of landscape and language, it interpreted that expansion, prescribing particular limits or ends.

In other words, the tale enacted the ideological conflicts over the role that self-interest and mobility should play within the structure of given hierarchies of class and value. One might find an ingenious man on the make battling a wealthy landowner, a genteel cowboy facing down an uncouth gunslinger, an earnest settler braving a tribe of savage Indians, a generous entrepreneur confronting an unscrupulous trader, a lone homesteader struggling against a powerful cattle baron, an honest tradesman striking back against a corrupt sheriff. The "class bias" evident in these tales was, as Henry Nash Smith reminded us, "one of the dominant forces shaping nineteenth-century attitudes toward the West" (51). But that bias was not simply an attribute of the upper classes, a striving to impose limits on the claims of the lower classes. Those "lower" and "middle" classes shared that bias, and even represented their own oppression as an infringement of the "opportunity" to attain entry to a higher class. The struggle, for the most part, was between those who preferred to maintain the given hierarchy and those who preferred a new hierarchy based on mobility. In these tales, the familiar images of rugged individualism stand alongside images of genteel aristocracy and privilege. The hero is the individual who has managed to incorporate these differences into a singular enterprise, and the villain is the individual who has attempted to manipulate one of the positions to his own ends, to turn privilege and mobility into opportunism and outlawry.

A characteristic example of this feature of the form is Owen Wister's characterization of the Virginian as a natural born aristocrat. Certainly Wister had no intention of attacking the self-interest and mobility of the Western movement. Indeed, the Virginian succeeds precisely because his aristocracy is embodied in his skills as a businessman and professional. Early in the book Wister defines the purpose of the Western adventure tale in precisely these terms of accommodation:

> All America is divided into two classes,—the quality and the equality. . . .
>
> It was through the Declaration of Independence that we Americans acknowledged the *eternal inequality* of man. For by it we abolished a cut-and-dried aristocracy. . . . [We] decreed that every man should thenceforth have equal liberty to find his own level. By this very decree we acknowledged and gave freedom to true aristocracy, saying, 'Let the

best man win, whoever he is.' Let the best man win! That is America's word. That is true democracy. And true democracy and true aristocracy are one and the same thing. (147)

Wister's aristocratic hero was just such a figure, a man whose natural nobility was neatly summed up in the admiring statement, "That man knows his business" (2). By such reasoning, the conflicting ideals of economic expansion became an essential part of the configurations of Western adventure tales, providing a narrative resolution to tensions of the emerging marketplace.[15]

Ultimately, the tales legitimated this resolution, and the expansionism it represented, by placing the adventures in the traditional typological context of America's mission. From the earliest explorer reports to the most recent horse operas, the focus of the narratives of Western expansion has been the establishment of an ideal America founded upon American ideals, the animating rhetorical principles of the mission and the marketplace. Every progressive act of expansion, every extension of the boundary separating East from West, civilization from savagery, was also a conservative act of self-definition, a continual resetting of those boundaries.

The boundary line thus simultaneously denoted the needs for limits and the need to overcome them. It is not surprising to find, then, that in these tales the conditions of expansion were generally represented by a series of treacherous boundary crossings. That such crossings mark the progress of the hero, and the narrative itself, indicates the privileged status accorded the task of expansion in the tale; that such crossings were dangerous indicates the degree of anxiety associated with that task. One of the most frequent occurrences is the crossing that is followed by defection: trappers joining foreign fur trade interests or adopting Indian ways, captives of Indians joining the tribes. If the mission to expand the American civilization required the movement of the boundary Westward, it also involved the crossing of that boundary into the realm of savagery, and so the very expansion that was to define the consolidation of American unity was also the potential source for its destruction.

During the Jacksonian period, these crossings became particularly associated with the expansion of the marketplace. The boundary denoted not just the line between civilization and savagery, America and the untamed wilderness, but also between self-interest and opportun-

ism, individualism and outlawry, mobility and recklessness. A general
concern of these tales, that is, was now the effect of marketplace
expansion, and particularly of the rise of self-interest and mobility, on
the future of the collective mission. The older divisions indicated by
the boundary had not disappeared, nor had the pattern of defection.
The American mission was still imagined as a journey across the
boundaries separating civilization from savagery, the sacred from the
profane, and trappers and captives were still "converted" into Indians
(in a parody of Christian conversion), crossing over into the savage
life. But now the rhetoric of these divisions was applied to the marketplace: the forces of civilization and savagery, of the sacred and profane,
now battled it out in the arena of economic expansion. The defections
still represented a betrayal of self, nation, and God, but they did so in
the language of the marketplace. The boundaries between hero and
villain were the boundaries between self-interest and opportunism,
mobility and selfish manipulation, hierarchy and rigidity.

This is not to suggest that the defectors and villains were no longer
perceived as the dangerous "others" to be overcome. As Richard Slotkin has explained, such

> fables. . .translate the Metropolitan strife of interest groups and classes
> into archetypal terms. Instead of interpreting history as a competition
> for power and resources by classes of fellow citizens, the Myth projects
> competition outward, and imagines the strife as that between a fully
> human entity—"civilization"—and an entity that is primarily inhuman.
> (1985, 79)

But these others on the far side of the boundary were, in this sense,
precisely the representation of those characters, or those characteristics,
within the culture that were deemed most troubling. In all of these
tales, the hero and villain parody and complement each other across a
border that must always separate them. In this way, the marketplace
remains pure, and the threats of and to its expansion are overcome.
From the mountain man to the cowboy, the pioneer to the outlaw, the
hero's most distinguishing feature is that he "knows his business," the
right and proper enterprise of the American adventurer.

During the Jacksonian period, these tales became enormously popular. In part that popularity can be attributed to these ideological
features: the tales seemed to express what Americans wanted to hear
about their interests and aims. But there were other reasons as well. If

the growth of the marketplace affected the form of these tales, it also affected their explicit subject matter and distribution. In short, they had become a part of the very marketplace they were representing. As Michael Gilmore has pointed out, "Literature itself became an article of commerce at this time, as improvements in manufacture, distribution, and promotion, helped to create a national audience for letters" (1). And that national audience wanted to read more about life in the Western territories. When Pike's report was published in 1810 it became an immediate success, and was followed a few years later by the equally popular publication of the Lewis and Clark journals edited by Nicholas Biddle.[16] By the early 1830s, the market had grown considerably.

This was the literary world to which Washington Irving returned after his prolonged stay in Europe, and he would take a keen interest in its operations. Many of his contemporaries, many indeed within his own literary circles, had already written on Western subjects, and, as his career decisions were to be motivated, in part, by his understanding of the extent to which literature had become a business, he would also take into account the ways in which the West had acquired a literary form. A brief look at a few works by these contemporaries will establish this context of the literary marketplace within which he would produce his own Western works.

James Kirke Paulding, one of the most popular writers of the day, was also one of the first popularizers of Western literature. In 1832 he published his successful novel *Westward Ho!*, bringing to culmination an interest in the subject that first found expression fourteen years earlier in his popular poem *The Backwoodsman*. That Irving had read both is likely since Paulding was related by marriage, and the two were not only friends but professional collaborators as well: in 1811 they worked together on *Salmagundi*, one of Irving's first efforts. In fact, Paulding was with Irving on the cruise up the Hudson in 1832.

In *The Backwoodsman*, much the same relation exists between adventure and enterprise as was embellished in Daniel Bryan's poem only a few years before: the familiar narrative formulation of the Western journey as national spiritual quest, as we follow "a true Yankee lad" as "he leaves his friends and home,/ Mid distant wilds and dangers drear to roam,/ To seek a competence, or find a grave,/ Rather than live a hireling or a slave" (1.45, 91–95). The adventures the hero faces are an integral part of his quest, for it is a journey in which "Glory and Danger ever are allied,/ And like twin eagles tower side by side;/

Rocky, and steep, and slippery to the tread/ Is the rough path that wins the mountain's head,/ Yet he who braves the dangers of the way,/ At every step attains a brighter day" (6.133–138). By conflating "competence" and "Glory," Paulding turned the hero's desire to be a self-sufficient farmer into a spiritual vocation, and placed that vocation into the adventurous context of moral and physical dangers to overcome. These adventures were then naturalized within the Western setting, a land of precipices and promise which accorded a national resonance to the spiritual quest. Western expansion was thus presented as an American adventure in the enterprise of self-sufficiency. While this "Yankee lad" is not directly identified in the poem as a hero of the marketplace —Henry Nash Smith (135) identified him as the first symbol of the Western yeoman in American literature—he is nonetheless one of the first heroes of marketplace expansion, for his virtues owe as much to the claims of economic mobility as they do to the ideals of settlement and subsistence farming.

These connections between adventure and enterprise are echoed fourteen years later in *Westward Ho!*, an anti-slavery novel about a Southern family settling in the Mississippi Valley. The book's moral stance derives from Paulding's dedication to "The free, daring, and adventurous life of the early settlers in this land of promise" (2:196):

> The result of their peculiar situation, habits, and modes of thinking has been a race of men uniting fearlessness of danger, a hardy spirit of enterprise, a power of supporting fatigues and privations, an independence of thought, which perhaps were never associated with the pursuits and acquirements of civilized life in any other country than the United States. (1:9)

Subscribing to the same logic which led Wister to describe *The Virginian* as a "colonial romance," Paulding sees in this "race of men" not only the new Westerners, but "our worthy ancestors" as well; in an essay written earlier, he had used almost the same language to refer to the first colonists:

> there is that in the peculiarities of their character; in the motives which produced the resolution to emigrate to the wilderness; in the courage and perseverance with which they consummated this gallant enterprise; and in the wild and terrible peculiarities of their intercourse, their adventures, and their contests with the savages, amply sufficient for all the purposes of those higher works of imagination which may be called Rational Fictions. (Ruland 134)

In these later works Paulding took the terms of the spiritual quest in *The Backwoodsman* and identified them explicitly with the American mission to expand into the West: "competence" and "Danger" became "enterprise" and "adventures," and "adventurous enterprise" became designated as the American national mission. This narrative formulation had become the most appropriate foundation for an American literature, a "Rational Fiction."

Another writer of Irving's acquaintance, the Reverend Timothy Flint, also traversed this same territory of adventurous enterprise. Like Paulding, Flint was immensely popular during this period, and for some time after. As late as the 1850s, as Bernard Rosenthal has pointed out (31), Harriet Beecher Stowe paid homage to his works in *Uncle Tom's Cabin,* mentioning them as part of a privileged array of writings that included the Bible, *Pilgrim's Progress,* and *Paradise Lost.* It was upon Paulding's suggestion, in fact, that Irving took a copy of Flint's *Recollections of the Last Ten Years* (1826) to read on his westward journey, a record of the Reverend's four-year travels through the Valley to plant the institutions of the church more firmly into the new soil. This book, along with Flint's popular *The History and Geography of the Mississippi Valley* (1832) and *Life and Adventures of Daniel Boone* (1833), and his edition of the fur trapper journal *The Personal Narrative of James O. Pattie* (1833), were later to become useful to Irving for the information they contained on the West. Paulding, too, claimed his indebtedness to *Recollections* in the foreword to *Westward Ho!,* noting its "most picturesque descriptions" (1:4).

Recollections was much like Paulding's books in form as well. Flint's observations consistently focused on the spiritual life the settlers were making in the West, and while he was often distressed by their aversion to "even the most necessary restraints"—one example he offers is that "they care little about ministers and think less about paying them" (vi) —he found in this "independence" "a coarse, but substantial morality" (vii) sound enough to stand as a foundation for the national spiritual expansion of which the settlers were forerunners. As Robert Berkhofer, Jr., noted in his introduction to a recent reprint of the book, Flint hoped his work would counter Timothy Dwight's recent attack on the settlers as unfit opportunists: "The business of these people," Dwight had written about early "pioneers," "is no other than to cut down trees, build log-houses, lay open forested grounds to cultivation, and prepare the way for those who come after them. These men cannot live in regular society. They are too idle, too profligate, and too shiftless to acquire either property or character" (*Recollections* v). In other words, these pioneers are villainous not because they are businessmen but because they are bad businessmen; their brand of business is bad for America. Flint disagreed, finding in their "hardy" expansionism a suitable foundation for solidifying, and even renovating, the nation's spiritual entitlements.

In one sense, though, the two men agreed: both saw acquisitiveness as the moving force behind the business of expansion. Were it corrupted, then the enterprise would be corrupted, but were it imbued with the properly acquisitive "spirit" of America, it would be the movement's salvation. As it was for Paulding, "property" and "character" alike were to be found, or lost, in the national adventure of the Western movement, and it was the writer's duty to point out the route that would draw the two together.

This mixture of spirit and economy can also be found in the works of another writer of Irving's acquaintance who visited the West, Charles Fenno Hoffman, a cousin of Irving's early employer Judge Josiah Hoffman and, like Flint, an editor of *The Knickerbocker*. A few months after Irving returned to New York from his tour, Hoffman left the city for his own trip, traveling through many of the same locations. His book about the experience, *A Winter in the West,* was published in the same year as Irving's *A Tour*; in fact, Irving read a copy of the book's sheets before his own was printed.[17]

While Hoffman was no less concerned than Paulding or Flint about the spiritual implications of Westward expansion, he conceived the strength of that spirit as residing less in character than in economic opportunity itself. His book is essentially a series of appraisals of Western resources in terms of their value for Eastern interests. For example, after noting the possibilities for canal construction in Michigan and the profitable commerce that would result, he added, "Did I not know how ignorant generally the people of the east are of the resources and conditions of this country, it would surprise me that the same New-York capitalists have not embarked in some of these works" (1:189). His book was designed to educate these businessmen—Dwight doubtless would have approved—and so he valued each settlement area as an "outlet for enterprise" in "want of capital" (2:61). Because Hoffman was more strictly an accountant of resources than a general observer, the settlers themselves were often absent from his remarks, as was any notice of the actual relation between labor and capital in these areas. Yet the book was not without at least one truly individuated portrayal of an enterprising individual: Hoffman himself, the hardy scout for business, the writer as financial planner, who conveyed his message to America despite the often severe traveling conditions and notwithstanding the support of only one leg (he had lost the other some years before). He called himself an "unambitious tourist" (1:1), but he might also have called himself a tourist of ambition. The adventure that had informed Paulding's and Flint's works, the "hardy spirit" of the settlers, was here the spirit of entrepreneurial vision, and the literary work a tool for its implementation.

Still another writer of the period who employed the adventure tales of Western expansion to identify the resources for economic opportunity was James Hall, whose reputation at the time has been neatly characterized by the subtitles of two twentieth-century biographies: "Literary Pioneer of the Ohio Valley" and "Spokesman of the New West." [18] Hall had become known in American literary circles through his part in the origination of the *Western Monthly Magazine*, [19] the first major literary periodical West of the Mississippi and a precursor of such devotedly regional journals as the *Southern Literary Messenger*. He also published many popular books on the West, such as *Letters from the West* (1828) and *Legends of the West* (1833). Along with Paulding and Flint, he was one of the most recognized popularizers of Western subjects, and along with Hoffman, one of the staunchest advocates of the wealth to be had in Western resources. He also claimed a legitimacy that none of the other writers could meet: he was a permanent resident of the West. His work, he would declare, was the national literature, the "rational fiction" for which Paulding had called.

Not surprisingly, one of the major differences between Hall's writings and those of the others was that his West was already established in its institutions, already settled, already within the boundaries of America. Still, like the America that all four men envisioned, it retained its "newness" and so continued to provide "*room* and *opportunity* for enterprise" (1828, 317). As Hall defined it, this enterprise contained both past and future, settlement and expansion. Early in *Letters from the West,* for example, the essential character os the West is represented in the "rapid rise" of Pittsburgh as a manufacturing town, an event that "may be adduced as a proud testimony of American enterprise" (34). Later in the book, Hall invoked this same enterprise, but now it had been transformed from an accomplished fact into a continually unfolding spirit of "slow and persevering industry" (317).

One consequence of this combination of accomplishment and desire, material and spirit, was an infusion of description with a call to action. Note that Pittsburgh contains its own rhetorical imperative as a testimony *of* American enterprise, and note the forces of the future implanted in the rigors of the settled West in the following Western landscape:

> from this land, so lately a wilderness, the savage has been expelled; towns and colleges have arisen; towns have been made; the mechanic arts cherished; the necessaries of life abound, and many of its luxuries are enjoyed. All this has been effected within the memory of living witnesses. Such are the fruits of civilization, and so powerful the effect of American enterprise! (165)

For Hall, then, the West was not only already part of America, the product of the enterprising spirit, but must still be cultivated by that spirit, the opportunities still pursued.

The effect of this approach on the work is a curious mixture of dramatic narrative and unembellished data, of "legend" and "fact," two terms that Hall saw as complementary, as he explained in the preface to his *Legends of the West,* a very popular work that began to appear in print the year of Irving's return to America: "The legends now presented to the public are entirely fictitious; but they are founded upon incidents which have been witnessed by the author during a long residence in the western states, or upon traditions preserved by the people, and have received but little artificial embellishment" (n. pag.). In order to draw the two sides together in *Letters from the West,* Hall organized his material by issue rather than by itinerary or geography, the more conventional formats of travel writing at the time. The overall impression, and perhaps Hall's intention all along, is a demonstration that the West was part of America, sharing characteristics with the rest of the nation. His chapter titles may seem to have no apparent relation to each other (he moves, for example, from "Names of Places" to "Shawnee Town and its Vicinity" to "National Character" to "Backwoodsmen—Daniel Boon—A Romantic Adventure"), but the adventures that he relates in his stories, and the economic opportunities he records in his descriptions, combine as expressions of the common traits of the nation and its people, traits exemplified in the West and Western expansion: "the same active, enterprising, and independent spirit; the same daring soul, and inventive genius; and that aptitude or capacity to take advantage of every change, and subsist and flourish in every soil and situation" (237).

In the end, Hall was both the only one of the four writers so far discussed who actually lived in the West, and also the least questioning of the "adventurous enterprise" of Western expansion. This uncritical perspective is not so surprising when one considers Hall's belief that any gap between the conditions as lived and as advertised was already eliminated in spirit by the presence of a progressive industrializing population. Since the West was already "settled" for Hall, then its potential lay in an insistent reiteration, not a critical foresight. It was just this assured insistence that led Melville to single him out as the spokesman of a West founded upon a genocidal expansionism. Focusing on Hall's nationalistic rationalization of a demented Indian killer in *Legends of the West,* Melville outlined "The Metaphysics of Indian Hating" in his *Confidence Man* by burlesquing the elegant disinterest of Hall's prose and prosaic pose for concealing a lacerating indifference to Indians. It was a criticism that could be leveled against any of the authors so far discussed, though Hall went the furthest in portraying Indians as impediments to the rightful claims of American economic expansion.

Paulding, Flint, Hoffman, and Hall were well aware of each other's works, often paying deference to the others in their own prefaces— Hoffman to Flint and Hall, Paulding to Flint—and Irving need not have been the close observer of the market that he was to be aware of their works as well. It would have been remarkable had Irving not considered writing on the West. In fact, this grouping of writers and works only partially suggests the saturation of the market with books on Western subjects.

To these writers with whom Irving was most directly related, there are still others to add before we can get a sense of the burgeoning marketplace in Western literature. Cooper's works, of course, must top that list. While both men had spent many years in Europe—Cooper returned to America after a seven year absence in 1833, the year following Irving's own return and subsequent Western tour—Cooper had continued to write books on American themes, cultivating a loyal American audience with three volumes of the Leatherstocking tales: *The Pioneers* (1823), *Last of the Mohicans* (1826), and *The Prairie* (1827). Irving, who had long appreciated Cooper's work, read *The Pioneers* just before his trip out West. He was no doubt aware that all three Leatherstocking books had become best-sellers in the United States, and was perhaps eager to discover why Cooper had gained such popularity during a period in which his own sales had slightly declined.[20]

While *The Pioneers* was not set in the West, its evocation of the frontier experience employed many of the same narrative tensions and underlying principles found in the writings of Irving's more intimate associates. The story's primary issue—the extension of private property and its accompanying laws and values into the unsettled wilderness—finds its dramatic resolution in the nostalgic deaths of three major characters from the "older" generation: Natty Bumppo, a half-savage frontiersman whose principal task in the book has been to protect an old landowner until he and his son, a sometime hunting companion of Bumppo's, can reassert their supposedly lost claim; Major Edward Effingham, the old landowner whose claim is finally found intact and then perpetuated in his son's good fortune and fortunate marriage to another landowner's daughter; and Indian John, better known as Chingachgook, an old Mohican chief whose own dismissed claim to the land has left him broken and in despair. Like Irving's use of nostalgia in his dinner speech and the introduction to *A Tour,* and like Hall's similar transformation of the past and present into the future in *Letters from the West,* Cooper uses these deaths to point the way to the inevitable, and necessary, expansion of economic interests into the West. Perhaps most telling is that this final entry in the Leatherstocking saga was also the first to be written. For Cooper, as for Hall, the settlement of the West was already a given. The nobility of natural man might be sacrificed in the process, and the ignobility of profit-seeking man might emerge in its place, but the adventure of that enterprise was finally a noble one in itself, bringing with it a new marriage of property and wilderness, "property and character."

To Cooper's works, one must then add the popular explorer reports, such as Pike's and Lewis and Clark's; the trapper journals such as James O. Pattie's *Personal Narrative* (1833), the Reverend Samuel Parker's *Journal of an Exploring Tour Beyond the Rocky Mountains* (1838), Zenas Leonard's *Narrative of the Adventures of Zenas Leonard* (1839); the autobiographies and biographies, such as those of Daniel Boone and Davy Crockett, including Filson's "The Adventures of Daniel Boon," the appendix to *The Discovery, Settlement and Present State of Kentucke*

(1784), and *A Narrative of the Life of David Crockett of the State of Tennessee* (1834); the travel narratives, such as Dana's *Two Years Before the Mast* (1840) and Josiah Gregg's *Commerce of the Prairies* (1844); the Indian romances, such as Charles Brockden Brown's *Edgar Huntly* (1799); and the almanacs, such as the popular Davy Crockett series. Far from being the mysterious "unstoried" land, the West was already "written," published and on the market. Even as early as the first Astoria expedition in 1811, Western travellers were "in the habit of taking notes and keeping journals," as Irving noted in *Astoria* (36). By 1826 Timothy Flint felt it necessary to justify his own entry into an already crowded marketplace of Western literature by opening his *Recollections* with a protest against the "showers of journals, and travels, and residences, and geographies, and gazetteers; and every person, who can in any way fasten the members of a sentence together, after having travelled through a country, is so sure to begin to scribble about it" (3).

Thus recorded, the Western journey became a narrative construct, prescribed as well as described in diaries, letters, newspaper accounts, guidebooks, as if journey and journal were inseparable. And the subject of that accounting, like the motivations of the travelers and writers themselves, was often the "business" of expansion. Indeed, with the emergence of a literary marketplace, these records themselves had become products that could be sold for profit. Even in those cases where the impulse of both writer and reader was to "escape" from the crippling atmosphere of business in the cities, the literary act of expansion was usually designed to resurrect that business in the wilderness, to determine and convey where and how to find that adventurous enterprise. As Frank Bergon has described it, "What brought many of the early pioneers West was not a dream of adapting to the land and creating a new, distinct society of equals, but rather the desire to transfer to the West society as they had known it in the East, with one difference: they would be at the top of the heap" (1978, 7). That desire shaped the way they imagined and wrote about their Western experiences. Hence it comes as no surprise when Turner, in an 1896 speech, described his mythic West as not only a place but a narrative, and a narrative that was itself an economic resource: "a bank account on which [Americans] might continually draw to meet losses" (Smith 254). The "*untransacted* destiny of the American people is to subdue the continent," proclaimed William Gilpin to the United States Senate in 1846 (130); but in the literature of the Western expansion, that untransacted destiny had long been fulfilled.

The uniquely American terms of this form of adventuring—the interweaving of mobility and hierarchy, the return to origins, the particular role of the boundary, and the particular boundaries of class, character, landscape, and language—become especially evident when one compares these American works with the European writings about Western expansion that were written during the same period. Like their antecedents, these European books continued to associate the sacred with the secular, the religious with the national and economic. And like the American works, they focused on the presence and potential of industry, and the industrious spirit, in the West. The image of America that had evolved in Europe since the colonial period had always included economic opportunity, a promise of success all the more resonant for its marked contrast to the increasingly abject conditions of the working classes in Europe. While not all of the books and pamphlets that began to appear in the 1820s were positive about the effects of these economic enticements, they all accepted the premise that the opportunities did indeed exist.[21]

The image was presented most positively in guidebooks. Many of the authors of these books, and the entrepreneurs who helped publish them, were connected to businesses, often American, that would benefit from emigration, such as land companies and, later in the century, railroads, and it was the agents for these businesses that distributed the books to an eager readership throughout Europe. Some of these businesses were legitimate, some not, but all profited from the anxious emigrants who paid large amounts of money in advance for travel expenses and a land allotment that would "inevitably" grow in time from a satisfactory subsistence farmship into a profitable large-scale business. In essence, it was not so different a hope than that shared by the Americans, as we see in Paulding's "true Yankee lad" and Irving's representative Yankee, Ichabod Crane, in "The Legend of Sleepy Hollow." This increase in productivity, the worker was informed, would result from the rapid settlement and development of the West of which his own emigration would be an integral part. The journey was depicted as safe, the land fertile, and the possibilities for advancement guaranteed, claims that were certified as authentic by authors who had seen the conditions "firsthand."[22]

Other firsthand accounts were not so positive, however. Like many American writers, such as Paulding in *Westward Ho!,* a large number of European visitors to the American West disapproved of the values that the image of unlimited opportunity engendered in both Americans and Europeans. They never claimed that the image was false, but perceived it as a temptation to selfishness and a potential threat to social order. American Westerners, they charged, were money-mad opportunists interested only in their own enrichment; as Harriet Martineau put it in 1837, they are the "busy and the sordid": the "Busy colonists. . .who come for other purposes than to meditate," and "those who would make haste to be rich; selfish adventurers who drive out the red man, and drive in the black man, and, amidst the forests and the floods, think only of cotton and of gold" (1:212–213). Another visitor, Francis Grund, stated the matter more broadly:

> Business is the very soul of an American; he pursues it, not as a means of procuring for himself and his family the necessary comforts of life, but as the fountain of all human felicity; and shows as much enthusiastic ardour in his appreciation to it as any crusader ever evinced for the conquest of the Holy Land, or the followers of Mohammed for the spreading of the Koran. (2:1–2)

For both writers, that selfishness was inseparable from the "adventure" of Western expansion, and was made all the more alluring by that adventure. It was precisely that allure they feared, for no less than the same exaggerated self-interest could be expected from the Europeans reading of such available opportunities. The appeal of free-market mobility would lead these readers, generally identified as the envious members of the lower classes, to become dissatisfied with the inflexible class divisions upon which the "stability" of their own societies depended; and the promise of personal profit would lead them to emigrate, thus depleting the work force necessary for these societies' survival.

Based upon what has been called the "safety-valve" theory, this latter criticism was first voiced as a comment upon American-European relations in 1755 (by Benjamin Franklin), gained much momentum throughout the next century, and was given the stature of "professional" historiography in 1893 by Frederick Jackson Turner, who himself traced it back in turn to a 1634 speech by John Winthrop and so to a rhetorical tradition of American expansionism. In fact, Turner's later reference to the West as a "bank account" was precisely a description of what he called the "safety valve for social danger." This notion, then, was not confined to the Europeans—James Hall, for instance, described the West as "the refuge of thousands, who have fled from poverty, from tyranny, and from fanaticism" (1828, 9). But while American writers used it to characterize the positive or negative effects of regionalism on America's national development, European writers used it to distinguish their own societies from the negative provincial enticements of the American "experiment." Frances Trollope, the mother of Anthony Trollope the novelist, voiced just this tactic in her acerbic *Domestic Manners of the Americans* (1832), announcing in her preface that her "chief object. . .is to encourage her countrymen to hold fast by a constitution that ensures all the blessings which flow from established habits and solid principles" (lxxvii-lxxviii).

But as with many other critics of American expansion during the nineteenth century, her strategy was in fact motivated by the very temptations the critique was decrying. Trollope was an opportunist herself who had met with great disappointment when she failed in her attempts, in 1827, to profit by the construction of a department store in Cincinnati, and by a venture into a Western museum.[23] Irving was well aware of such motivations, and had described them at length in his essay "English Writers on America" in *The Sketch Book*. Those writers most critical of America were likely "disappointed in some unreasonable expectation of sudden gain":

> They may have pictured America to themselves, an El Dorado, where gold and silver abounded and the natives were lacking in sagacity; and where they were to become strangely and suddenly rich, in some unforeseen, but easy manner. The same weakness of mind that indulges absurd expectations, produces petulance in disappointment. Such persons become embittered against the country on finding that there, as every where else, a man must sow before he can reap; must win wealth by industry and talent; and must contend with the common difficulties of nature, and the shrewdness of an intelligent and enterprizing people. (44)

That Irving, who had met Trollope in England in 1823 and had read her book in 1832 on his journey toward the Western territories, would have recognized the profound disappointment underlying her cynicism is more than likely, since he himself had briefly ventured into unsuccessful land speculations in the West with high hopes for a quick fortune.[24] Both positive and negative images, then, from both European and American works, arose from this same assumption, that the American West was a land of adventurous opportunity promising danger and success to the brave and industrious settler.

The America revealed by these tales was a country of adventurous enterprise, a marketplace of the imagination compelled to expand its boundaries and conquer all that was brought within its purview. Western American literature had become a part of the marketplace of Western expansion, and its adventure form had become the vehicle for the discovery, exploration, and cultivation of the American enterprise. Yet in this act of expansion was a setting of familiar boundaries. Whether these were adventures encouraging mobility or fixed hierarchy, individual self-interest or the common good, they were the adventures of the marketplace in the enterprise of American expansion. When Irving returned to America, then, he found not only a new America but a new calling as well. He would enter that marketplace himself in search of the American tale of adventurous enterprise.

2

Irving, the West, and the Work of the Imagination

"Irving on the prairies! . . . The very idea has a novelty about it" (Hall 1835, 332). James Hall's skeptical review of Washington Irving's *A Tour on the Prairies* was an apt response to an image Irving himself had cultivated in his early works as Geoffrey Crayon, Gent. It was difficult to imagine this middle-aged gentleman of ruffled sleeves and exquisite temperament deep in Indian territory cutting out the tongue of a buffalo he had just killed; and just as difficult to picture this sensitive sketcher of scenery, pre-romantic purveyor of the romance, writing a history of the American fur trade. But Irving did travel through and hunt in the West, and he did write about the American business that operated there.

Such facts would indeed seem odd were one to proceed from the assumption that it was the gentle appreciator Geoffrey Crayon and not the rapacious historian Diedrich Knickerbocker who went West, that there was no connection between this Geoffrey Crayon and the Washington Irving who made his living by such literary creations as both Crayon and Knickerbocker, or between Irving's activities as a writer and the prevailing Jacksonian sensibility by which the nation was beginning to move Westward with the violence of absolute certainty. By focusing instead on such connections, between the civilized man and the Indian adventurer, the self-styled aristocrat and the bourgeois capitalist, the man of letters and the professional writer, one sees an Irving emerge whose presence in the West was no novelty at all: an American writer in a Jacksonian America. From his Western experiences and his Western books, we can learn more about Irving, more about the role of the writer in Jacksonian America, and more about the role of literature in the economic expansion of that America into the West. Of particular significance are the conditions surrounding his literary career at the time of the tour: his attitudes toward the emerging market in Western writings and the professionalization of American literature in general. From these concerns, he shaped his own version of adventurous enterprise, a version that came to define much of the literature of Western expansion throughout the nineteenth century.

Irving and the West

When Irving returned to America in May 1832, he was celebrated and prosperous. The international success of *The Sketch Book* had firmly established his renown as an author, and as he was the first American to achieve such stature in Europe, his career was a focus of special attention. Yet Irving was insecure about his reputations as both a writer and an American. His most recently published books—*The Life and Voyages of Christopher Columbus* (1828), *A Chronicle of the Conquest of Granada* (1829), and *Voyages and Discoveries of the Companions of Columbus* (1831)—sold fairly well but were not met with the ecstatic popular or critical praise of his earlier successes. And if his identity as a writer was in doubt, so, inevitably, was his identity as an American writer. It was a critical commonplace of emerging nationalism that literary skill depended upon and reflected the resources of the nation; and in the case of the literature of an emerging America, the commonplace was exercised with particular zeal, by Europeans and Americans alike. Because *The Sketch Book* was published while Irving lived in

Europe, and his literary persona and reputation developed during this period, this popular American writer found his works considered largely as evidence in debates of national resources and affiliations. European critics often located Irving's successes in his acculturation to European society, and American critics, while eager to claim this same success as an outgrowth of native talent, as frequently attributed his lesser work to a waning of his native identity.

In a speech on the night of his return to New York, Irving took up the debate from the diplomatic position of an apologist denying he had done anything wrong. He focused less on the reasons for his long absence than on the feelings evoked by his return, thus indicating the program of identification by which he would ingratiate himself with his American readers. "I had been led at times," he began, "to doubt my standing in the affections of my countrymen. Rumors and suggestions had reached me that absence had impaired their kind feelings; that they considered me alienated in heart from my country. Gentlemen, I was too proud to vindicate myself from such a charge." Upon his return to his "native place," his pride would allow him only to attest to the strength of his previous attachments, to "the friends of my youth. . .[and] others, whom though personally new to me, I recognize as the sons of the patriarchs of my native city" (*MW*2:59–60).

Yet the past was hardly where Irving hoped to situate himself in the minds of his listeners; his nostalgic perspective was only the first step in his gradual reintegration into the present moment. He needed to tie the past to the present, to reshape it to fit the rhetorical formulations of current political conviction. And so, though now fifty years old, he spoke of experiencing his return with the anticipation and anxiety of a prodigal son returning to the fold, thus turning nostalgia into rebirth, personal loss into national gain.

This stance of a bereft and fearful child was a common one for Irving, and deeply felt, as any cursory reading of his works reveals. But when he claims these sentiments once again in his dinner speech, he is also using them deftly as a plea for national recognition. His nostalgia for the "scenes of his youth," which recasts his subsequent alienation as a period of longing for an earlier America, also allows him to recover his sense of childhood and so his attachment to a later America; and his sense of troubled exile allows him to identify with an America still uneasy with its new-found independence. Certainly his listeners at the dinner would have understood the comments as such, for the image of the return to childhood had long been part of the American rhetoric of progressive idealism.

Not surprisingly he would employ this stance a few years later in his introduction to *A Tour on the Prairies,* the book by which he hoped to be reborn as a best-selling American writer. He begins that introduction with a quotation from *The Sketch Book,* once again cultivating the reader's sense of nostalgia: Geoffrey Crayon watches "the last blue line of my native land fade away" upon his leaving for Europe, and ends with his fear "whether it may ever be [my] lot to revisit the scenes of [my] childhood" (3). A few pages later, he transforms this nostalgia into promise by charging its anxiety of loss with a hope of renewal: "Was [I] to be taken as a favored child. . .or repulsed as a stranger, and a changeling?" (6).[1]

With such sympathies identified to his dinner hosts, this "child" of the new age then directly asserts his connections to the "progress" he finds upon his return, and he does so in economic terms. He notes the "changes of rapid improvement and growing prosperity," the "vast commercial emporium" (*MW*2:60) that New York had become. He tells of only one reservation, but it is registered less as a doubt about this commercialism than as a reaffirmation of his intention to reinstate himself in this new society: "but my admiration was cold and ineffectual, for I was a stranger and had no property in the soil" (60). By calling upon the principal assumption behind the American "pursuit of happiness," that owning American property is what "makes" an American, Irving left no doubt as to his intentions to transform himself into that very property. "Is this not a land in which one may be happy to fix his destiny," he asked, "and ambitious, if possible, to found a name?" (60). Before that time came, however, he could only reassert his "birthright in the brilliant scene before me" by calling, ironically, on lines by his European colleague and friend, Walter Scott: "This was my own—my native land!" (60). And so Irving leaves his European writing career in the past tense, and so he presents his native identity, now embodied in his identity as a writer, as a property yet to be acquired, an economic endeavor allied to the progress, the narrative, of his age.

But Irving was at a loss where to begin. His most recent book, *The Alhambra,* was soon to be published in England, but its exotic subject would hardly satisfy those critics who questioned the strength of his national allegiance. With no new projects in mind, he decided to travel, an activity to which he had always been drawn at moments of personal stress and creative sterility. In his present situation, it offered a particularly appropriate solution. While thus becoming reacquainted with his "native land," Irving could discover not only new but American material for a book. He had no firm itinerary but chose to set himself a path broad enough for a subject perhaps to find him. First he visited friends in Washington D.C., reintroducing himself to native "society" and explicitly identifying himself with the new powers; while there, at another dinner in his honor, "He came out a Jackson man," a guest observed, "and his encomiums on the character of the President were exceeded in warmth and enthusiasm only by those of Swartout the Collector, who is always warm and enthusiastic on that subject" (Hone 1:63).[2] Then he began his education, his growth into this new America, by traveling through locations familiar from his childhood, upstate New York and New Hampshire; echoing his New York dinner address, he wrote of experiencing "the renovated feelings of a schoolboy" (L2:716). This boyhood, however, was to be brief, as he was soon heading across Lake Erie on one of the country's new steamboats, learning just how far and fast he had to travel to keep up with the times.

During this voyage, the possibility of visiting the West first appeared to Irving in the form of an invitation from one of the other passengers. Henry L. Ellsworth, an influential man in Connecticut society, had recently been appointed by the Jackson Administration as a commissioner of the newly formed Board of Indian Affairs, for which his first assignment was to report on the progress of the "Indian Removal" plan in the Oklahoma territory. Responding to Irving's interest in the trip, he invited the writer, and his two current traveling companions, an English tutor and the young man in his charge, to accompany him. Irving quickly accepted. It seemed the ideal journey with which to reacquaint himself with the American landscape, and the ideal location in which to gather the "native" American materials for his literary reintroduction to his American readers.

Irving had long felt the necessity of writing an American book. In a letter written in 1829 he noted: "I feel the importance. . .and I may say the duty, of <writing> producing some writings relating to our own country which would be of a decidedly national character. It. . .would be at the same time very gratifying to my feelings and advantageous to my literary character at home" (L2:412). Writing is his business, in other words, and "producing" an American work (rather than simply "writing" as he had originally written) would be advantageous for that business. He had made one unsuccessful attempt, while in Europe, to write a book on "American themes," but now, in the West, where America saw itself as being reborn, Irving could labor to issue himself as an active participant in that process.

This interest in the West as an economic resource was not new to Irving, nor was he unfamiliar with the "wilderness" experience. When he was twenty, he took a journey through the undeveloped Hudson Valley and into Canada with Judge Josiah Hoffman, his employer, who wanted to examine his property and fur trade interests; Irving went along, at least in part, to scout the business opportunities for his family. According to Henry Adams, this region was at the time a "frontier" area: "New York was still a frontier state; and although the city was European in its age and habits, travelers needed to go few miles from the Hudson to find a wilderness like that of Ohio and Tennessee" (Myers 1972, 3). Irving's experiences along the way attest not only to the accuracy of Adams' assessment, but to the potency of this conception of the land as a "frontier," a borderland of beckoning promise and promising danger.

His journal entries, along with accounts by some of the other travelers, construct the adventures of such a frontier excursion as a crossing of the boundaries separating the commercial and the "cultural," the interests of individual mobility and class hierarchy. The close connections between these two sides are most evident in the two personae that are gradually distilled on the trip, two personal inclinations that would later develop into the writer's two most pronounced alter egos, Knickerbocker and Crayon. On the one hand, we see an aggressive Irving who would certainly have surprised James Hall: a hunter in an uncultivated landscape, a Jacksonian hostile towards constraint. At one point in the journal, for instance, he wrote of the abandon with which he dove into the Hudson after a wounded deer to *"get in at the death"* (J1:15). And in another incident, which he chose not to report, the writer, after flirting with an Indian squaw, was knocked down by her Indian husband, who, in exasperation and under restraint, called the stunned Irving a "damned Yankee" (Pierre Irving 1:57).

At the same time, we also see the conventional Irving, the gentle and privileged appraiser of a composed nature, a Federalist disdainful of the "common rabble" the travelers meet along the way. He mentions being particularly offended by two men named Sharp with whom they were forced to share a hut furnished in the "rudest style." One of the two men, whom he notes was "the most impudent chattering forward scoundrel I ever came across," makes the major blow at decorum by entering the hut with his foot bleeding from an axe wound, thus leading one of the women to faint "almost immediately." "I now gave up all hopes of getting along We were here in a wilderness. . .among a set of men rough and some of them insolent (the Sharps) with ladies of delicate minds and constitutions sinking under fatigue and apprehension" (J1:21–22). Finally the Sharps begin "to play cards for liquor," driving one of the women to tears and the others to despair, and Irving places himself in between the men and the women. Thus he identifies himself as not only the protector of the women but also the arbiter of the boundaries of decorum itself, separating the rude wilderness from the civilized tourists.

While this genteel Irving may seem to stand in opposition to his more aggressive counterpart, both sides of his proprietorship during the tour share the premise that the landscape is a product to be possessed—by force or force of sensibility. This stance was also revealed in his exposure to the business of the region. During these initiations into the more exacting demands of wilderness life, Irving also became acquainted with the presence of the fur trade in the wilderness. In Canada, he wrote later, he "had seen much of the Magnates of the North West Company, and of the hardy trappers and fur-traders in their employ, and had been excited by their stories of adventurous expeditions in the 'Indian Country'" (L4:273). If these tales provided Irving with his first glimpse of the interpenetration of the Western experience and economic expansion, they also provided him with examples of how that experience might be of the most profit to him. The very principle of marketable resources that had led the fur trade to the West Coast would, twenty years later, lead Irving into the Oklahoma territory, and into the business of producing Western books. "I was sure," he later wrote of his decision to take on the *Astoria* project, "that a narrative, treating of [the trappers] and their doings, could not fail to be of stirring interest, and to lay open regions and races of our country as yet but little known" (L4:273). Like the explorers and settlers he was to describe in *A Tour,* like the trappers and businessmen he was to describe in *Astoria* and *The Adventures of Cap-*

tain Bonneville, like so many people in the nation who endorsed the Western movement as the destiny of an economically mobile chosen people, Irving brought the enthusiasm of economic endeavor to his own chosen craft, his writing.

Irving had remained interested in the wilderness throughout his European sojourn, during which time that wilderness had become specifically identified with the Western territories, the "Indian Country." Several times he requested that books on Indians and frontier life be sent to him from America, apparently already contemplating writing on the subject. The strength of this interest can best be explained by his attraction to particular literary properties in the West, such as the mutability of the landscape and its indigenous populations. Writing of his decision to travel with Ellsworth, he noted that

> The offer was too tempting to be resisted: I should have the opportunity of seeing the remnants of those great Indian tribes, which are now about to disappear as independent nations, or to be amalgamated under some new form of government. I should see those fine countries of the "far west," while still in a state of pristine wildness, and behold herds of buffaloes scouring their native prairies, before they are driven beyond the reach of a civilized tourist. (*L*2:733–734)

One might expect that this mournful view of progress as reminder of a cherished past—Irving's most customary theme—would place his vision of the West in opposition to the progressive expansion then occupying Americans. Indeed, it was that very "progress," the prescriptions of that narrative movement, that was largely responsible for the imminent "disappearance" of that "pristine" West. Such is the implication of Perry Miller's remark that Irving, especially in *The Sketch Book,* was "only" a nostalgic writer providing American readers with "a welcome interlude from the strenuousness of prosperity, after the reading of which they could return, with refreshed enthusiasm, to the making of more money" (1961, 378). Yet for Irving, and for a large number of Jacksonian Americans, that nostalgia was neither escapist nor regressive. He was less concerned in this case with the threat to the West than to the "civilized tourist." In that figure's defense he would become the tourist as pathfinder, preserving the lands and cultures that were destined to be lost by transforming them into resources, both moral and economic, for those destined to take their place. Far from the "mere spectator of other men's fortunes and adventures" whom

Irving declared himself to be (in his persona as Geoffrey Crayon) in the epigraph to *The Sketch Book,* he would become a participant in that "enthusiasm" of Western expansion. As he made clear at the welcoming dinner in New York, he could thus bend his customary nostalgia to the notion of economic progress, imbuing that progress with the rationale of inevitability.

One motivation for Irving's identification with the prevailing rhetorical stance of his time was that he was well aware of the suitable currency of such a project on Western "themes." He had read many of those Western works written by such friends and acquaintances as Paulding, Flint, and Hoffman; and, as his working notes for the Western volumes indicate, he was also well read in everything from the writings of Lewis and Clark and Cooper to the European volumes that had been published during his European sojourn. He was also prepared to make use of his considerable business acuity to enter that marketplace. In this sense, he would become a Western pioneer himself. James Hall celebrated Timothy Flint in just these terms: as the "chief pioneer of this useful art [of bookmaking] in the west, and. . .the very Daniel Boon of our bookmakers" (1833, 264). Hall's conflation of Western pioneer and Eastern writer, and his substitution of "book-maker" for "writer" (like Irving's substitution of "producing" for "writing" in his letter of 1829), were national inclinations, and Irving intended to incline himself in that direction.

The circumstances surrounding the tour itself are worth noting as they highlight this conjunction of economic expansion and literary expression. In 1830, Jefferson's plan for the removal of Indians from the East into Western reservations was passed into law under Jackson, who had become famous for his own Indian removal policy in Florida, a policy that was to lead to the Seminole Wars which began a few years later. All Indians east of the Mississippi River were to be relocated to the west. Some of the more disruptive consequences of the law were soon evident, when tribes refused to be moved or when the new arrangements violated earlier claims. After two years, in July 1832, Congress established a Commission of Indian Affairs to monitor and regulate the progress of the policy under the jurisdiction of the Secretary of War, Lewis Cass, a military man who was also a previous governor of the Michigan territory and a published author of writings on the "Indian question."[3]

Among the first three commissioners Cass appointed was Henry

Ellsworth, and the tour on which Irving was to accompany him was the first action of the commission. Ellsworth was to meet the two other appointees at Fort Osage in the Oklahoma territory and travel through the area monitoring Indian location and strength for the military, and diminishing hostilities, whenever possible, between tribes. At the close of the "tour"—significantly a word that could indicate both a civilian and military exercise—Ellsworth was to report his observations to Cass. What Irving described as a "civilized tour," then, was really an instrument of the War Department in service of Indian removal, a function which was in turn tied to the expansion of the marketplace into the West.

In *A Tour*, Irving invokes this hidden purpose in his general use of the word "excursion" to describe the journey. Like the word "tour," it has both military and civilian meanings. On the one hand, it means "an issuing forth against an enemy"; on the other, "a ramble from one's home" (*OED*). In both cases it involves a crossing of boundaries. The intention of that crossing, however, is not to defy the boundaries but rather to reestablish them: an excursion always ends with the return home; or, as the *American Heritage Dictionary* defines it, "A short journey made with the intention of returning to the starting point." Once again, then, we see the affiliation of the civilized tour with expansion, in this case with a narrative form of expansion, the movement of a civilized party into dangerous Indian territory, with the implicit military purpose of reconnoitering that territory as a pathway for later settlement, for the "return home."

In the end, the true focus of concern of this "Indian" commission, and of Indian removal in general, was finally not Indians at all. From the first the object was the acquisition of land, an object more directly revealed in 1849 when the commission was shifted to the jurisdiction of the newly formed Department of the Interior, entrusted to regulate the sale of federal lands. And it was, of course, this acquisition upon which the expansion of the marketplace into the West depended.

This policy was represented not only by the commission but by the commissioner. Ellsworth was, in Paul Wallace Gates' words, one of the nation's "great nineteenth-century prairie landlord[s]" (118). He owned enormous tracts of land in Indiana and Illinois—by 1838, a few years after the tour, his holdings amounted to over 220,000 acres—on which he established large scale farming units. Sometimes he ran the units himself, but most often he acted as an agent for other Eastern investors. In either case, the farms were essentially investments; the profit came from rentals to settlers for small sections of the land and the equipment to work them. This tenancy relationship proved very profitable indeed for the absentee owners.

One of Ellsworth's primary activities was promoting the land to both the entrepreneurs and the farmers. He wrote advertising pamphlets, similar to those popular in Europe, in which he outlined the range of concerns that were, in his mind, essential to the task of Western business expansion; in one such work, for instance, entitled "Valley of the Upper Wabash," he advised landlords to "employ smart, enterprising young men" (Gates 241). These pamphlets, in conjunction with his other promotional activities, were influential enough to make Ellsworth, the businessman as author and author as advertiser, "the principal protagonist of, and leader in, the movement to bring settlers to the prairies" (Gates 172). This authorial opportunist was certainly prepared for his "literary" responsibilities as commissioner.

There are many connections to be made between his efforts as an author of promotional material for Western land sales and of military reports for Indian removal. Both represented the activities of acquisitive interests, both surveyed the landscape in the name of enterprise and expansion, and both embodied the observations in an implicit narrative of risk and adventure. Just as the military's role in protecting the economic interests of the investors and settlers was disguised as a policy of concerned assistance for the Indians, so Ellsworth's role as a recorder and scout for those interests was disguised as patriarchal concern for, and curiosity about, the Indians. One finds his intentions revealed in a journal of the tour he kept for his own uses, an extensive record amounting to 116 pages which he later transcribed as a lengthy letter to his wife. While he never intended this letter to be used for publication or promotion, it exhibited the same fundamental acquisitive vision of the West as the other literary forms.[4] The West had become fodder for the curiosity of the encroaching "tourist," the speculator as spectator. In all these forms, the literature of expansion was a participant in the expansion of the nation's marketplace.

Ellsworth was not the only other author besides Irving on the tour, nor were military reports, promotional pamphlets and private correspondence the only ways these Western "properties" were exploited by the literature. The two European gentlemen with whom Irving had been traveling at the time of his meeting with Ellsworth took advantage of the West, as Irving did, as a resource for later publication. Charles Latrobe, a thirty-one-year-old Englishman, was already an accomplished traveler and travel writer. He had been made a member of the Alpine Club for his many unguided mountain-climbing expeditions, had made a walking tour of the Tyrol, and had written about both experiences in *The Alpenstock* (1829) and *The Pedestrian; A Summer Ramble in the Tyrol* (1832). During this trip to America he was gathering material for a new travel book. The result was *The Rambler in North America,* published in London in 1835, the same year as Irving's *A Tour*; in fact, Irving rushed his book into print for fear that Latrobe's version would come out first and diminish the marketability of his own projected volume.[5]

Latrobe's literary industriousness was not lost on the other member of the tour, Count Alexandre de Pourtalès, a nineteen-year-old Swiss aristocrat and Latrobe's tutee. Pourtalès' voyage to America was something of a reverse of the traditional young man's visit to the continent in search of culture and antiquity. He wanted to see the new world, not the old, and to have adventures, not acquire an education; his intention, according to Ellsworth, a somewhat prudish observer, was "to sow his wild oats in a foreign country" (Ellsworth 68). An avid reader habitually drawn to romantic literature, he decided to follow his tutor's example and keep a journal to supplement the many letters he wrote to his mother detailing the journey.[6] Those details mostly consisted of his "exploits," for, in Pourtalès' imagination, the tour's primary function was as a forum for his own adventuring, and any geographical or anthropological discoveries made along the way were merely fortuitous benefits.

Among this list of author-tourists one must finally include Irving, the writer who produced the most successful work from the tour. Like the other three, he hoped to mine the tour for benefit to his career; like Latrobe and Pourtalès, he searched for adventures to record, and like Ellsworth, for a profitable way of articulating a profit-seeking national expansion. All four were engaged by the economic interests that were driving that expansion forward, and connected, in their works, the adventures of economic and national expansion. The West they described was a testing-ground for the adventurous and enterprising American character.

So here was a touring party originated by a military man who was also a published author (Cass), designed for the gathering of material for reports by an commissioner of Indian Affairs and landowner who was also a published author (Ellsworth), and further constituted by two other published authors (Irving and Latrobe), and a young man whose entry to this fraternity of authorship was accomplished within the course of the tour itself. Their literary interests combined Indian removal, national expansion, and wilderness exploration into a scheme of adventure and enterprise. Taken together, their writings suggest the extent to which, and forms by which, literature was to take part in Western expansion. As anthropological and geographical record, as promotional advertisement, as military monitor, as propaganda, as private correspondence, as historical accolade, as property in its own right, their literature claimed the territory in the names of adventure, business, manifest destiny and civilized tourism, and made that claim through the form of the tale of the enterprising adventurer in the land of promise. In keeping with the typological vision of American expansionism expressed by Turner, here was an actual journey into the center of the American continent that was also a literary journey into the heart of America, a crossing of boundaries that was also a setting of boundaries.

When Latrobe described his charge's literary habits as "forming opinions from observations" (Pourtalès 4), he was offering a revealing model from his experience as a tutor, for that "forming" was the impulse of expansion under ideological tutelage. These travelers were not only witnessing and recording expansion from the perspective of civilized writers. They were also writing the script for that expanding civilization to follow, and their authorship was part of their authority as civilized men. This authority, finally, resided not so much in their talents as observers of Western conditions—though the writings they produced were, and indeed remain, valuable for the information they offer—but in their ability to convey through those observations the values motivating Western economic expansion. They were particularly attuned to these values since they were the same values motivating and governing their literary productions in the first place. In his own contribution, *A Tour,* Irving explored this relation between economic expansion, literary authorship and cultural authority by which the nation defined the prerogatives of its Western venture.

It was only appropriate that Independence, Missouri, was the point of departure for the last leg of the party's journey before the tour. For Americans this town was already well-known as a signpost of Western expansion. The first white man to site the location was Daniel Boone, who was deep on his Westward march in search of profitable property. By Irving's time it was "the starting place for all kinds of adventurers," to use the words of Irving's nephew, John Treat Irving,[7] who later also traveled in the Oklahoma Territory with Ellsworth. Its name alone brought with it the apt rhetorical resonance with which to begin an adventure so tied to America's economic expansion into the West. In a sense, the tour became—as all adventures became in the contemporary rhetoric of the American "enterprise"—a re-commencement of America, in which the "tourists" acted the parts of "adventurers" in that enterprise, and their writings identified the narrative form appropriate to the economic values behind it.

This narrative form emerged, then, at precisely that cultural moment when business became an inseparable component of the literary imagination, and when Western economic expansion was beginning to take on the impetus of a national prerogative. In Irving's responses to this conjunction of events, both personal and professional, we find clues as to how the work of the imagination was to be defined for the remainder of the century.

The Work of the Imagination and the Imagination of Work

In the introduction to *A Tour on the Prairies,* Irving followed the persuasive strategy of his welcome home speech and placed what he called his "foray through the Pawnee hunting grounds" in two related contexts: his own reemerging nationalism as an upwardly (and westwardly) mobile American writer, and the nation's emerging commercialism. His first intention was to appear a loyal American, motivated by the same devotion to nation and profit. So he noted that he will use his literary efforts to earn both financial independence and his way into public favor. But he was also suggesting a closer connection between literature and business. If his financial success will depend upon his writing, his success as a writer will depend upon the world of business. American literature and American economic expansion were fast becoming inseparable.

But if Irving seemed generally pleased by the prospect of literature becoming a business, he was uneasy about the consequences of that merger. His own experience in the business world, and his fragile temperament, had made him wary of its enticements. Every effort at financial independence seemed to lead to failure and despair. Much of his concern was the expression of personal fears and desires, but his disastrous introduction to business while in Europe, and to the commercial America he found upon his return, confirmed his sense that these problems were cultural as well. Turning the national literature into a business was as dangerous as it was necessary, and required as stable and secure a financial world as it did an artistic intelligence and educated readership. As the introduction to *A Tour* suggests, Irving will design his Western tour as an examination of this conjunction of imagination and vocation; and by extension, of the nation's own adventurous enterprise toward financial independence, the exploration and settlement of the West.

Financial independence had always been an obsessive goal of Irving's, and one of his greatest fears. Until well into his thirties, he had remained dependent upon his family, particularly his brothers, for money and work, a position he found simultaneously appealing and repellent. His brothers were aware of his divided feelings, and it was, in fact, by their suggestion that he found himself traveling to Europe in 1815, ostensibly to decide upon an occupation. A few years earlier, they had made him a partner in their import-export hardware business, and now they sent him to London to help his ailing brother Peter with the Liverpool end. For two years he helped out on the "books" but preferred, characteristically, to travel and socialize. In the end, despite some diligent efforts on his part, the business collapsed altogether, a loss Irving experienced as devastating; he always referred to it as an "ordeal," "Detestable" and "horrible" (Williams 2:259). The strength of Irving's reaction can best be explained by his long-held fear that now he would have to fend for himself and so would be separated from the care and comfort of his family. While he had hoped for financial security, he feared the independence that it produced: such security would be tentative at best, and generally threatened abandonment and loss. He felt that fear even at the most successful point in his career, in 1821, after the enormous popularity and high sales of *The Sketch Book*. He wrote then to his friend and sometime business associate Henry Brevoort: "I have by patient & persevering labour of my most uncertain pen, & by catching the gleams of sunshine in my cloudy mind, managed to open to myself an avenue to some degree of profit &

reputation—I value it the more highly because it is entirely independent and self created; and I must use my best endeavours to turn it to account" (*L*1:614). His labor is persevering, but his pen is uncertain, thus producing an anxiety that, set up in opposition to an apparently valued "independence," is turned "to account," evaluated in economic terms.

This same anxiety, in fact, was the principal motivation behind his greatest literary achievements. Very shortly after the death of his betrothed Matilda Hoffman in 1808, which he experienced as a devastation dooming him to a lonely independence, he began to travel, a form of retreat that he would later describe as "a kind of succedaneum for matrimony" (*L*1:340). Soon he produced, in collaboration with his brother Peter, *A History of New York*. And very shortly after the bankruptcy, he began producing the first number of *The Sketch Book* for publication in the United States. Now he felt himself again threatened with an undependable literary capability and a panic of financial independence, and again he felt drawn to traveling and writing. His anxiety was increased in this case, however, because he also felt himself threatened by the emphasis on financial independence in the commercial culture to which he was returning, a culture he saw governed—as he saw himself—by the uncertain rhythms of labor, exchange, profit, and loss. Once again he felt himself surrounded by the "cares and sordid concerns of traffic" (*L*1:515).

By this association of financial independence with the dangers of excess and loss, he linked his own interests as a writer in traveling West to the interests of the nation in its westward expansion. These dangers were, according to Irving, as crucial a part of the economic expansion of Jacksonian America as they were of his own. While self-interest was a dependable social posture if affected in moderation (as in the measured vocation of the writer), it could also become destructive of both self and society if embraced too vigorously. Irving rarely made this criticism directly, for he felt too dependent upon the acceptance of his reading public. Such critiques as can be found in his writings are generally in vague and ambiguous forms, as in the self-deflating satire of Diedrich Knickerbocker's attacks on Yankees, or the same narrator's critique of the disputatious new republic in "Rip Van Winkle." But in a few works written soon after his Western tour, he makes his position clear.

The most direct expression of his concern can be found in a short

sketch entitled "The Creole Village" (1837), a meditation on the imminent transformation of a small Western village by an encroaching
commercialism.[8] He begins by offering a nostalgic vision of an ideal
Western community. In a sly twist, Irving associates the community's
utopian Americanness not with its American traits at all, but rather
with the strength of its "old world" traditions: "In no other part of our
country. . .are the customs and peculiarities, imported from the old
world by the earlier settlers, kept up with more fidelity than in the
little, poverty-stricken villages of Spanish and French origin which
border the rivers of ancient Louisiana" (*WR* 22). Soon, though, it
becomes evident that the community stands as the more American
ideal by its very resistance to its rapidly developing American neighbors. Following the formula of Irving's earlier gestures to nostalgia,
these villages are doomed to pass away. This time, however, Irving
does not transform that collapse into a positive homage to the new
commercialism. In fact, it is just that commercialism which will destroy
the most special feature of these "poverty-stricken" places, their har-
mony. Further, the nation has nothing to put in its place, or at least
nothing of true value:

> In a word, the almighty dollar, that great object of universal devotion
> throughout our land, seems to have no genuine devotees in these pecu-
> liar villages; and unless some of its missionaries penetrate there, and
> erect banking houses and other pious shrines, there is no knowing how
> long the inhabitants may remain in their present state of contented
> poverty. (23)

Not long, the argument assumes. However much Irving may hope that
they "retain their happy ignorance, their absence of all enterprise and
improvement, their respect for the fiddle, and their contempt for the
almighty dollar," his "prayer is doomed to be of no avail," for nearby
he finds an "American town, just springing into bristling and prosperous existence" (27). The America that had been for John Smith a new
Eden of "industrie" had apparently suffered a long and unfortunate
fall.

The key phrase for Irving is "almighty dollar," as he indicates when
he repeats it once and then again in a satirical retraction:

> This phrase used for the first time, in this sketch, has since passed into
> current circulation, and by some has been questioned as savoring of
> irreverence. The author, therefore, owes it to his orthodoxy to declare

that no irreverence was intended even to the dollar itself; which he is aware is daily becoming more and more an object of worship. (27n.)[9]

The joke hides a complex criticism of the marketplace, and is particularly concerned with the role of literature in the marketplace. Its premise, a common one at the time, is that the nation's spiritual enterprise, now infused with the values of competitive commercialism, was in danger of being replaced by the worship of money and self. Irving's strategy for revealing that threat is to implicate even his own profession, and thus the complacency of the reader in that transaction. First he implies that his phrase has become a kind of circulated currency, an ironic condition for a criticism of empty materialism, for now the phrase itself has become a valued material object. He then compounds the irony by suggesting, under the guise of a retraction, that this "object" has also become an object of worship among his "orthodoxy," the book-buyers and readers who worship *him*. But then he quickly retracts the retraction by once again declaring the dollar an unworthy object of worship. His contemporary audience, well aware of the dangers in the shifting ground of belief from success as a sign of grace to money as a sign of success, would recognize the hidden simile to the traditional religion of the communal enterprise by which Irving underscores the falseness of this new religion of self-interest. And the better readers might also recognize the point of their own ironic complicity in that falseness: that in this commercial era, one must be aware of the professions in professions of faith.[10] Ignorance may be a happy state for the inhabitants of the creole village, but it could not protect them from the America of the nearby town, a

> community. . .torn to pieces by new doctrines in religion and in political economy; there were camp meetings, and agrarian meetings; and an election was at hand which, it was expected would throw the whole country into a paroxysm. Alas! with such an enterprising neighbor, what is to become of the poor little creole village! (28)

Once again, it seems, Rip Van Winkle must awaken.

Irving echoed this sentiment in other writings at the time. In an essay entitled "Sleepy Hollow," first published in 1839, Irving described his return to the site of his early famous story. At first he sees it, happily, as "but little changed":

> The march of intellect, which had made such rapid strides along every river and highway, had not yet, apparently, turned down into this favored valley. Perhaps the wizard spell of ancient days still reigned over the place, binding up the faculties of the inhabitants in happy contentment with things as they had been handed down to them from yore. (*MW*2:110)

And yet such enchantment only serves to dissolve his own: "Alas! alas! to me everything now stood revealed in its simple reality. The echoes no longer answered with wizard tongues; the dream of youth was at an end; the spell of Sleepy Hollow was broken!" (111). What now stands revealed to him, in fact, is not a sleepy hollow at all but a busy town caught up in the "hand of improvement": "The spirit of speculation and improvement had seized even upon that once quiet and unambitious little dorp" (111). After hearing that a bank is soon to be established, he concludes with sadness that "The fate of the neighborhood is, therefore, sealed. I see no hope of averting it. The golden means is at an end. The country is suddenly to be deluged with wealth" (113).[11]

This seemingly unavoidable marketplace expansion was of special concern to Irving because of its implications for his literary career. The economic developments and new economic attitudes that were soon to overcome Sleepy Hollow were also soon to envelop the arts as well. Irving shared with many writers a fear that the environment of the marketplace was becoming increasingly inimical to the cultivation and appreciation of quality literature, and even to workings of the literary sensibility itself.

One often articulated grievance was that the marketplace did not value art, failed to reward its artists, and so diminished the production of art: "the fine writer," Irving wrote in an 1813 review, "if he depend upon his pen for subsistence, will soon discover that he may starve on the very summit of Parnassus, while he sees herds of newspaper editors battening on the rank marshes of its borders" (*MW*1:52).[12] The artist might be able to keep himself separate from the "herd" and preserve those achievements of sensibility, but he will be poor and publicly disgraced.

Underlying this view was the larger assumption that art was simply incompatible with the conditions and values of the marketplace. As the attack on newspaper writers suggests, the art would be equally dimin-

ished if the artist decided to join the marketplace. Either the artist
would become dulled by the routine, the "sordid dusty, soul-killing. . .way of life" (*L*1:316) that Irving once angrily characterized as the
lot of the businessman, or he would become overwhelmed by temptation. Self-interest would become the writer's primary motive and profit
the final arbiter of value. In both cases, the artist would become a mere
craftsman, and his art a mere commodity for mass-market consumption. The very "invention of bookmaking" which James Hall had
praised in his review of Timothy Flint's *Lectures* would become a sign
of the denigration of literature. For instance, many writers criticized
the emerging marketplace of Western writings in just these terms,
claiming that the exploitation of national resources for the purpose of
producing marketable books was a desecration of the literary calling.
In "The American Scholar," Emerson denounced authors who "follow
trappers into the prairie. . .to replenish their merchantable stock" (*Essays* 61). The remark may, in fact, have been directed at Irving, whose
Western books were popular at the time (Todd 1965, xviii). The same
assessment was later voiced by Charles Dudley Warner when he criticized Irving's *Captain Bonneville* as "a specimen of a very prevalent
practice of late years, viz. of book-making" (Rees and Sandy xxvii).

In short, the world of business and the world of culture were
mutually exclusive: "This world is usurped by the plodder & the
moneymaker and the labourer," Irving wrote in his journal, "so Scarce
a quiet corner is left in it for the poet" (*J*3:665). And now even the
"quiet corners" of the West were beginning to become busied by
commerce. As Emerson noted in his own journal, "This invasion of
Nature by Trade with its Money, its Credit, its Steam, its Railroad,
threatens to upset the balance of man, & establish a new Universal
Monarchy more tyrannical than Babylon or Rome. Very faint & few
are the poets or men of God" (7:268). Irving's almighty dollar was
Emerson's universal monarchy; for both men, the expansion of the
marketplace threatened the very foundation of its cultural assets, the
workings of the imagination.

The source of this division between business and the imagination
was twofold. First, the culture's inclination toward utilitarianianism
had been accompanied by a deep suspicion of the imagination. According to this view, the practice of writing "constituted something of a
repudiation of the. . .values of practicality and industry" (Hedges 14).
Second, the culture's essentially religious temperament had been ac-

companied by a deep suspicion of any work unsanctified by larger contexts of purpose.[13] According to this view, the world of business was associated with mere labor, and the world of art with purposeful leisure. As Irving put it in the 1813 review, "Absorbed in politics, or occupied by business, few can find leisure, amid these strong agitations of the mind, to follow the gentler pursuits of literature, and give it that calm study, and meditative contemplation, necessary to discover the true principles of beauty and excellence in composition" (*MW*1:50). Both of these views were prominent during the late eighteenth and early nineteenth centuries, when business and "culture" were considered discrete realms divided neatly along class lines. By the 1820s and 1830s, though, that division was no longer so certain or so clear. The emergence of the national marketplace, the rise of the middle classes, and the transformation of literature into a business, were redefining the relationships between the two realms.

Irving himself was of two minds about the situation. On the one hand, he feared that the conditions of the marketplace, such as the emphasis on profit and the demand for increased production, might indeed lead writers to create lesser forms of literature. At the same time, however, he favored the process. On the practical level, he had chosen to make writing his career, and he hoped that the opening and expansion of a literary marketplace would provide him not only with a means of support but profit as well. On the ideological level, he also felt that American literature would maintain its value as an integral element of American life only if it succeeded in adapting to these new conditions, only if the literary calling became a literary career. The problem, then, was how to bring the practice of writing into the marketplace without diminishing the writer's capacity to recognize and express "excellence and beauty."

To solve this problem, though, one would first have to overcome the hostilities toward both the marketplace and the imagination, as well as between them, and that would be no easy task. Insofar as both marketplace and imagination were equally suspect as realms in which individual interest was likely to overpower social endeavor, neither alone could provide suitable terms for reconciliation. Irving had, in fact, long taken the stance that both should be equally criticized. For instance, in his first published work, *Letters of Jonathan Oldstyle*, Irving created a satirical pose by straddling his own ambivalences toward the social styles of both aristocrat and Yankee: the former is represented as the curator of culture but also of artifice, the latter, as the leveller of privilege but also of refinement. As William Hedges has noted (17), even the two parts of the name evoke the conflict between eighteenth and nineteenth century "style": Jonathan, the common but redolent Yankee, and Oldstyle, the sophisticated but outdated aristocrat. In *A History of New York,* Knickerbocker criticizes equally the upper classes and the middle classes, the rich and cultured and the acquisitive and uncultured. In *The Sketch Book,* the traffic of the marketplace is as omnipresent and subtly satirized as the leisurely pursuit of culture that is offered as a refuge.

Perhaps the most precise articulation of Irving's uneasiness about both business and culture can be found in a sketch from that book, "Roscoe," an examination of the nature of a career in literature. The sketch is basically a description of a venerated author, Mr. Roscoe, whose achievement, according to Geoffrey Crayon, lies not just in the quality of the books he has produced, but in his ability to produce those books in the marketplace. This is a subject of deep interest to Crayon because it bears precisely upon his (and Irving's) desire to bridge the gap between English culture and American practicality, and thereby forge a respectable American literary marketplace. At first, though, any such connections are disturbing. Upon seeing the elderly writer at the Athanaeum, Crayon is made momentarily uneasy by the rude conjunction of business and culture: "To find, therefore, the elegant historian of the Medici, mingling among the busy sons of traffic at first shocked my poetical ideas" (16). Those ideas, while never specified, seem to consist primarily of an assumption that the market-place is itself an affront to any fineness of sensibility. Soon, though, he comes to modify his views. Roscoe's achievement, he claims, is pre-cisely his ability to thrive as a poet in the marketplace:

> Born in a place apparently ungenial to the growth of literary talent; in the very market place of trade; without fortune, family connexions or patronage; self prompted, self sustained and almost self taught, he has conquered every obstacle, achieved his way to eminence, and having become one of the ornaments of the nation, has turned the whole force of his talents and influence to advance and embellish his native town. (17)

But if Roscoe has succeeded in the marketplace, he is not finally a part of the marketplace. While he has "effected [a] union of commerce and intellectual pursuits" (18), there yet remains "something in his whole appearance that indicated a being of a different order from the bustling race around him" (16). The tenor of these passages, and of the sketch as a whole, is as sorrowful as it is admiring. The loftiness of Roscoe's achievement is inseparable from its isolating effects. It is also fragile on both counts, for when the marketplace itself eventually fails him—as it must, in the world of Irving's imagination—he is driven back into a strangely alienated realm of imaginative compensation:

> Those who live only for the world and in the world, may be cast down by the frowns of adversity; but a man like Roscoe is not to be overcome by the reverses of fortune. They do but drive him in upon the resources of his own mind, apt sometimes to neglect, and to roam abroad in search of less worthy associates. He is independent of the world around him. He lives with antiquity and with posterity. With antiquity, in the sweet communions of studious retirement, and with posterity in the generous aspirings after future renown. The solitude of such a mind is its state of highest enjoyment. It is then visited by those elevated meditations which are the proper ailment of noble souls, and are like manna, sent from heaven in the wilderness of the world. (18)

The passage is filled with apparent contradictions. While ostensibly ejected from the marketplace, Roscoe turns his isolation into a marketplace of the imagination: he mines the "resources" of his mind, and produces books for posterity (and presumably for the marketplace). While "independent of the world," he is more fully alive than most. While his greatness lies in his commerce with the world, his artistic achievement is the consequence of a "solitude of. . .mind." In the end, though, these are not so much contradictions as ambivalences. If, for Irving, the marketplace offered only the sad choice between a "bustling and disputatious" world and almost certain isolation—the marketplace was, in short, the "wilderness of the world"—it was also the only realm wherein the true success of art could be measured.

The example of Roscoe's career, then, offers little as a model for producing a commercial culture that honors the claims of both commerce and culture. Even his particular role as historian suggests that such resolution is more a dream of the past, or the reverie of distanced contemplation, than a stance of active participation in the world. But perhaps Roscoe's biggest problem is that there is finally no place in the marketplace for the kind of work he does. While he may be a nineteenth-century businessman, he has remained an eighteenth-century author.

As the sketch indicates, Irving neither expected nor wanted writers simply to adapt their art to the conditions of the marketplace, nor for those people participating in the marketplace to abandon their principal motivations of self-interest and profit. Rather, he wanted to bring the practice of writing into the marketplace in such a way that preserved its virtues by incorporating them into the marketplace; literature would become a profitable cultured pursuit, and the marketplace, a cultured arena of profit. In brief, he wanted to construct a viable popular culture. But as the confusions at the end of "Roscoe" suggest, he was concerned that the self-interest implicit in both business and imagination was likely to undermine that task. Success depended upon two conditions: the people in the marketplace must learn to appreciate the pursuit of "excellence and beauty" in art, for only then would they become capable of curbing their self-interest and supporting, even encouraging, a national literature and a national literary marketplace; and writers must learn to accept the pursuit of self-interest in the marketplace, for only then would they become capable of making their imaginations as useful as they might be profitable. For Irving, these two tasks were inseparable. In his criticism of excessive self-interest, for instance, he often linked imagination and business as joint causes, characterizing bad writing as a dubious business practice, and business as a dubious exercise of imagination.

This connection finds its most marked presence in Irving's discussions of the new forms of exchange emerging in the marketplace. His language is particularly telling in an early journal entry in which he uses much the same logic he would later employ in his criticism of the "almighty dollar." In this case, his purpose is to identify the most threatening elements of the marketplace:

> Credit—paper currency—a whole system built upon promises—A community promising each other great sums, multiplying the aggregate Myths & fancying themselves rich. The Banks great manufacturers of promises where they promise by wholesale & buy & sell promises—But if a time comes to cash those promises then one fails after another & the failure of one promise authorizes the forfeiture of another—
> Words coined into cash—and every one knows how inexhaustible the coinage of words is. This may be called a land of promises[.] (*J*5:317)

The problem here is not commercialism per se—certainly not the exchange of money for goods, or the regulation of the marketplace by the profit motive. As in both "The Creole Village" and "Rip Van Winkle," Irving is less concerned about business itself than about the lack of restraint evident in many business practices. In this case, he specifically points to the increasing reliance on credit and paper money, both of which prescribe "value" by the conditions of the marketplace alone, and he characterizes the threat of this reliance as a problematic interweaving of imagination and business, of "words coined into cash." Through this new culture of capitalism, America, the land of promise, is in danger of becoming merely a land of promises.

In an 1840 article, "A Time of Unexampled Prosperity: The Great Mississippi Bubble,"[14] Irving narrows the focus of his attack to the particular mode of exchange that had become most identified with the use of credit and paper money: speculation. As in the earlier sketches and comments, Irving distinguishes between a marketplace based on business and one based on speculation. Business itself was not the source of danger; properly engaged, the spirit of enterprise could help America recover its principles. But the speculative arena in business, with its emphasis on competition among individuals and its potential for division and loss, could destroy those principles. "Foundations of a traders credit," he explained in a journal, "are propriety[,] integrity, punctuality, industry, prudence, firmness of dealing[,] freedom from Extravagance from wild spirit of Speculation & from vice" (*J*5:312). This is the very "spirit of speculation," one assumes, that had "seized upon" his beloved Sleepy Hollow; the first proddings of its presence can be found even in the original story, "The Legend of Sleepy Hollow," in the attempts of Ichabod Crane, extravagant speculator, to impose his vision on the land.[15]

According to this conception, business, which was based on work, led to genuine earnings, while speculation, which was based on investment, could lead only to lucky gain; business, which operated on an exchange of money for goods, led to a stable economy of mutual benefit, while speculation, which operated on the exchange of money for the promise of money (credit), could lead only to an unstable and divisive society. Business was thus the more moral activity because it equated effort with gain, and individual profit with community enterprise. This reasoning is the basis for Irving's article, a recounting of the

story of a seventeenth-century land swindle in France. While the incident is remote in time and place, it is clearly a warning for the America
of 1840 with its own recent economic debacle, the depression of 1837,
resulting from its expanding speculative land industry: "Now is the
time," Irving writes in the preface to the story, "for speculative and
dreaming or designing men" (*WR* 95).

The article focuses on an independent entrepreneur, John Law, who
attempted to entice the people of France, with the approval of the
greedy Regent, the Duke of Orleans, to buy land in the Mississippi
Valley in America. The more people he could get to buy the land, the
more the land was worth. Gradually more land was sold than existed,
and more money was proffered in credit than was actually possessed,
and the relationship between land and money as a foundation of value
ceased to be functional: first inflation, then panic, then total loss. The
land deeds became as valueless as the money with which they were
bought. The ultimate cause of the disaster, according to Irving, was
not so much the greed of the original swindlers as the mania for
speculation that gripped everyone involved: "Wealth was to be ob-
tained instantly, without labor, and without stint" (105); "Honest
tradesmen and citizens. . .had been seduced away from the slow accu-
mulations of industry, to the specious chances of speculation" (119).
The word "specious" suggests that speculation deludes the investor,
turning self-interest into social catastrophe: "Could this delusion always last, the life of a merchant would indeed be a golden dream; but
it is as short as it is brilliant. . . . Let but a doubt enter, and. . .the
whole superstructure, built upon credit, and reared by speculation,
crumbles to the ground, leaving scarce a wreck behind" (96). Irving
offers a final warning: "When a man of business, therefore, hears on
every side rumors of fortunes suddenly acquired;. . .when he sees adventurers flush of paper capital, and full of scheme and enterprise;. . .when he hears of new regions of commercial adventure; of
distant marts and distant mines, swallowing merchandise and disgorg-
ing gold," then let him "prepare for the impending storm" (96).[16]

One of the most striking features of the passage in the article is the
extent to which Irving implicates his own profession in that self-
interest. Speculation is described as a practice of characters from books,
"adventurers" in "new regions of commercial adventure," or even as
authors who turn "enterprise" into "scheme." ("It tempts of adventur-

ing" [*J*5:313], he noted in his journal.) In the most telling formulation, he declares that "Speculation is the romance of trade, and casts contempt upon all its sober realities. It renders the stockjobber a magician, and the exchange a region of enchantment. It elevates the merchant into a kind of knight errant, or rather a commercial Quixotte" (*WR* 96). The criticism here is not of the practice of literature, or even the exercise of the imagination per se, but of the merger of imagination and the marketplace which threatens to distort both.

Just as the transformation of literature into a business threatened the integrity of the art, the transformation of the marketplace into a realm of romance threatened the integrity of the nation. In both cases, the excessive or speculative imagination becomes the metaphor for a self-interest that has become the axis of authority and the source of power. It is only fitting that in the lexicon of the marketplace, speculation was defined as a form of "fictitious dealing"; that is, a deal which is produced by promotion of an illusion, and the success of which is determined by the extent to which that illusion becomes accepted as a real condition of the marketplace.[17]

Irving's concern about the power of this fictive process is finally a concern about both the imagination and the marketplace, for the process draws on the resources of both and ultimately befuddles both; it places the self and self-interest rather than the community and communal obligation at the center of the determination of value, and seduces those selves into believing that they have in fact created a community out of their shared interests. But the result is as unstable as it is unsettling. When Irving criticized Ichabod Crane's spirit of speculation, for instance, he did so by focusing on Crane's extravagant imagination; and if Crane himself is ultimately defeated by that very imagination, it would not be long before more successful Cranes arrive to "seize upon" America's Sleepy Hollows with an extravagance of imagination matched by a power to persuade. In Emerson's words, "The rapid wealth which hundreds in the community acquire in trade or by the incessant expansions of our populations & arts, enchants the eyes of all the rest" (*Journals* 7:431).

Irving's solution to these dangers—to the incompatibility of business and literature, the antithesis of business and imagination, the conflicts between self-interest and the common good, labor and leisure, profit and purposefulness—was to take shape in what he saw as the most congenial meeting ground for business and culture: the professionalization of a national literature. The terms of this merger were founded on models drawn from the practices of both the marketplace and art. Irving saw in certain the operations of business a "sober reality" that provided the necessary restraint and decorum to curb the excesses of the speculative imagination, and he saw in certain operations of the imagination an appreciation of "excellence and beauty" that provided the necessary restraint and decorum to curb the excesses of the marketplace. The model of professionalism as Irving imagined it succeeds in merging business and imagination because the professional is both man of business and man of the imagination, and as both, is capable of resisting the temptations of speculation. As a man of business, who engages in commerce through work, he is superior to the speculator, who produces only the "hocus pocus of trade," as Knickerbocker described it in *A History of New York* (596), and as a man of the imagination, who engages in art through work, he is superior to the speculative artist, who produces only illusion and falsehood. The professional is at once the writer as businessman and the businessman with an artistic sensibility. And he prospers as both, profiting by his craft even while he endows the marketplace with taste, coherence, and discipline.

The basis for this happy merger is not always consistently identified, however. It is difficult to tell, for instance, whether Irving's concept of professionalization was drawn more from the world of business or art. On the one hand, he generally associated the qualities of professionalism—the capacity for decorous appreciation and appreciation of hierarchical restraint—with art alone, and particularly with an eighteenth-century aestheticism, and pictured the businessman as either a dullard or a mercenary. On the other hand, he associated those same qualities with the practice of business, and pictured the artist as an extravagant child requiring the discipline of strict business habits. These contradictions seem to be generated by a conflict in perspectives: as a member of the merchant class and a man of the marketplace, he looked to business for the model upon which to base his concept of professionalism; and as an aspiring member of the leisured class and an artist, he looked to art for the model. But while these contradictions often led him to write elaborate justifications of both his art and his business, and just as often to write equally elaborate justifications of the need to subordinate one to the other, they did not deter him from his dedication to the professional ideal. He continued to see his task as adapting the cultured imagination to the culture of the marketplace.[18]

It is not surprising that in imagining the terms of his entry into the marketplace, Irving focused on the "professional" aspect of his craft. The 1820s and 1830s saw the professionalization of many disciplines, including writing; and, according to William Charvat, it was Irving himself, along with Cooper, who "established the American literary profession" (1968, 47). Both writers' works were endorsed by the marketplace and supported by the profession's self-regulating institutions, the magazine and book publishers, and both writers were able to earn enough money by their writings to support themselves. The two men were also in competition for sales as well as imputed literary reputation. Their sometimes stormy relationship along these lines reveals much about the state of the profession at the time.

Given Cooper's preference for class hierarchy, and his simultaneous commitment to the marketplace of literature, one might expect him to look favorably on Irving as a fellow professional. But in fact he felt a lifelong hostility toward Irving's success as a writer. Irving's very acuity in business, in fact, brought from Cooper a characteristic show of wrath: "What an instinct that man has for gold!" he complained to his wife after hearing of Irving's financial relationship with John Jacob Astor (*Letters* 5:330). Generally his criticisms followed class lines: Irving was of the merchant class, and so lacked the breeding necessary for the refinement of a literary sensibility; at the same time, he was also eager to sacrifice what talents he had for fame and profit. So we find Cooper criticizing Irving for a "Vulgar Ignorance" which had been tolerated only because it had been "kept down by concentrated knowledge and taste" (*Letters* 4:167). In the context of Cooper's own upper class, these criticisms were as logical as they were perfunctory, but in the context of the new profession of writing, they were largely ironic. Despite the differences in their backgrounds, Irving shared the same class bias, and defined his professionalism in the same terms as Cooper. Both writers saw their work as preserving a hierarchical society threatened with displacement by an expanding marketplace, and as a source of income and personal profit. Both saw books as the repositories of social value, and both were willing to subordinate a book's quality to its potential value as a commodity. Irving, for instance, repeatedly refined the "decorum" of his works and softened his social criticisms in subsequent editions. Cooper was to go even further and determine the nature and extent of his revisions by the amount of extra money he could negotiate from his publishers. In a letter to one such publisher, he declared what Irving would never assert without qualification: "It is necessary to speak of these works. . .as mere articles of trade" (1:165). What emerges even from their differences is a common vision of a literary career as a professionalism fine-tuned to the demands and threats of the expanding marketplace.

Of the two, Irving was perhaps the more celebrated American author of his time, and also the shrewder professional, making more money on his writing and the celebrity it brought him. His attentiveness to the profitableness and details of subscription sales is well known, as is his interest in the frequent reissue of works in revised and uniform editions. This business sense was evident in his dealings with his Western writings as well. He was well aware, for instance, that the public interest in his Western travels could be of value in generating pre-publication publicity, keeping his name current while he searched the terrain for a suitable shape for a book. He let enough people know of his travel plans, and soon both the Eastern and Western press were reporting each major stop, and noted in enthusiastic expectation a desire that from the trip Irving would produce a major work confirming the native literary resources of the "new" territories. Finally, the touring party itself, while under Ellsworth's direction and ostensibly for his purpose as commissioner of Indian Affairs, quickly became known as "The Irving party." While Irving did not consciously choreograph the tour as a road show strictly for his economic benefit— indeed, he was often horrified and intimidated by the attention he received, as when, in a Cincinnati theater, he slipped out after he was announced and hailed by the audience—he did pursue his craft as a business, and was eager to take advantage of his opportunities as a professional writer.[19]

This perception of the professional as both a man of culture (committed to restraint, decorum, taste, community, and hierarchy) and a man of the marketplace (committed to acquisitiveness, individual interest, and mobility) places Irving squarely in a debate about professionalism and self-interest that has existed since the inception of the institution. While critics and historians have generally agreed that the emergence of the professions was a consequence of industrial capitalism and the expansion of the marketplace, few have agreed on the relation between them and the prevailing conditions of capitalism. For the most part, the debate has centered on the role of the professions in regulating the self-interest of the marketplace. According to some writers, the professions were essentially a means of promoting individual self-interest; according to others, they were a means of restraining self-interest in the service of a communal ethic. In the former, the institution simply reflected the marketplace ethic of economic individualism, and in the latter, it functioned in response to that ethic; in both, it furthered the interests of the marketplace. These different perspectives also led to quite different interpretations of the purpose and function of such features of professionalization as regulation by self-determined standards, the process of self-credentialling, and the posture of detachment. Magali Larson has recently argued, for instance, that professions "organized themselves to attain market power" (x); while Bernard Barber has characterized the "primary orientation" of that organization as directed to "the community interest rather than to individual self-interest," and perpetuated through a system of rewards "that is primarily a set of symbols of work achievement and thus ends in themselves, not means to some end of individual self-interest" (Lynn 16).[20]

Irving's position in the debate was once again in the middle: professionalism enabled the individual to profit even while it restrained the profit-seeking impulse, thereby honoring the interests of both individual and community, commerce and culture. Such a view required a certain kind of individual, of course, as well as a certain kind of social organization. For Irving that individual was the same natural aristocrat who was later to become identified as the archetypal Western hero, a man of initiative yet also a man of restraint, capable of harnessing that initiative to the benefit of the community. Correspondingly, that social organization was a flexible hierarchy based on distinctions not of blood but of work and character. Anticipating Wister's comments about "the quality and the equality" in *The Virginian*, Irving wrote in his notebook:

> Of Distinctions in Society—We may talk as much as we please about equality—There is an equality of rights in nature, but none of conditions. Strength, talents, &c &c give continual superiority—as in the trees of the forest—
>
> We have no hereditary distinctions, but we have classes of society

arising from talents, manners, wealth &c. This is a natural aristocracy—
Wealth is respectable as implying talents in its acquisition. The rich man
is important in society as having great means of usefulness[.] (*J*5:311)

He ends the passage, though, with a warning: "The mere vanity of
wealth is contemptible." This aristocratic capitalism may indeed reconcile the interests of business and culture, mobility and hierarchy, the
individual and the community. But the temptations of the marketplace
remain, and one needs proper guidance to achieve true success. The
best man for the job is the professional, for only he can cross such
boundaries while still respecting them.

Such a view enabled critics and celebrants of capitalism alike to
share in a vision of the American marketplace. Cooper, for instance, no
champion of capitalism, employed much the same rhetoric in his harsh
critique of American democracy, *The American Democrat* (1838). First
he condemns "a community governed by men in trade, or which is
materially influenced by men in trade" on the grounds that it is "governed without any fixed principles, every thing being made to yield to
the passing interests of the hour, those interests being too engrossing
to admit of neglect, or postponement" (169). Yet, he goes on, such a
community may succeed if directed by a "real" merchant: "The real
merchant is a man of high pursuit, and has need of great general
knowledge, much firmness of character, and of far-sighted views, to
succeed in his objects. He is a principal agent in extending knowledge
of civilization, and is entitled to a distinguished place in the scale of
human employments" (170–171). Like Irving's professional, Cooper's
merchant brings culture to the world of business, and business to the
world of culture.

This formulation of the professional "code" had, in fact, long been
celebrated in American culture. From the colonial period through the
nineteenth century, Americans had chosen their heroes by their enterprise as well as their adventurousness. The greatest of these heroes
excelled in both: they were professionalized adventurers. George
Washington, for instance, was valued for his decorum, bravery, and
shrewd business sense; he was cheered in just the terms Irving identified as those of the natural aristocrat. Like that later Virginian of
Wister's novel, the secret of these heroes' success lay in their ability to
"know their business" and do their job well, whether that job be as a
pioneer, merchant, politician, or writer. That ability, in turn, depended

upon a capacity for restraint and a concern for others; in all, a balance between self-interest and the common good. When that balance was absent or distorted, the figure of the professional became a fraud or villain, such as one finds in the crooked lawyers, landlords, cowboys, and politicians of the popular novels and plays of the nineteenth century—what Irving called "loose adventurers" in *Astoria* (7). The villainy of these latter figures confirms the code by warning of the potential for unfair advantage that remained within the marketplace regardless. So powerful was this code that it continued to be celebrated long after the possibilities for professional success had themselves become restricted to a privileged few; the heroes then became the failures who maintained their faith in the principal of integrity, a professional code of honor.

The code, though, did not finally champion fairness. Like all ideologies it simply provided a system of justification whereby success or failure were transformed into the natural and the inevitable. Hence the culture was perfectly capable at the middle of the century of making heroes out of the "robber barons," men who succeeded precisely by exploiting the principles of professional behavior. The code thus became a self-fulfilling prophecy—or, rather, a prophecy of self-fulfillment—managing to perfect that merger of which Irving was so critical in "The Creole Village": the merger of professions with professions of faith. Irving was not unaware of this potential for abuse, but hoped his own model of professionalism would overcome it.

For Irving, that code was perhaps nowhere more necessary than in the profession of writing. If the marketplace must become professionalized, then so too must the literary marketplace, but the literary profession held a special responsibility in this process. Insofar as the arts were, according to Irving, the primary preserver and cultivator of culture, professionalization was ultimately an education of imagination. The writer must educate the reader, and, by extension, the society as a whole, in the values to be inculcated in the marketplace. As Irving's remarks in "A Time of Unexampled Prosperity" suggest, the code of professional conduct applied first to the writer and his text. For instance, the speculator's failure could be perceived in two lights: first, as a character in this tale of capitalism, he was nothing but a self-deceiving adventurer, an anti-American villain; second, as a tale-teller or writer himself, he was the deceiver of others, the creator of a house of cards or land of enchantment (in this case an endangered America). But it is finally the reader who must learn to defeat the character, reject the tale-teller, and revise the tale; as the analogy suggests, such critical discernment as a reader is the model for professional conduct as a man of commerce. The terms of success for the "honest merchant" are modeled on the exchange between writer and text, and between text and reader. Here is the restrained but active businessman who turns speculation into an act of observation and moral insight.[21]

By just such analogies between imagination and the marketplace, in which "value" is revealed as determined by the fluctuations of self-interest, Irving sought to define the role of the imagination in Jacksonian America. In his published writings and private letters and journals, Irving presented himself as a professional above all, adapting the form of his art to the values of the marketplace, while at the same time protecting it from its pressures and distortions. The formula seems clear enough, and yet it was fraught with difficulties. For one thing, Irving had still not eliminated his fear, expressed in his sketch of Roscoe, that the business environment and the production of art were incompatible. How can the imagination succeed as an educator of the marketplace if to do so it must first succeed in the terms of the marketplace?

Throughout his career, Irving felt it necessary to explain how he could be both a good writer and a paid one. He found himself in a particularly difficult position when he accepted Astor's patronage to write *Astoria*. In that case, as in many others, the critics charged that he had exceeded the boundaries of professional conduct, had become a writer for hire who could only falsify and delude. Generally, Irving defended himself by reasserting his allegiance to the profession: "I have shewn that I do not throw things off in a slovenly way and for the mere love of filthy lucre" (*L*4:735). The emphasis here should be put on the qualification "mere" and not the more emphatic "filthy lucre," for Irving was not claiming he was no businessman; indeed, this quotation comes from the same letter in which he considered ways to get *A Tour on the Prairies* in print before Latrobe's book.

The writer as businessman must walk a fine line indeed. When writing about a railroad executive who had lately taken up "A little gentleman like exercise of the pen" while negotiating for an enormous railroad consolidation, Irving noted with some scorn: "I know he takes pride in shewing the world that a literary man can be a man of business; but in my humble opinion a literary man on a locomotive is worse than a beggar on horseback—and will bring up at the same end of the journey in half the time" (*L4*:526). In other words, the man should stick to his own business, and leave the business of writing to those who write well, and who can, without pride, show the world that a literary man can indeed be a man of business.

The pressures of the marketplace could do more damage than simply tarnishing the integrity of the writer, or diminishing the quality of his work. Irving felt they could also have a crucial influence upon the shape of the imagination itself, limiting its capacity for capturing and conveying the truth. In his discussions of his works as "romances," he expressed two contradictory views about this influence corresponding to his ambivalence over the demands of his professional obligations and entitlements. As we saw in his comments about the romance of speculation, he tended to belittle the romance as the work of a falsifying imagination in search of profit alone; and yet in other writings he described his own works as romances, by which he meant the work of an honest and penetrating imagination in search of a profitable truth.

Irving's various comments on *A Chronicle of the Conquest of Granada*, a work published a few years before his return to New York, are characteristic of his view of the marketplace in which "romancing" and the "romance" acquire their significance as both falsifiers and enhancers of truth. On August 31, 1828, he wrote to his friend Colonel Aspinwall that the "chronicle" of *Granada*, as he was determined to characterize the book,

> is founded on facts diligently gathered by my brother Peter & myself out of the old Spanish Chronicles, which I endeavoured to work up into an entertaining and popular form, without sacrificing the intrinsic truth of history. . . . With all its romantic colouring I really believe it will give a more full and correct idea of that rugged and singular war, than any work extant; many of the details having hitherto existed in manuscript —and all being dressed up with an eye to the scenery of the country and the customs of the times. It is an attempt, not at an historical romance, but a romantic history. (*L2*:330–331)

Romancing, in this instance, is only a "dressing up" of reality, a "colouring" but not "sacrificing" of "the intrinsic truth of history." It is significant that before the word "idea" Irving had begun to write "account" but decided to cross it out: romancing discovers an abstract or essential truth bound to, but not limited by, historical accuracy. Yet

Irving was also careful to distinguish his work from an "historical romance," a merely fictional representation set in an historical period. Romancing, then, may highlight reality, but the romance invents its own. Such romancing, while in a questionable relation to the profit motive—as is evident in his concern that his "work" toward a "popular form" may interfere with the writing's "intrinsic truth"—may nevertheless manage to arrive at that truth precisely because the reality has been "worked up." The romance, on the other hand, may distort that truth in the name of the same "entertainment," the same profitable popularity: the "account" revealed as financial record.

Irving's determination to distinguish between "romance" and "romancing" was in part a response to what he saw as the potential for profit-making to obscure or even eliminate the boundaries between truth and falsehood, to translate such moral distinctions into the amoral realm of economic advantages and disadvantages. Such an apparent preference for "interest" over "truth" could be found, for instance, in a contemporary review of *Granada* from an English journal, the *Monthly Repository and Review*: "So well told a tale, whether of truth or fiction, we scarcely remember to have read; and we doubt whether any historical romance can be named which can compete in interest with this romantic history" (Williams 2:331). While Irving may have accepted the cultural distinction between historical romance and romantic history, he was also concerned about the marketplace values underlying that distinction. He was determined to imbue the literary judgment with the moral sense of professionalism.

While Irving was often concerned that his renown as a fiction writer would be likely to undermine the public's faith in his histories, one would be mistaken in seeing his comments about *Granada* as nothing more than the defensiveness of an historian anticipating that his work will be criticized for inaccuracy. Rather, Irving is attempting to defend a fidelity to the truth that *distinguishes* his work from the historian's. It is, in many ways, a necessary defense, since in this work Irving is representing the historical period through the "literary" device of the limited narrator. The "author" of the "manuscript" of which the book is supposedly comprised is Fray Antonio Agapida, and it is through the configurations of his Catholicizing vision that Irving hoped to reveal the true figure of the era. Irving revealed how important this device was to his overall conception of the book when he angrily responded to his publisher's decision to include his own name on the title page of the first edition:

> You must have perceived that this was a Nom de Guerre to enable me to assume greater freedom & latitude in the execution of the work, and to mingle a tinge of romance and satire with the grave historical details. By inserting my name in the title page as the avowed author, you make me personally responsible for the verity of the facts and soundness of the opinions of what was intended to be given as a romantic chronicle. (*L*2:414–415)

For Irving, and for many of the more romantically inclined American authors of the period, the operative distinction implied by the terms "romancing," "romance" and "imagination" was not between fact and fiction, nor between reality and imagination. Instead it was between truth and falsehood, a formulation that did not so much oppose imagination and reality as emphasize their interdependence. In this sense, Irving's literary romanticism was distinctly pre-romantic—as, one might argue, was true for most of the American "romantics" of the early nineteenth century. He saw the limited narrator as a device that illuminated the reality around it rather than questioned the nature of reality itself; he never allowed his limited narrators to dominate and draw reality itself within the endlessly questionable sphere of their own individual perception. Unlike the romanticism of Poe, Hawthorne, and Melville, Irving's vision stipulated a given and stable truth outside of the acquisitive machinations of interpretation. According to the terms of this scheme, then, the reader must be trained to recognize the "work of the imagination" itself, within which must be included the imagination of work, the pressures of the marketplace that influence the writer's judgment. By such an education, the reader can learn to distinguish between the false, and ultimately profitless, history dedicated to profit alone and the true history dressed up in appealing and profitable form.

But such a task called for a delicate balance between reality and that "work" of the imagination, between the search for truth and the search for profit. In still another comment on *Granada*, Irving is less sure where to locate the boundary separating the two: "But I have made a work out of the old chronicles, embellished, as well as I was able, by the imagination, and adapted to the romantic taste of the day. Something that was to be between a history and a romance" (*L*2:396). In his questioning of his abilities, and his qualification of "romantic" as a strictly public and external aspect of style, there is a discomfort with "romancing," as we saw earlier in his use of the term "liberties," suggesting that while "romancing," like the "romance," allowed the writer to find the truth, it could also lead him to lose or distort it.

Irving's uneasiness is evident in many of the comments he made about his own work. About *The Alhambra,* for instance, he felt it necessary to claim that "Everything in the work relating to myself, and to the actual inhabitants of the Alhambra, is unexaggerated fact. It was only in the legends that I indulged in *romancing*; and these were founded on materials picked up about the place" (*L*4:639); and about *The Life and Voyages of Christopher Columbus* he explained to his publisher that "My brother will be of much assistance to me in my researches, and in the examination and collation of facts & dates, about which I mean to be scrupulously attentive & accurate, as I know I shall be expected to be careless in such particulars & to be apt to indulge in the imagination" (*L*2:193). "Indulging" is a dangerous posture to take in an era of self-interest and marketplace expansion; mostly it is a rejoinder to an overexposure of self. But it was an unavoidable posture for a writer who saw his task as treading the line between truth and profit.

When pressed Irving could go either way. Sometimes, as in letters justifying his own speculations, he opted for profit as the basis of truth, but more often he chose the path of the genteel imagination, as is illustrated in a letter he wrote in the early 1840s:

> When I think what revelry of the mind I have enjoyed; what fairy air castles I have built—*and inhabited*—when I was poor in purse; and destitute of all the worldly gear on which others build their happiness; when I reccollect how cheap have been my most highly relished pleasures; how independent of fortune and of the world; how easily conjured up under the most adverse and sterile circumstances; I feel as if, were I once more on the threshold of existence, and the choice were given me I would say, give me the gilding of the imagination and let others have the solid gold—let me be the "easily pleased Washington Irving," and heap positive blessings on others, until they groan under them[.] (*L*3:350)

Yet even here Irving seems uncomfortable with his choice. The word "gilding" is intentionally ironic only on a superficial level, and hides a deeper yearning for that solid gold that is beyond the disquieting conjuring of both imagination and speculation.

Irving's decision to focus on the genre of the Western adventure tale in particular grew out of these concerns. Because Western literature was as much a part of the marketplace as the economic expansion it was representing, Irving applied to it the same standards of professionalism. As a Western writer he could simultaneously profit as a professional and reconsider the narrative form with which the nation was endorsing that profit-making system. We have already seen how the Western movement had, from the first settlements, been considered as a narrative form; Irving has, in this case, merely taken the trope one step farther and defined Western expansion as an expansion of imagination.

Insofar as his model for this process was the relation among writer, text, and reader, his attention would naturally be directed at the narrative forms associated with expansion. In his choice of subject and genre both, we find the professional imagination at work. He wrote first about the Indians, considered the most conspicuous impediments to economic expansion, and next about the fur trade, the preeminent Western business, along with land sales, until the silver and gold strikes and the railroad monopolies of the 1850s. And he employed most of the major genres connected with these subjects: the Indian adventure tale, exploration report, tourist account, fur trapper narrative, and romantic history. But Irving was not satisfied with simply reproducing Western literature as he found it upon his return from Europe. Both subject and genre needed closer examination. Irving's strategy throughout his Western books would be to explore these subjects by examining the way they were expressed in the literary forms, the enterprise in the adventure.

Irving's major concern was with the promotion of self-interest implicit in these narratives. As he saw it, such formulations as white man hero versus Indian villain, and the conquering of Indian and landscape in the name of civilization and progress, were designed to valorize the white man's expansionism, and obscured or denied many of the less favorable or less adventurous elements of the Western movement. The most excessive and cruel behavior on the part of these heroes was justified, excesses that abused not only the Indians and the wilderness but the heroes themselves and the mission they represented. The manifest destiny of Western expansion may have been written by God, but the literature representing that expansion had been written by human beings for human purposes, and required human restraints. By revealing the "true" nature of the Western experience through a contrast to the "false" adventuring of the Western adventure tale, Irving hoped to adjust the boundaries of the American literary sensibility to the boundaries of its expanding commercial culture. He would infuse the tale of adventurous enterprise with the spirit of professionalism, and so infuse economic expansion itself with the social and moral equities of culture. In short, Irving would ally what he describes in *A Tour* as the "expansion of feeling" (*T* 97) experienced by Americans in the West with the feelings of expansion that brought them there.

He would not, though, seek to reconsider the premises upon which that commercial system of values rested, the values of self-interest and social cohesion, mobility and hierarchy, that were the basis for adventurous enterprise. Rather, he would seek only to bring those values into a more direct and responsible dialectic with the experience they engendered. By educating his readers to the inadequacy of certain of these cultural fictions, he would also reacquaint them with certain true and necessary ideals. The unquestioned villainy of the Indians and the heroic excesses of the white men would give way to the heroism of disciplined opportunism. Such an education would lead finally not only to a more accurate but also to a more productive imaginative approach to the facts of expansion, a popular and profitable Western literature providing a truthful examination of the realities of Western business.

For this approach to succeed, the tale teller must beware of the tendency to use tale-telling itself in the service of self-aggrandizement and justification. Interestingly, it is Irving's co-traveller Latrobe who, in his own Western adventure tale, most directly points to the essentially self-interested nature of the act of tale telling: "In narrating the events of a battle or a hunt, every man is, to a certain degree, of necessity an egotist, for the simple reason that he knows perfectly well his own resolves, and the part which he plays, and next to nothing about those of his comrades. So I must make the narrative of my own feelings and movements, the thread whereon to weave a notice of those of others" (71). Latrobe does not go so far as Irving in indicting American society for this egotism, but like Irving he conceives of the imagination as potentially divisive, exaggerating the independence of the self and blinding it to a true accounting of its relation to others. It is a view that was shared also by many other writers of Western literature of the period. However varying in tone their depictions of the consequences of such nearsightedness, from the comic to the grave, these writers all commented upon the dangers of the "diseased" or deluded imagination in the westering experience.[22]

On the more comic side we find a passage in Lewis Garrard's trapper journal *Wah-to-yah and the Taos Trail* (1850) which considers the role of daydreaming in Western life:

> At night, the rain fell and the wind blew, driving the smoke in our faces: all went to bed early, leaving me sitting by the fire. It was my favorite pastime to take a blanket and lie on the ground with it wrapped around me, with back to the wind, apart from the noisy camp, to read, or scrawl a few words in a blank book of the events of the day, or think of friends far away; or, perchance, nodding, and, in a dreamy state, with the warm sun beaming on me, build castles in the air. Many object to this idle run of thought, as it exerts, say they, a pernicious influence on the mind; that it drives away rational, sober thought, and distracts the mind from business; but what satisfaction it is, especially on the prairie, where there is no mental occupation, to think of things not in our power to possess; for, during the brief moments we indulge in this train, we are as much gratified and happy as if in actual possession; and why deprive one of this *poor* luxury? With myself it was like the two-mile heats in races— "once around and repeat;" for, on every opportunity, I endeavored to resume the thread of the last reverie, and dream away, sometimes in a conflict with the Indians, or rescuing a fair maiden from the hands of ruthless savages; or, again, chasing buffalo and feasting of the fat of the land. Anyone, in the Far West, is romantically inclined.
>
> We awoke in the morning, again drenched, cold, and uncomfortable, with saturated clothes hanging on us. A kettle of beans was on the fire cooking when the men went to bed; and, while I was punching the savages in imagination, I had punched the fire too much. The consequence was a mess of burnt beans; some tough, stringy, old steer meat, emitting such an unpleasant smell, which to eat seemed almost a sin. Maybe the fellows didn't swear at me! Tell it not in Gath! but I laughed until their woe-begone faces relaxed into good-humored smiles. (40–41)

Garrard may seek to defend the "*poor* luxury" of such daydreaming, but the comedy of its consequences can only emphasize its poverty of perception. These western travelers lose themselves in adventure tales and lose track of their surroundings, of their true "business" as tourists and trappers. Significantly, it is the Westerners themselves who are most "romantically inclined": in the midst of a "region of adventure," to use Irving's phrase from *A Tour,* they find it necessary to draw on popular formulations they bring with them.[23]

In *Two Years Before the Mast* (1840), Richard Henry Dana inadvertently makes a similar point when he describes his desperate need for good books while traveling at sea toward the West coast. After months of unrelieved boredom, he finds a copy of Bulwer's *Paul Clifford,* and spends all his time "below" reading it: "The brilliancy of the book, the succession of capital hits, and the lively and characteristic sketches, kept me in a constant state of pleasing sensations. It was far too good for a sailor. I could not expect such fine times to last long" (229). The implication of both passages is that there are no true Western adventurers, nor any real Western adventure, at least as described in the adventure tales. The true adventures are decidedly less "romantic," more suited to the business of the ordinary trapper and sailor, and more likely to draw the men together into a community of workers than separate them into isolated individuals.

Kit Carson's *Autobiography,* dictated a few years after Garrard published his book, throws a darker light on the consequences of such daydreaming. In one striking incident, Carson confronts his own myth as an Indian fighter, only to find that myth undercut by delusion and failure. A Mrs. White and her child had been captured by Indians, and Carson had been hired as a tracker by the army rescue party. After finding the Indian camp, he advised the party to attack immediately, but the officer in charge decided to follow instead the advice of another, less famous guide, who suggested they wait to see if the Indians wished to parley. This decision proved a grave error, for the Indians seized the opportunity to escape, killing Mrs. White in the process. That her death was even more lamentable because of the failure of the officers, Carson makes very clear; he claims vigorously that he was not responsible, that it is beyond question that if "my advice had been taken, the life might have been saved, for at least a short period." But as indicated in the last phrase, Carson was also doubtful of his own ability to meet the expectations placed upon him. When he discovered the body, he found more than simple evidence of his failure as a scout; he also found his failure as an adventure hero:

> In about 200 yards, pursuing the Indians, the body of Mrs. White was found, perfectly warm, had not been killed more than five minutes, shot

through the heart with an arrow. She evidently knew that some one
coming to her rescue. She did not see us, but it was apparent that
was endeavoring to make her escape when she received the fatal shot.

In camp was found a book, the first of the kind I had even seen,
which I was made a great hero, slaying Indians by the hundred and I
have often thought that as Mrs. White would read the same and knowing that I lived near, she would pray for my appearance and that she
might be saved. I did come but had not the power to convince those
that were in command over me to pursue my plan for her rescue. They
would not listen to me and they failed. (94–96)

On one level, of course, Carson is attempting to validate the myth:
Mrs. White would have been saved, and he would have been the very
hero described in those books, had the others only listened to him.
The fault is all the more clearly theirs because they do not accept the
myth. But at the same time, he is also revealing his discomfort with the
power of that myth to mislead her into a false hope. It is possible, for
instance, to read in the passage that Mrs. White's fatal decision to
attempt an escape to her "rescuers" was prompted by her faith in that
myth. In any case, the event ended tragically because of a myth, a
distortion of imagination, and because the party failed to trust a man,
specifically a professional, who was capable of seeing beyond the myth
to the real dangers. As in Garrard's book, the real world provides a
rude interruption for the men seeking to rescue "a fair maiden from
the hands of ruthless savages," and an even darker surprise for the
maiden herself.[24]

A failure of imagination, then, can bring about a failure of expansion. By imagining Indians as less than completely villainous, the
rangers seal Mrs. White's fate and fail as heroes. Many Western tales
offer this word of caution to the "civilized" imagination; generally, as
in this case, the reader is warned against underestimating Indian villainy. But in many tales, the reader finds it equally dangerous to
overestimate that villainy. In Charles Brockden Brown's *Edgar Huntly*
(1799), the narrator's imagination has become unhinged by the early
experience of the slaughter of his parents: "You will not be surprized
that the fate of my parents, and the sight of the body of one of this
savage band, who, in the pursuit that was made after them, was
overtaken and killed, should produce lasting and terrific images in my
fancy. I never looked upon or called up the image of a savage without
shuddering" (173). While Edgar certainly has a justifiable reason for his

later unhappiness, his "fancy" is depicted as no less diseased. His sanity is questioned, and so his status as a civilized man.

This notion of Indian hating as a disease of imagination and an inseparable, and troubling, part of Western expansion, was explored by Robert Bird in his popular *Nick of the Woods* (1837). In his 1853 preface to the book, Bird defined the social and literary poetics of the tradition:

> The whole object here was to portray the peculiar characteristics of a class of men, very limited, of course, in number, but found, in the old Indian days, scattered, at intervals, along the extreme frontier of every State. . .; men in which the terrible barbarities of the savages, suffered through their families, or their friends and neighbors, had wrought a change of temper as strange as fearful. That passion is the mightiest which overcomes the most powerful restraints and prostrates the strong-est barriers. . . . No one conversant with the history of border affairs can fail to recollect some one or more instances of solitary men, bereaved fathers or orphaned sons, the sole survivors, sometimes, of exterminated households, who remained only to devote themselves to lives of ven-geance; and "Indian-hating" (which implied the fullest indulgence of a rancorous animosity no blood could appease) was so far from being an uncommon passion in some particular districts, that it was thought to have infected, occasionally, persons, other wise of good repute, who ranged the woods, intent on private adventures, which they were careful to conceal from the public eye. (9)

Like Irving, Bird associates the workings of imagination with the work of expansion: Nathan's Indian hating is conceived as an "infection" of both mind and society. His desire for vengeance has taken on a life of its own, independent of the savage cause that generated it—"a ranco-rous animosity no blood could appease"—and this independence not only leads him away from his social commitments but has led others to do the same. In short, he has turned national conflict into "private adventures," and has even concealed them from "public view." Like Irving also, Bird uses the language of Western narrative to chart this "change of temper": Nathan has crossed the boundaries of restraint, has "prostrated" those "barriers" that define the "border" land of the frontier. The Indian hater thus became the emblematic figure in deter-mining where those boundaries were to be placed, and how they were to be maintained, in the adventurous enterprise of Western expansion.

Perhaps the most representative figure in this tradition is James Hall's Indian-hating Colonel John Moredock from *Sketches of History*,

Life, and Manners in the West, a work published in the same year as Irving's *Tour*. In a narrative plotting common in Western literature since the first captivity narratives, Moredock, like Brown's Huntly and Bird's Nathan, has come to hate Indians because they have slaughtered his family: when he is young, his mother, who had already lost a number of husbands to Indian attacks, is killed along with his siblings. When he grows older, he hunts down and kills those Indians responsible, but he is not satisfied with so surgical a vengeance. Indian killing soon becomes "the ruling passion of his life": "He thought it praiseworthy to kill an Indian; and would roam through the forest silently and alone, for days and weeks, with this single purpose" (2:81). Hall's discomfort with Moredock's obsessiveness is obvious; that it is an obsession of imagination is indicated in the opening to the story, a discussion of the role that tales of atrocities, in addition to the actual events, play in such cases on the frontier. "From the cradle, [the pioneer] listens continually to horrid tales of savage violence, and becomes familiar with narratives of aboriginal cunning and ferocity" (2:77).

It is all the more remarkable, then, that Hall proceeds to praise Moredock as "a man of determined courage, and great coolness and steadiness of purpose," and even compliments him as a decent and kind human being:

> The reader must not infer. . .that Colonel Moredock was unsocial, ferocious, or by nature cruel. On the contrary, he was a man of warm feelings, and excellent disposition. At home he was like other men, conducting a large farm with industry and success, and gaining the good will of all his neighbours by his popular manners and benevolent deportment. (2:81–82)

At home, perhaps, but in the wilderness Moredock was different from other men, even dangerously close to not being a man at all. He had almost become a savage, incapable of successful industry and community spirit.[25]

We find this concern over the diseased imagination more explicitly articulated in Hall's depiction of another Indian hater, the "Pioneer," in his *Tales of the Border*, also published in 1835. Once again we find a character driven to obsessive hatred because his family has been killed or carried off by Indians. In this case, however, the savagery of that hatred makes it impossible for him to go "home" again. As the Pioneer explains, hatred had "rendered me moody and unsocial. It kept me estranged from society, encouraged a habit of self-torture, and perpetuated a chain of indignant and sorrowful reflections" (Pearce 1967, 228). He is rescued from savagery when, about to kill an Indian squaw, he discovers that she is actually his sister, and further, that she is happy as an Indian. These revelations paradoxically restore his civilized values by reminding him of the boundaries between the civilized and the savage. What the Pioneer comes to realize is that, as Roy Harvey Pearce has noted, "Only as a savage had he the right to such vengeance; for only as savages did the Indians have a right thus to protect themselves from the white man and their ways" (1967, 229). The "sorrowful reflections" of his diseased imagination become the serene understandings of a man who has learned to adjust his imagination to his experiences. Upon recovering his civility, he returns home to put to proper social use what he has learned by his experiences in the world of savagery: he becomes a preacher.

If Hall thus defended this disease of the imagination, he also recognized that such tale-telling challenged the white man's community of belief. In a revealing passage in *Sketches,* he implied his dilemma: "The valley of the Mississippi has been the theatre of hardy exploit and curious adventure, throughout the whole period of our national existence, and its fertile plains present at this time a wide field of speculation. If we trace the solitary path of the fearless Boone; if we pursue the steps of Shelby, of Clarke, of Logan, and of Scott, we find them beset with dangers so terrible, adventures so wild, and achievements so wonderful, as to startle credulity" (1:17). Hall may not go so far as to claim that these tales are in fact exaggerated or distorted, but his comment suggests an uneasiness that the tales could lose their efficacy as a mode of social cohesion. For the adventurous tale of Western expansion to succeed, it must be believed by its listeners; the crossing of the frontier must be accompanied by the crossing of the frontier of credulity. Yet this approach is not without its dangers, as Hall acknowledges by pointing to those unsettling frontier tales which, by extending those boundaries of credulity, lead the white settlers into threatening situations.

Irving's response to this problem differed from Hall's. While Irving sought to adjust the imagination to fit the experience, Hall intended to adapt the reader's sense of experience to the heroic imagination of adventurous enterprise. Both, however, were conceiving problem and solution in the terms offered by their culture, placing the imagination as paramount component of the Western movement. The role of the imagination ranged from seeing to envisioning, from acknowledging the real to creating the believable, from relying on shared experience to inspiring individual exploit. In the former camp stand such works as Irving's *Tour* (1835), Garrard's *Wah-to-yah* (1850), Dana's *Two Years Before the Mast* (1840), James Paulding's *Westward Ho!* (1832), George Catlin's *Letters and Notes on the Manners, Customs, and Conditions of North American Indians* (1844), and Samuel Parker's *Journal of an Exploring Tour beyond the Rocky Mountains* (1838); in the latter, such works as Hall's books, Filson's *The Discovery, Settlement and Present State of Kentucke* (1784), James O. Pattie's *Personal Narrative* (1833), and Charles Fenno Hoffman's *A Winter in the West* (1835). As we have seen, this range is framed by the language of adventurous enterprise, in which the polarities of tension were defined as self-interest and the common good. But by focusing on the work of the imagination as the principal mediator between the new commercial values that were leading America westward and the traditional values that unified it as a republic, these works revealed a larger premise of the culture: America itself was a dramatic form, and its culture a faculty of imagination. According to this scheme, the success of the American adventure in the West had indeed come to depend on the success of the tale of adventurous enterprise. Beginning with *A Tour on the Prairies,* Irving would prescribe what he felt were the proper, professional boundaries to the shape of that tale and the work of the imagination that produced it.

3

A Satire of Western Economic Expansion: *A Tour on the Prairies*

When Irving's first Western book was first reviewed, it was immediately recognized as a particular kind of American literary work, a work of Western economic expansion. In a review in the *North American Review,* the well-regarded and widely circulated critic Everett Emerson praised the work as an illustration of the establishment of a "classical" American literature through the effective and profitable use of native American materials. "We thank [Irving]," Emerson stated, "for turning these poor barbarous *steppes* into classical land" (1835, 14); that is, for endowing the West itself with a classical literary form. This view of the book was confirmed, in part, by Irving's placement of it as the first text in a three volume series entitled *The Crayon Miscellany.* The second volume included *Abbotsford* and *Newstead Abbey,* accounts of Irving's visits to the estate of Walter Scott and Lord Byron's mansion, and the third volume was *Legends of the Conquest of Spain,* a collection of tales about the conquest of Spain by the Saracens. In conjunction with these

others, *A Tour* appears as another evocation of a classical land associated with a rich literary past; and, in this sense, the book does indeed
transform the American wilderness into America's classical land. But
Emerson's definition of "classical" has less to do with the mutabilities
of a literary past than the exigencies of an economic present. The
success of this classical form, in Emerson's terms, lay in its economy,
the economy of the American imagination asserting itself in the West.

Irving's chief accomplishment, it would seem, lay in his ability to
use the West as a resource for his, and the reader's, profit. In a lead up
to a quotation from the book, for instance, Emerson implicitly con-
nects his own informing metaphors of economics and rebirth ("labored"): "The following example will show more forcibly, than any
labored comments, how much Irving has made of his materials" (7).
When he later compliments Irving by noting his ability to enliven even
those materials more properly belonging to "the dull round of business" (13), he is not so much attacking business itself as praising Irving
for making that business, the American round of business, profitable.
"We behold with delight his easy and triumphant march over these
beaten fields, but we glow with rapture as we see him coming back
from the Prairies, laden with the poetical treasures of the primitive
wilderness,—rich with spoil from the uninhabited desert" (14); and
finally, "No matter how cold, and barren, and desolate the scene,"
Irving manages to "fill it with life and motion, with interest and
passion." That this "interest" is a gauge of economic as well as literary
value becomes clear at the end of the review when Emerson states his,
and what he sees as Irving's, underlying objectives directly:

> Let him write on; he can write nothing which will not be eagerly
> anticipated and cordially welcomed; and we trust, we may add, well
> paid. If it be not, it is a scandal to the country. If, in these times of
> overflowing prosperity; when princely fortunes are daily built up in the
> country; when, under our happy institutions, an energy and enterprise,
> elsewhere unexampled, are in a state of the intensest action, and are daily
> reaping a golden harvest, in all the fields of prosperous industry, if there
> is not, on all hands, the disposition,—the resolute and affectionate
> purpose,—to make the talents and accomplishments of a man, like
> Washington Irving,—who is an honor to his country,—the source of
> fortune to himself, then we shall deserve, that he once again leave us
> forever. But we indulge no such sinister anticipation. We believe a better
> day is dawning on American letters, that our republican princes are

beginning to understand, that of all sordid things sordid affluence is the meanest[.] (27)

In this context of literature as a source of personal and national fortune, Irving's book has the capability, if read and appreciated properly—that is, with "interest"—to keep America away from the path of "sordid affluence" and on the right path of "prosperous industry."

This double use of the term "interest" was popular at the time. For instance, another contemporary reviewer of *A Tour* noted that "the author has invested every incident and picture with a high interest" (Dula 71). And a few years later Edgar Allan Poe explained, in a review of Cooper's novel *Wyandotté,* that the writer best serves his own interests by cultivating his reader's:

> In saying that the [reader's] interest depends, *first,* upon the nature of the theme, we mean to suggest that this theme—life in the Wilderness —is one of intrinsic and universal interest, appealing to the heart of man in all phases; a theme, like that of life upon the ocean, so unfailingly omniprevalent in its power of arresting and absorbing attention, that while success or popularity is, with such a subject, expected as a matter of course, a failure might be properly regarded as conclusive evidence of imbecility on the part of the author. (*Poetry* 479)

Emerson's use of the term differs from Poe's only in the moral component that he sees as part of that act of engagement between writer and reader in the marketplace. For Emerson, Irving's book succeeds not just because it is entertaining or useful or profitable—that is, captures the reader's "interest"—but because it also uses that interest to instruct the reader in recognizing certain prescriptions for moral action, such as the proper guidelines for the exercise of economic expansion.

Emerson's conception of the work as a cautionary endorsement of expansion is, in fact, an accurate rendering of Irving's overall purpose. Irving did use his tourist's appraisal of the Western territories as a means of exploring the nation's movement West, and he did find much to champion as well as criticize in that movement. But his book was far more troubled about American commercialism than Emerson thought. For Irving, the enterprise of Western economic expansion was in grave danger, and found its greatest threats not in such outside forces as Indians or a harsh landscape, but in the forces of commercialism itself.

Irving explored these dangers by focusing on one of the popular imaginative forms that his culture had adopted as a way of expressing and representing its expansionism, the Indian adventure tale. Throughout *A Tour* he examined the tale's accuracy and underlying values as a text of expansionism. Against its narrative form promoting Western economic expansion, he placed the conditions of expansion he found on his journey; against its confident formulations of white heroes and Indian villains he placed the characters he met along the way. *A Tour on the Prairies* thus became a tour not only of the nation's movement West, but of one of the principal literary forms by which it represented that expansion to itself.

The end result was satire. Through each conjunction of experience and imagination, expansion and tale of expansion, Irving revealed the illusory and self-serving values of capitalist expansion that the white men had brought with them.[1] The enterprising American had fooled himself into believing his own self-portrait as adventurer, and was failing to measure up. Instead of conquering Indians, he had become a victim of his own savage greed; instead of doing business he had become a thief; instead of cultivating resources he had become an exploiter; instead of becoming a worthy man of adventure he had become a foolish and frightened and dangerous adventurer. The path to prosperity was fast leading to a sordid affluence, if affluence at all.

But if Irving thus offered a critique of the false tale of adventurous enterprise, he did not abandon its underlying tenets. In the end his satire was largely comic, designed not to undermine but only to revise that tale, to curtail its reckless celebration of unfettered expansionism. As a mode of adjustment he offered an economic aesthetic that would produce success in the Western experience through a series of restraints based upon the exercise of "professionalism" in both the doing and the telling. Expansion itself would thus acquire built-in boundaries, such as the recognition of a class hierarchy in the West, the "composition" and "diversification" of the landscape, the mastery of the figurative and descriptive uses of tale-telling and language. This new aesthetic and ethic of professionalism is represented as an antidote to the misleading tale-telling on the one hand, and the failed experience on the other. The result is a joining of experience and imagination, tale of expansion and expansion itself, self-interest and the common good: a renewed tale of America's adventurous enterprise. Like all satires, in other words, this was a book which sought to educate the reader. While Irving's characters were confronted with their illusory preconceptions about the Western venture, while his own narrative persona was confronted with the illusory preconceptions of the Western adventure tale he had come to write, the readers were led to recognize the inadequacies of their own economic idealism and the tales they read to confirm it.

Irving begins this process of education by explaining to the reader up front that this is no ordinary adventure tale. In the book's "Introduction," he warns his reader that while he was "expected to write about a region fruitful of wonders and adventures," he has "nothing wonderful or adventurous to offer," and that his book is nothing more than "a simple narrative of everyday occurrences" (8–9). The denial is true enough on one level: the West he saw was indeed the unadventurous West of the everyday, and his work would record it as such. But his denial also tells us to be wary of that record, for in the phrase "simple narrative of everyday occurrences," he is placing his account within a tradition in American literature in which the focus of the narrative in fact shifts *away* from these literal occurrences to the writer's, and reader's, interpretations of them. William Hedges has described it concisely: "One of the chief concerns of American fiction. . .is with the irony embodied in the seeker, searcher, viewer, sometimes virtual voyeur, whose observations or researches end by revealing, to the reader if not to the protagonist himself, more about the onlooker than about an observed world" (151). In part a reflection of the culture's suspicion of imagination (which, in the minds of some writers, was an unwitting exercise of imagination in itself), this perspective sought to explore the relation between the imagination and individual self-absorption.

A writer who used this approach with great effectiveness was Edgar Allan Poe, and one of his stories, "The Black Cat" (1843), throws some light on Irving's seeming disclaimer. In the opening of the story, the narrator denies that there is anything fanciful or invented in the tale he has to tell; it is merely an objective scrutiny of "a series of mere household events" (*Poetry* 597). A close reading of the story reveals otherwise, however, as we discover that his household events take place in a house of madness, and his objective scrutiny consists of delusions representing a variety of pathological terrors. The narrator's denial, that is, is really Poe's invitation to the reader to look beyond the tale to the telling. For Poe, and many other American writers of this period, the "truth" was hidden in, and by, the ways the characters constructed the stories they tell—or, in the case of this narrator and many of his others, deny they are telling—to give order to their everyday lives. We must "analyze" these stories if we are to understand the psychological and cultural forces that direct those lives.

Irving employed this strategy many times before writing *A Tour*. In the opening to *Bracebridge Hall,* for instance, he noted that "I am not writing a novel, and have nothing of intricate plot, or marvellous adventure, to promise the reader" (9). And early in the first edition of *The Alhambra* he explains that he is "not writing a regular narrative, and do not pretend to give the varied events of several days' rambling over hill and dale, and moor and mountain" (*Al* 26). While these disclaimers work slightly differently in each of the books, they produce much the same general effect of introducing some concern over the exercise of imagination, suggesting that the relation between the imagination and the world around it is tenuous at best. On the simplest level, Irving may be hoping to defend himself against the expectations of his readers for a more fully realized work, thus preventing loss of both critical support and a profitable readership. He may also hope to diminish his self-exposure by adopting a posture of diffidence and gentility, a characteristic style of evasion one finds throughout his career. He notes both of these concerns in *A Tour* when he explains that "I have always had a repugnance, amounting almost to disability, to write in the face of expectation" (8). But Irving is also announcing his intention to explore one of his most characteristic subjects, the relation between reality and perception.[2]

This is just the strategy signaled by Irving's opening to *A Tour*. The narrator's "simple narrative of everyday occurrences" will operate much like "The Black Cat" narrator's "ordinary succession of very natural causes and effects" (*Poetry* 597), albeit with some modifications. Irving would not go so far as Poe in making reality itself contingent upon the interpretations of individual perception. Where for Poe the world outside was inevitably obscured by the acquisitive powers of imagination, for Irving the dialectic between reality and imagination would remain the primary means of identifying the truths of both the world and the psyche. In this case in particular, Irving was less interested in the properties of individual madness than with the perversities of culture-bound self-interest. Specifically, he wanted to explore the self-justifying shape of the American commercial imagination, a shape that was both revealed in and perpetuated by the stories it told. However suspicious Americans might have been about the workings of the imagination, they were nonetheless powerfully influenced by the imagination of the marketplace, particularly as embodied in those cultural fictions relating to the economic expansion of the Westward movement. In *A Tour* Irving would seek to remove that suspicion even while debunking those fictions; he would align the interests of the imagination with the interests of the marketplace.

To this end, the book begins with a central irony. The tour by which Irving hoped to reacquaint himself with his "native land" is characterized as a journey through Indian territory, a "native" land in itself as yet "uncharted" (if not unclaimed) by the "white man" (here meaning the Americans). Irving's pun on "native" quickly brings into question the basic premise of that designation, that the true natives in and of this land are the white Americans. In Irving's formulation, the identity of this commercially expanding America was to be defined not by its own claims to ordained and indigenous possession, but by its response, both actual and imaginative, to the native Indian populations then living in those territories, natives with equal if different claims to possession. By charting the popular adventurous representations of that relationship between white man and Indian—as hero to a real foe or alarmist to an imagined one, as civilized man to savage or savage man to noble savage, as parent to an errant child or spoiled child to a wise father, as cultivator of property or usurper of both nature and the child of nature—Irving set out to reveal both the basic cultural assumptions behind, and the actual consequences of, expansion.

The Indian Adventure Tale

If, for many Americans during this period, the "Indian wilderness" was America, then the Indian adventure tale was the tale of their mission, their enterprise.[3] This conception was popular well to the end of the nineteenth century, when, once again, Turner summarized the position by identifying "the effect of the Indian frontier" as a "consolidating agent in our history": each frontier of Western expansion, and thus each stage of the "winning of the West" and the creation of the American republic, was "won by a series of Indian wars" (42, 46). As early as the first settlements, according to Richard Slotkin, the Indian war became "a metaphor for the entire secular history of the society, and as a link with the sacred mythology of the Bible." Soon both Whites and Indians were transformed into a "cast of characters representative of the important social and political tensions within the colony" (1985, 55).

By the nineteenth century, these tensions had become largely associated with the marketplace of Western expansion, and the economic enticements of expansion had, in most instances, come to provide the terms of the drama. Within such forms as captivity narratives, guidebooks, almanacs, fur trapper narratives, and travel journals, the Indians were cast in two related roles: as impediments to and as martyrs of expansion. In both cases they were the characters conquered in the march of civilization. As prior residents of the land, they inhibited the settlers from free and peaceful access to that requisite foundation for their economic success. As Michael Paul Rogin has pointed out, land "was the major economic resource, the major determiner of social status, and the major source of political power in early America," a condition by which, in the nineteenth century, the Western lands in particular had become "the most important single source of American economic development from 1815 to 1845, the decades during which market capitalism transformed America" (79–80). The dispossession of Indian land thus became an integral "part of the history of American capitalism" (13).

This transformation of land into property, and the Indian into the illegitimate holder of that property, was a fundamental principle in the rhetoric of expansion as far back as the first settlements. John Winthrop declared that the deaths of Indians (by smallpox) "cleared our title to what we possess" (Pearce 1967, 19), a title granted the colonists by their divine appointment as spreaders of the American civilization. In a self-justifying twist of logic, the notion of property thus became the boundary separating civilization from savage, white man from Indian, and the justification for any acts of dispossession committed in the name of that boundary: Indian property was American property simply because Americans, as civilized people, saw its value as property. Indians, as savages, only saw it as a stage for their "wandering," an activity which, in the language of the villainous "other," was the savage version—and thus repudiation—of the civilized act of expansion. The acquisition and cultivation of that property—and generally, the acquisition was considered to be an act of cultivation in itself—was an indisputable necessity since the expansion of civilization depended upon it. This circular logic persisted over the next two hundred years and played as central a role in the settlement of the Far West. James Hall, for instance, invoking the Lockean reasoning of the *Declaration,* claimed that the Indians had no "rights" to their land because they were savages, and that they were savages because they had no notion of property: "The proposition is well understood, as applied to ourselves, that *security* of person and property, is the basis of all our rights, and is the chief cause of all our civilisation. Why should not the converse of that proposition be true of the Indians: that the insecurity of property, or rather the entire absence of all ideas of property, is the chief cause of their barbarism" (*Sketches* 1:128).

Irving had satirized just this relation between the treatment of Indians and the notion of property as a product of civilization in *A History of New York*. In his discussion of the colonists' clashes with Indians, Knickerbocker outlines the three basic "rights" by which the land was claimed by the immigrants: the rights by discovery, cultivation, and extermination (this last otherwise termed the "right by gunpowder"). Knickerbocker's satire acquires its power not by exaggerating such reasoning but only by mimicking it:

> In entering upon a newly discovered, uncultivated country therefore, the new comers were but taking possession of what, according to the aforesaid doctrine, was their own property—therefore, in opposing them, the savages were invading their just rights, infringing the immutable laws of nature and counteracting the will of heaven—therefore they were guilty of impiety, burglary and trespass on the case,—therefore they were hardened offenders against God and man—therefore they ought to be exterminated. (416)

Such "reasoning" was virtually impossible to undermine. To question the rights of Americans to dispossess Indians of the land was to challenge not only the superiority of the American civilization but the sanctity of its mission. Certainly the logic of the Indians themselves was unacceptable. "My reason teaches me that *land cannot be sold,*" said Black Hawk in 1834: "The Great Spirit gave it to his children to live upon, and cultivate, as far as is necessary for their subsistence; and so long as they occupy and cultivate it, they have the right to the soil" (101). This point of view was generally considered as dangerous as it was wrong; certainly it was never considered worthy enough to debate.

But it was also considered the Indians' only argument, and thus an unarguable justification for transforming Indian land into American property.

This reasoning was elaborated along a number of similar lines. For instance, if Indians were characterized as unable to understand the principles of "civilized" property—the individual right to acquire property, the concept of transferable title, and the legality of buying and selling land—they were also deemed unable to understand how land should be treated as property; that is, cultivated for profit. "By nature," according to Lewis Cass, Indians have "that unconquerable aversion to labor, so characteristic of all savage tribes" (1830, 71). That it is unconquerable does not mean that Indians themselves cannot be conquered, only that they cannot be so civilized as to appreciate the need to work, to turn nature into a product of civilization.

By such an association between property and civilization, the soil itself became infused with the values of both while the system of market capitalism was strengthened. Ralph Waldo Emerson stipulated the cultural imperatives behind this process when he identified property as "the motive to industry" (*Journals* 10:312). The economic principles underlying this rhetorical stance were later explored by Rosa Luxemburg:

> Capital in its struggle against societies with a natural economy pursues the following ends:
>
> 1. To gain immediate possession of important sources of productive forces such as land. . . .
> 2. To "liberate" labour power and to coerce it into service.
> 3. To introduce a commodity economy.
> 4. To separate trade and agriculture. . . .
>
> Since the primitive associations of the natives are the strongest protection for their social organizations and for their material bases of existence, capital must begin by planning for the systematic destruction and annihilation of all the noncapitalist social units which obstruct its development. (Takaki 69)[4]

Certainly not all of the Americans who moved into Indian territory were as open and deliberate about their intentions. There were many who perceived the threat to the Indians as well, and called for the alternative of bringing them within the boundaries of the civilized world by instilling them with a *"love of property,"* to use Timothy Dwight's phrase (Rosenthal 44). Of course, they would still be dispossessed. But even though this alternative was consistent with their basic reasoning, most Americans found it unacceptable. Were Indians to be thus civilized—that is, if such civilizing were even possible, which, as the rhetoric suggests, was deemed unlikely at best—they would then be able to make claims to that property by the same logic. As Ronald Takaki has pointed out, what these American enterprisers, and Jackson in particular, desired as part of the marketplace "was the Indian's land, not the Indian himself as a Lockean farmer" (99).

These same arguments were also directed against Blacks during this period, and for many of the same reasons. Many of the Indian wars, in fact, were nothing more than attempts to deny to fugitive slave an access to land for either ownership or security. Jackson's Seminole Wars were a case in point: General Philip Jesup, one of the principal military leader of the second of these wars, declared the confrontation of 1836–1837 to be "a negro, not an Indian war; and if it not be speedily put down, the south will feel the effects of it on their slave population" (Rogin 238). Ronald Takaki places the connection on a more fundamental level when he notes that "The removal of Indians and the expansion of black slavery made possible the Market Revolution" (78).

The connection between Indians and Blacks also manifested itself in the rhetoric as Indians were commonly identified as Blacks and even "niggurs" during this period. We find a characteristic example in fur trapper Long Hatcher's description of a skirmish with Indians: "I takes tother Injun by the har and makes meat of him *too. Maybe* thar wasn't coups counted an' a big dance on hand [even] ef I was alone. I got old bull-thrower [his rifle], made medicine over him, an' no darned niggur [Indian] kin draw bead with him since" (DeVoto 1947, 44; the bracketed information is DeVoto's). Irving himself describes the origins of this rhetorical practice in a passage in *A History of New York* in which Knickerbocker explains that "being of a copper complexion, it was all the same as if [Indians] were negroes—and negroes are black, 'and black' said the pious fathers, devoutly crossing themselves, 'is the colour of the Devil!' Therefore so far from being able to own property, they had no right even to personal freedom, for liberty is too radiant a deity, to inhabit such gloomy temples" (414).

But Indians did not become the villains of Western adventure tales because they prevented easy acquisition of land by white "Americans"; in fact, the Indians were actually present only in a very small proportion of the Western lands available to Whites. To be sure, many white

feared that Indians would impede economic expansion regard-
n ironic consequence, in part, of the very tales of Indian terror
intransigence that white culture had produced to confirm the
⌐ ⌐riority of its own expansionism. But to discover the sources of
these prejudices in the context of economic expansion, one must also
seek out less literal relations between motivation and image.

At this early stage of marketplace expansion, many Americans were
troubled by their new-found independence, and especially by the advent of economic individualism. This concern, though, did not generally express itself as an enlightened sympathy for the Indians as victims
of excessive acquisitiveness. Instead, the Indian became another kind
of villain, a dark double of the American enterpriser. The images
themselves remained the same—the Indian as savage, as primitive, as
"natural man"—but where, in the cases discussed above, these images
were used to characterize the essence of Indian villainy as an anti-
capitalism, here they were used to characterize it as a capitalism gone
mad in the wilderness. In projecting the fears of their own independence and acquisitiveness onto the Indians, the Americans thus managed both to express those fears and to preserve the distinction between savage and civilized, heroic self and villainous other, that prompted
the dictates of their expansionism in the first place.

We see the foundation for this displacement most vividly in the
frequent incidence of disguise and mistaken identity in captivity accounts, trapper journals and dime novels. In these narrative patterns,
white men and women adopt Indian ways and thus exhibit an alarming
propensity to become Indians, to become savage in the wilderness. The
actions of such Indian haters as Bird's Nathan Slaughter and Hall's
Colonel Moredock represent, in this context, a grim identification
between Indians and Whites. "In the figure of the dangerous Frontiersman," writes Richard Slotkin, "the ideology of ruthless commercialism
is associated with the doctrine of savage warfare derived from the
Puritan polemics of Mather and Nowell" (1985, 79). Revealed in these
images of ruthless white men and ruthless Indians is not only the
hidden "Indian" in the white man but the hidden "white man" in the
Indian as well, an ironic commentary on the notion that the white
man's mission was to possess the wilderness in the name of civilization:
in fact the white men in these stories are really discovering the savagery
they have brought with them, the perseverance and shrewdness and

exuberance of commercialism. The adventures of economic expansion were transforming the white man into a savage opportunist.

But if this pattern of imagery voiced a concern over economic expansion, it did not indicate a rejection of expansion. In fact, this displacement of fears was also an expression of displaced desires. In response to the threat of this breakdown in boundaries between the civilized capitalist and savage Indian, the images of the Indians themselves became exaggerated precisely along the lines of the white man's hidden desires. The conventionally assigned Indian virtues thus became Indian vices: the Indian's perseverance became his rabid possessiveness (the avenger), his shrewdness in bartering became his unreliability (the betrayer), his exuberance became his dissipation (the drunk). By thus displacing their own acquisitive desires onto the Indians and identifying these Indians as the villainous other, the Americans could protect those desires, and eliminate the guilt and fear that attended them, by then displacing the Indians in turn, "removing," murdering, idealizing them out of existence.

While such a narrative strategy was certainly successful in legitimizing the dispossession of the Indians, it was not always so successful in eliminating the feelings of guilt that came along with it. Another image of the Indian consequently appeared: the martyr. This figure represented the innocence, purity, and naturalness that Americans feared they were in danger of losing in their expansion into economic independence as a nation. We find this figure most decisively rendered in the leading character of Washington Irving's "Philip of Pokanoket," in *The Sketch Book*. Irving recognized that ennobling so controversial a man required great sensitivity, especially a man generally considered to have posed the gravest threat to the success of early New England and to have caused the most damage and grief. Yet Irving not only turned him into a hero, but into a typological representation of the original American, and by extension of the America sacrificed to the ideals of expansion and progress.[5]

But the complexity of Irving's characterization was hardly the norm. Generally the martyr figure was simply a victim, and one more of his own inadequacies than of the incontinence of his conquerors. So while the martyr may at first seem to indicate a different role for the Indian in this drama, in an odd way he too was a villain, an "other" who must be conquered if the hero is to succeed in his mission. While dignified within the boundaries of a cultural primitivism, he was yet doomed to fall before the divinely ordained expansion of the American way of life. The image of his dignity—his "simple" beliefs and "primitive" relation to the land—finally represented the absence of civilization, just as, in Renaissance Christian theology, evil was defined as a distance from good. As Francis Parkman baldly reported, "He will not learn the arts of civilization, and he and his forest must perish together" (*Conspiracy* 44).[6] James Fenimore Cooper was even more direct in his reference to the implicit dramatic formulation. In Roy Harvey Pearce's words, "savage heroism, as [Cooper] called it, was doomed, even in the west, to go down before civilized heroism." And, in his own words, "As a rule, the red man disappears before the superior moral and physical influence of the white" (Pearce 1967, 201). However sad their demise, the Indians were never finally portrayed as the true heroes of the tale, for that rightness and goodness, that right and privilege for unlimited acquisition and possession, were properties of the civilized man alone.

This is not to say that Indians were never accorded the status of "hero" in the popular imagination, but rather that this Indian heroism was of a different order than the heroism reserved for the white man. The Indian hero might be represented as a figure of great conviction, courage, and perseverance, and might even be depicted as superior in spirit to the white adversaries that have come to defeat him. But those adversaries were never, in these cases, heroic in themselves, for the Indian hero would never be able to defeat a white hero. In the end, he must even suffer defeat at the hands of his inferior adversary, a stipulation that limits his heroism to his doomed nobility.

Still, some writers considered even this assignation of heroism to Indians as an attack on civilized values. Just as Indians were associated with fears about the fragile boundaries of the ethics of economic enterprise, so too were they associated with fears of revolutionary violence. With the memory of the Revolution still vivid, with revolutionary activity still present in Europe, and with a national ideology that seemed to ordain the revolutionary sentiment as the foundation of liberty, many Americans felt that the nation needed to protect itself from a process of continuing revolt within its own boundaries. The idealization of any outsiders, then, especially in the terms ratified by the culture, such as an oppressed self striking out against a tyrannical, authoritarian society, was perceived as a threat to the cohesion of the union. Commenting during the second Seminole War—the same war that other writers used to represent the necessary massacre of Indian villains—the writer James Paulding criticized the making of such "Indian heroes":

> I say heroes, for it seems only necessary for a bloody Indian to break his faith; plunder and burn a district or two; massacre a few hundred soldiers; and scalp a good number of women and children; to gain immortal honour. He will be glorified in Congress; canonized by philanthropists; autographed, and lithographed, and biographied, by authors, artists, and periodicals; the petticoated petitioners to Congress will weep, not over the fate of the poor white victims, but that of the treacherous and bloody murderer, who will receive his apotheosis in the universal sympathy of all the humble echoes and by poetical flowers of that prince of hypocrites old Johnny Bull. (*Letters* 215–216)

Once again, the Indian "hero" is placed up against the white hero and transformed into the dramatic other. Even the hero has become, in this sense, a villain—and a self—in disguise.

These are only some of the images of Indians that were common during Irving's time.[7] Given the popularity of these images, as well as their richness as vehicles for exploring the implications of economic expansion, it is not surprising that Irving would shape his first book on Western themes as an Indian adventure tale. The form of the adventure became both medium of entertainment and principal subject; or, more precisely, the medium became the subject. In the end, Irving's use of the form was satirical, exposing these Indian tales as misadventures of the expansionist American imagination.

Irving's Foray into the Pawnee Hunting Grounds

The most basic "adventure" of the Indian adventure tale was the Indian attack, and so this becomes a primary focus of Irving's satirical approach to these tales—the satire established by the pun on "native land"—and a central structural motif in *A Tour* by which Irving evaluates his culture's expansionist sensibility. The book begins with a chapter subtitled, first, "The Pawnee Hunting Grounds," establishing the expected suspense narrative as the touring party heads into this "dangerous neighborhood"; the book maintains this suspense throughout with a mention of the Indian threat in virtually every chapter, climaxing about two-thirds of the way through with an alarm in camp; and it ends with the same insistent characterization of the tour as a typical Western adventure: "and thus ended my foray into the Pawnee Hunting Grounds" (122).

At first glance, this is an unsurprising structure for a Western adventure tale. Yet, as Irving forewarned in the introductory denial, he had nothing adventurous to offer. The book, in fact, contains not a single incident with Indians: not one Pawnee is seen, and the climactic Indian alarm is nothing more than a burlesque of mistaken identity. Far from the "simple narrative of everyday occurrences" that Irving promised in the introduction, the book becomes, by this device, an adventure tale without the customary adventures, a complex narrative, that is to say, directed precisely at "those who look for a marvellous or adventurous story."

Irving did not, however, mean to suggest that there was no need to fear Indians in the West. Just before the tour Irving wrote to his friend William Jordan, with a curious combination of whimsy and apprehension, that he hoped "to escape unscalped or toma hawked" while on the trip; he wrote to his sister Catherine that he hoped "that we may be able to fall in with some wandering band of Pawnees in a friendly manner, as I have a great desire to see some of that warlike and vagrant race," a race "continually on the maraud"; and, after the tour, he wrote to his brother Peter that he had been lucky in avoiding the Pawnees, "the terror of that frontier" (*L2*:722, 727, 735). Such fears were common enough at the time. Only recently had gross distortions of the size and intent of movements by the Sauk and Fox tribes led to the Black Hawk War, which was also grossly distorted in the subsequent reportings. The army's "victory" did little to allay concern. Irving, in fact, had met Black Hawk, only recently incarcerated, on his way out West. While he wrote to Catherine that he found the old chief surprisingly "emaciated and enfeebled" (*L2*:723), he acknowledged that Black Hawk had been associated with many acts of violence. And these anxieties had been intensified in the area by the rumor that there had been a series of recent Indian wars in nearby terrain—between the Gros Ventres and the Crows—which Irving had confirmed when he met up with the fur trapper and trader Milton Sublette on the way to Fort Gibson. Sublette had only just returned from a dangerous encounter with the Gros Ventres, whose faces were still painted and whose talk was still hostile.[8]

Yet Irving chose to leave these details out of his own published account. His intention was not to deny the reality of the threat but to maintain his focus on the unstable responses of the men in the face of it. When he notes that "Thus in traversing these perilous wastes every foot print and dint of hoof becomes matter of cautious inspection and shrewd surmise" (*T* 61), and that "It is at passes like this that occur the most dangerous ambuscades and sanguinary surprises of Indian warfare" (64), he is making the reader aware of very real dangers in Western life. But he is also suggesting that one should learn to match that fear to the reality of the danger, and not indiscriminately project it onto Indians in general. Hence the book often shifts unexpectedly from real danger to false alarm and back again, leaving the reader to reconsider the literary formulae by which that danger is translated into justifiable action.

We find the first of these shifts in the second chapter when Irving establishes his motif of a passage into Indian territory with an image not clearly aligned with the narrative of danger he has just established. The party's entrance into that territory is marked by its crossing of the Verdigris River; while the men are not here entering the most dangerous hunting grounds of the Pawnee—that will come later with another river crossing—they are still entering unknown Indian lands. And soon they notice a mysterious Creek Indian on horseback watching from the opposite shore as the party crosses the ford. "He had paused to reconnoitre us from the brow of a rock," Irving writes,

> and formed a picturesque object, in unison with the wild scenery around him. He wore a bright blue hunting-shirt trimmed with scarlet fringe; a gaily colored handkerchief was bound round his head something like a turban, with one end hanging down beside his ear; he held a long rifle in his hand and looked like a wild Arab on the prowl. (14)

For all the specific details, one is hard pressed to know just what to make of this "object": is he dangerous, friendly, or merely "picturesque"? is he a mere impediment or a mysterious omen? The sense of caution and indecision apparent in Irving's search for a comprehending set of allusions and similes is echoed in the greeting offered by one of the guides: Tonish calls out to the Indian in "his Babylonish jargon" (14), the mixture of tongues representing the mixture of perspectives possible, and the unsure role of tale-telling, in that tangle of impression.[9]

Irving leaves the mystery unsolved, as "the savage having satisfied his curiosity tossed his hand in the air, turned the head of his steed, and gallopping along the shore soon disappeared among the trees" (14). The first Indian that Irving sees, then, on this tour into dangerous Indian territory, is presented as an inscrutable icon; one might say that his allusive iconography signifies inscrutability itself. Irving's similes may invoke an ostensibly pacifying romantic primitivism, but in the end it is the Indian's curiosity, and not Irving's or ours, that is satisfied.

This vision of the Indian as exotic can be found in many works of the time. Henry Nash Smith traces the origin of the figure to the perception of the Indians as uncivilized nomads of the American desert: "Although regions too dry for farming could be inhabited by migratory tribesmen following their flocks and herds, such people were considered uncivilized. They could not be integrated with American society and were therefore perpetual outlaws. The analogues were often mentioned—the Bedouins of the Arabian desert, the Tartars of Asiatic steppes" (176–177). In Irving's version, though, the figure is modified: he represents not an uncivilized outlaw, and not even an outsider, but a mysterious insider demarcating the threshold to America's "native land." Hence the very metaphor designed to exclude the Indian is transformed into a force of mystery that excludes the white man. And the mystery is not easily solved. In the chapters that follow, a narrative rhythm is quickly established between reiterations of the Indian threat and comic defeats of that threat; his portraits of Indians likewise varying from depictions of brutal savagery to honorable, if primitive, nobility. The problem, it seems, is not in the Western experience at all, not in the villainous Indians ready to attack, but in the disposition of the white man to fictionalize Indians according to the terms of their adventurous enterprise. In this way, Irving indicts not only the Western adventurers but writers and readers of Western adventure tales as well.

In the sixth chapter, he explicitly discusses these dubious workings of the imagination:

> In fact the Indians that I have had the opportunity of seeing in real life are quite different from those described in poetry. They are by no means the stoics they are represented; taciturn, unbending, without a tear or a smile. Taciturn they are, it is true, when in company with white men, whose good will they distrust, and whose language they do not understand; but the white man is equally taciturn under like circumstances.

> When the Indians are among themselves, however, there cannot be
> greater gossips. (26)

"As far as I can judge," he concludes, "the Indian of poetical fiction is
like the shepherd of pastoral romance, a mere personification of imaginary attributes" (27). By focusing the reader's attention on the literary
formulations of the Indian, Irving is first suggesting, of course, that
there is a reality that the American imagination has misperceived or
distorted. The Indians, that is, are more "human" than these formulations allow. But he is also directing his reader's attention to the source
of those formulations, the imaginative process whereby Indians are
made into these "mere personifications."

He points to that process when he locates the Indians' "personhood"
in their capacity for self-expression, and when he notes that the white
man may have arrived at his misconceptions because the Indians were
unable to understand the white man's own form of self-expression, his
language. The effect of such a passage (and there are many like it) is to
lead the reader to reevaluate the validity and purpose of his or her
traditional imaginative perceptions. But Irving is not suggesting that
the imagination itself be mistrusted or abandoned in favor of "reality."
Rather he is leading the reader to question the hidden purposes behind
those perceptions that may have led to the distortion. This way the
national imagination will be regenerated, able to register the world as
it truly exists.

Early in the book there is a passage in which Irving sets up the
terms of his examination of the white man's confused imaginative
conceptions of the Indian. He describes at length an Osage visitor who
rides for a time with the party, only to disappear with much the same
mystery as the earlier Creek overseer. The travelers first meet the young
Osage as he rides up to the party with "open, noble countenance and
frank demeanour" (20), a guilelessness that is emphasized by a contrast
to the "sinister visage and high-handed conduct" of a "frontiers-man"
who had also just joined the party. It seems that one of the frontiersman's horses had recently been stolen, and that "he was sure it had
been stolen in the night by a straggling party of Osages encamped in a
neighboring swamp—but he would have satisfaction! He would make
an example of the villains" (19). The timely appearance of the Osage
would provide him with that example.

Irving's attitude toward this confrontation illustrates his intention to revise the traditional white hero/Indian villain formulation. He notes the superficial nature of the white man's sense of that justice: the instrument of justice would be the unsubtle rifle, "that invariable enforcer of right or wrong upon the frontiers" (19), and he would exercise that instrument with blind vindictiveness, with "the frontier propensity to charge every thing to the Indians" (19). Upon seeing the Indian leading what he identifies as his horse—the Indian claims he is looking to return the horse to its owner, but the owner claims it is an old Indian trick to acquire reward money—he calls "for tying [him] to a tree and giving him a sound lashing; and was quite surprised at the burst of indignation which this novel mode of requiting a service drew from us." "Such, however," Irving comments,

> is too often the administration of law on the frontier, "Lynch's law," as it is technically termed, in which the plaintiff is apt to be witness, jury, judge and executioner, and the defendant to be convicted and punished on mere presumption; and in this way I am convinced, are occasioned many of those heart burnings and resentments among the Indians, which lead to retaliation, and end in Indian wars. (20)[10]

As it turns out, injustice is diverted, and the white man sent on his way. He does get the horse, however, and without paying any reward money. On this last point, Irving offers no censure. He had defended the Indian on the grounds that the accusations were based on false images of Indians in general; he had not, however, claimed that the Indian had any right to the horse or the money. Despite his concern for the Indian, Irving shared his culture's view that these rights were reserved to the civilized white man. If, in this case, the frontiersman was less than civilized, the horse was still more his property than the Indian's.

The focus of the passage, though, is not on the issue of property but of injustice. It is designed to lead the reader to question this making of Indian "villains," the unquestioning assent to the authority of romantic literary depictions untempered by experience and a disciplined imagination. Further, it leads the reader to question the makers of these tales, who, like the "hero of La Mancha," as he describes the frontiersman, "are equally bent on affairs of doughty enterprise, being about to penetrate the thickets of the perilous swamp, within which the enemy lay ensconced" (20). It is precisely at this point that Irving notes that his party had "wandered from our true course" (19).

This deflation of the Indian as villain occurs throughout the book, and is generally accompanied by just such a commentary on the role that tale-telling plays in creating the false expectations. When, after a third of the book has passed by and the party has finally entered the much dreaded Pawnee territory, the only Pawnees to be seen are the imaginary Pawnees of the party's imagination. He hears them described in a campfire discussion on the first night after the crossing: "The conversation now turned upon the Pawnees, into whose hunting grounds we were about entering. There is always some wild untamed tribe of Indians who form for a time, the terror of a frontier, and about whom all kinds of stories are told" (42). As we have found before, Irving is not denying that there may indeed be some "wild untamed tribe" to be feared, but chooses to focus instead on the way that threat is perceived; and, in this case, that threat seems to present itself only in the insistence of the white man's adventuring imagination, in his "fearful stories." In the seventh and tenth chapters he describes how both Indians and white men tell stories of Indian violence—presumably different stories, though Irving does not clarify the point. The Indians "chaunt all their exploits in war and hunting" (26), and the white men tell "old frontier stories about hunting and Indian warfare" (35). In other words, both "sides"—and it is significant that Irving includes the Indians in this conception—construct and confirm the danger of such clashes through their telling of adventure tales, through their unwitting reliance on the formulations of self-referential and self-justifying narratives. His own adventure tale would reveal just this self-referentiality, and the consequent inability to overcome the misapprehensions that result. Those examples that he offers support both claims: that the dangers of true adventure indeed exist, but that they are being distorted by the vain and fearful projected "adventures" of the white man. The mysterious Pawnees remain a mystery, but still there seems no end of discussion about them.

The Pawnees, as the rangers "represented" them, are "admirable horsemen, and always on horseback; mounted on fleet and hardy steeds, the wild race of the prairies" (42). They "sometimes engaged in hunting the deer and buffalo, sometimes in warlike and predatory expeditions, for like their counterparts, the sons of Ishmael their hand is against every one, and every one's hand against them" (42). In other words, they are sometimes peaceful, sometimes not, both bold instiga-

tors and mere respondents, and always adventurous opponent or counterpart. But the rangers are not content to rest with so unjudgmental a
view. The conversation quickly focuses on the Pawnees' "mode of
fighting" and on the "Luckless. . .band of weary traders or hunters
descried by them in the midst of a prairie" (43). Then follows "Several
accounts. . .of the secrecy and caution with which they will follow and
hang about the camp of an enemy, seeking a favorable moment for
plunder or attack" (43). No wonder, then, that the Captain tells the
party, "We must now begin to keep a sharp look out" (43). Once
again, then, the danger seems real enough, despite Irving's warnings
about the tendency to misread the signs. But still the uncertainty
remains. The rangers may not be so different from the earlier frontiersman, anxious to tell stories and "blame everything on the Indian." The
party may indeed have crossed into a "region of adventure" (48), as
Irving describes it in the next chapter, but has anything really changed?

Up to this point in the book, there have only been fears and rumors
about the threat of Indian attack; nothing has been confirmed, except
in the men's own active imaginations. During one incident, for instance, the men panic at the appearance of an Indian dog. First they
fear that the savage foe is lurking nearby, and, when that turns out to
be wrong, they fear that the animal is vicious: a cry of "mad dog" rings
throughout the camp. As it turns out, though, the dog is blind and
helpless. In such scenes, Irving deflates the Indian attack just as he had
deflated the Indian villain: a false "reading" leading to a false alarm.
Yet the effect is also only temporary, for the next alarm might as easily
be real. By building suspense, Irving can take an even closer look at the
nature of these fears. Eventually, he provides us with a suitable climax:
suddenly, the cry of Indian attack is heard throughout the camp. . . .

The panic begins when the rangers fail to read the signs of the
wilderness accurately and assume that the danger is real and immediate.
The Captain, while out scouting, notices "something on the edge of a
parallel hill that looked like a man" (75). He watches, and it remains
motionless, like himself; and when he moves, it also moves like himself,
"in a parallel direction" (76). Soon another "form" joins the first, and
this mirroring movement continues. The mirroring is broken, however, when the Captain offers a signal that he had arranged with the
rangers—his cap waved at the end of his rifle—and the "forms" do
not respond. The Captain strongly suspects that they are Indian spies,
and when he sees them leave the hill and head toward the camp, he

rushes ahead and warns some rangers to warn the others. This is the
origin of the alarm, and as such seems a reasonable enough basis for
fear and defensive measures. But the facts, when revealed, tell a different story.

In fact the men the Captain had seen were only two rangers returning from a hunt. The enemy thus turns out to be the rangers themselves, or more precisely, their propensity to see Indian enemies in
every shadowed "form." Irving makes the point explicitly when he
recounts the discussion in which this mistaken identity is revealed. As
the two rangers enter the camp, the others begin to ask them excitedly
about the lurking menace they believe is stalking them:

> "Well, but the Pawnees—the Pawnees—where are the Pawnees?"
> "What Pawnees—?"
> "The Pawnees that attacked you—?"
> "No one attacked us."
> "But have you seen no Indians on your way?"
> "Oh yes, two of us got to the top of a hill to look out for the camp,
> and saw a fellow on an opposite hill cutting queer antics, who seemed to
> be an Indian."
> "Pshaw! that was I!" said the captain. (77)

The rangers, in their craving for Indian adventure and their fear of
Indian attack, have peopled the wilderness with that craving and that
fear; their Indian adventures have been reduced to a burlesque of
mistaken identity. In a way they have become Indians themselves
precisely by failing to recognize that their deluded imaginations have
brought them "parallel" to the very savagery from which they distinguish themselves. As a result, the boundaries between the civilized man
and the Indian, the self and the other, have broken down.

While Irving may have hoped that this shattering of boundaries
would lead his readers to consider Indians in more humane, and
human, terms, his primary intention was to make those readers more
aware of the civilized values that had become blurred and distorted in
the Western experience. If America, as represented by the presence of
these rangers, was to survive its adventures in the enterprise of Western
expansion, then a more discriminating sense of those boundaries would
have to be developed.

Irving demonstrates the danger of this failure of discrimination by
representing the rangers' panic as a breakdown not only of social form

but literary form as well: "There was now a scene of clamour and confusion that baffles all description" (74). That scene is beyond description because it consists of the collapse of the adventure form itself, a moment beyond either glorification or satire. The adventure tale, in other words, which has given form to the rangers' mistaken sense of their own identities as civilized men, has also destroyed the very notion of form itself, the "bounds of respectful decorum" (*A* 7) that Irving defined as the essential attribute of civilization. The preservation of form, then, depended upon the boundary-making facility of the imagination, which Irving defined as the essential means of being civilized.

Such is the point when, in his conclusion to the event, Irving notes that the ranger's mistake lay not in their fear of Indians but in their acceptance of the *tale* of Indian danger: "Here the bubble burst. The whole alarm had risen from this mutual mistake of the Captain and the two rangers. As to the report of the three hundred Pawnees and their attack on the hunters, it proved to be a wanton fabrication, of which no further notice was taken; though the author deserved to have been sought out and severely punished" (77). Significantly, this "author" is never identified: *this* identity must not be mistaken. The villain here is not an Indian spy, or even the deluded rangers, but all the tellers and listeners, the believers, of the adventure tale, the self-proclaimed "heroes" who lose much more than their lives to their "villains." They lose their very capacity to be heroes. If the Indian villain ceases to exist, then so too does the white hero.

Irving pursues this logic of his satire by placing in the position of his hero not the brave white man Indian fighter, but instead a number of men who fail, at crucial moments, to succeed as the very heroes they claim themselves to be. Irving himself, of course, as the author/narrator would seem the first logical candidate for hero. But for a number of reasons, Irving diminishes his own presence and directs his readers' attention to the men of action on the tour. He may have felt that his satire depended upon an undermining of the "author" as romantic hero, or that a focus on the author might shift attention away from his exploration of the relation between the adventuring imagination and the actual adventures of expansion. He might also simply have felt that such a direct examination of a developing self would have been inappropriate for this book, or even for his art in general.[11] In a general sense, though, the narrator's very remoteness from this world of engagement may be seen as the foundation for the true heroism his other characters lack. Unlike them, he will learn to master his culture's fictions, and thus become if not a man of action himself then at least a man of a properly adventurous imagination. As author of this new tale of adventurous enterprise, he will provide the proper vehicle through which that action may take place.

First, though, he must be educated. For much of the book, the narrator is as prone to a misguided imagination as the other figures. In one of the rare events when he places himself at the center of an adventure, he discovers just what the men of action discover: the limits and consequences of the pursuit of heroism. The scene is a buffalo hunt, a much treasured experience of the prairies that was also a staple of the Western adventure tale. Its function in both cases was to test the courage and skill of the hero. The narrator begins the hunt with the proper exhilaration, and for a while everything seems to fulfill one's expectations: the galloping chase, the misfiring pistols, the final triumph. But upon dismounting, the narrator sees another story unfold:

> I am nothing of a sportsman: I had been prompted to this unwonted exploit by the magnitude of the game and the excitement of an adventurous chase. Now that the excitement was over I could not but look with commiseration upon the poor animal that lay struggling and bleeding at my feet. . . .
>
> To add to these after-qualms of conscience the poor animal lingered in his agony. He had evidently received a mortal wound, but death might be long in coming[.] (102)

The heroism of the prairies, it would seem, demands more than a passion for adventure. It demands the appropriately engaged skills of the sportsman, the professional. Such a sportsman, we must assume, would have been a more accurate shot, saving the animal from agony while producing a legitimate trophy of Western life. What the professional knows, in other words, is the difference between self-interest and greed, false adventure and true adventure. To fail at such knowledge, to fail at heroism by misperceiving oneself as the hero, is to be the cause of needless violence. As he states directly in an earlier passage, "Man is naturally an animal of prey, and, however changed by civilization, will readily relapse into his instinct for destruction. I found my ravenous and sanguinary propensities daily growing stronger on the prairies" (51). The narrator's experience on the buffalo hunt shows him that the heroics of the civilized adventure tale are created precisely out of these uncivilized propensities.

This is the lesson that the substitute heroes of the book must learn, those men of action who, by repeatedly failing as typical heroes of the adventure tale, provide telling examples of the failure of the adventure form and the adventuring imagination in the Western experience. Because Irving has diminished his potency as the hero, these failings threaten to leave the tale without a hero altogether. That gap is pointed out to the reader by the delusions associated with each substitute. In place of himself as romantic protagonist passing through disillusionment to heroic maturity, Irving places the young Count de Pourtalès, well fitted for the role by age and temperament. But Pourtalès fails, his goals misguided, even his failures unheroic. In place of himself as romantic protagonist passing through exploit to heroic triumph, Irving places one of the tour's scouts, the irritating Tonish, but he too fails for he is all talk and no true achievement. In place of himself as romantic patriarch passing through danger in order to offer munificent protection, he places the pompous Ellsworth. But this hero fails to understand the Indians, to protect them, and even to recognize his own ineffectuality. Finally, in place of the romantic community of heroes passing through danger by means of a disciplined system of support and shared values, he places the lazy and inexperienced rangers, and they fail to help themselves, each other, or learn anything from their experiences. With all their differences, these figures share the central flaw that leads to their failures as heroic figures: they see themselves in romantic perspective as heroes, and this self-interest, because ill-adapted to the true westering experience, leads them to undermine and possibly endanger both themselves and the community enterprise in which they are ostensibly engaged. Their failures are designed to help the reader understand the true limits of selfhood and accept the necessary demands of social dependency and given forms of hierarchy as the requisites of order and meaning. This is a decided revision of the romantic narrative formula.

It is a revision, though, well in keeping with the already established tradition in American humor of burlesquing self-serving heroism, especially in the depiction of the frontiersman. In much humorous writing of the seventeenth and eighteenth centuries, the fast-talking Yankee out-thinks the slow-witted frontiersman. Irving had earlier offered his own variation in "Sleepy Hollow," in which, as in *A Tour,* he elevated the frontiersman over the tenderfoot. His modification turns the tale from a contest of cunning and manipulativeness versus simple faith and practicality to one of blind conceit versus the cleverness borne of true experience. Irving's humorous heroes think of themselves as heroic frontiersman, pathfinders for civilization in perilous Indian country, but they are really just deluded Yankees.

Pourtalès is perpetually described as an overanxious and self-glorifying adventurer: he is "prone to every kind of wild adventure" (11) and has a distinctly "romantic ardour" (22); he has a "game spirit that seemed always stimulated by the idea of danger" (22), and hopes to "achieve great exploits" (23); he has even, "with the sanguine anticipations of youth, promised himself many hardy adventures and exploits" (24); he has, finally, a "passion for adventure" (105) which makes him susceptible to the tales of "Indian braves and Indian beauties, of hunting buffaloes and catching wild horses" that Tonish directs his way. Influenced by these tales, the count comes to see the purpose of the tour as a "dash into savage life" (11). He will spend his time "mingling among the Indians and participating in their hardy adventures" (12), sharing in those "delights he had promised himself in mingling with absolutely savage life" (13). Specifically, he wants to join an Osage hunting party and, according to Ellsworth, acquire an Osage wife.[12]

Most often Irving's attitude toward Pourtalès' adventurism is gently but firmly satirical. He chides Pourtalès for his dandified posturing. Note, for example, in the passages above, the absurd gap between such frivolous words as "dash" and "delights" and the more severe "savage life." In another scene he contrasts the count's imagined "knight errantry" (27) with an Indian visitor's true exoticism. The effect of such a strategy is to undermine the traditional role of Indian adventurer whereby the hero is placed comfortably above the Indians in both ingenuity and stamina. Such superiority is hardly in evidence here where even the Indians make fun of what Irving significantly calls Pourtalès' "eagerness for Indian enterprize" (26). The implication is that he has abdicated the white-man enterprise to which he should more properly belong, an enterprise of shared community values rather than individualistic adventuring. Pourtalès' imaginative yearning clearly does not prepare him for the test he is to face in the Indian country.

That test comes a number of times, but two incidents in particular stand out. The first occurs early in the book when he decides against the judgment of virtually everyone in the tour to join an Osage hunting expedition; and the second, a more serious event, when he rides ahead of the others during a buffalo hunt "with his usual eagerness and

impetuosity" (103). In referring to the first, Irving notes that the "rash-
ness of the enterprize" (22) was no small thing, as the count could
easily become lost on the inhospitable prairies. Only narrowly does he
escape such a fate. He is not so lucky, however, in the later incident.

In both cases the danger to the count resulted from the self-interested priorities of his adventuring imagination: he was foolish to separate from the company; he was even more foolish to reject the wisdom
of experience represented by that community. For instance, he knows
nothing of the skills of "woodcraft" necessary for survival on the
prairies alone. Pourtalès fails these tests because he is no true "sportsman," which is to say he lacks the quality of "professionalism" that
distinguishes the accomplished and undeluded adventurer from the
posturing "hero." The cost is that he is forced to spend a night on the
prairies alone and truly frightened, for he is in real danger of falling
"into the hands of some lurking or straggling party of savages" (105).
He is found soon enough, however—the quickness of the rescue
serves to diminish the likelihood that this failure of heroism could be
interpreted as a heroic adventure in itself—and he finally seems to
learn his lesson: "It was a joyful meeting to [all] parties," Irving notes,
"for much anxiety had been felt by us all on account of his youth and
inexperience, and for his part, with all his love of adventure, he seemed
right glad to be once more among his friends" (107). Thus Pourtalès
comes to recognize, if only in a limited way, the danger of his adventuring imagination, and the importance of confining his exploits within
the adventures of the community.

Another of Irving's substitute heroes, Tonish, learns a similar lesson
by a similar deflation of hyperbolic posturing. Irving did not care much
for Tonish, as the crudeness of the incessantly emphasized nickname
indicates. "Tonish" was not, in fact, his real name but one given him
by the tourists; he was really one Antoine Deshetres, a Missouri-born
guide, cook, and general worker. Irving's use of him in the book as a
figure of satire has little of the gentleness and compassion directed
toward Pourtalès. These differences in treatment have much to do with
Irving's attitudes toward their class backgrounds. From the initial
introduction of Tonish to the reader, Irving bases his satire on the
peculiar deficiencies of class:

> Having made this mention of my comrades, I must not pass over un-
> noticed a personage of inferior rank, but of all pervading and prevalent

importance: the squire, the groom, the cook, the tent man, in a word, the factotum, and I may add the universal meddler and marplot of our party. This was a little swarthy, meagre, wiry French creole, named Antoine, but familiarly dubbed Tonish; a kind of Gil Blas of the frontiers, who had passed a scrambling life sometimes among white men, sometimes among Indians. Sometimes in the employ of traders, missionaries and Indian agents; sometimes mingling with the Osage hunters. We picked him up at St. Louis, near which he has a small farm, an Indian wife, and a brood of half blood children. According to his own account, however, he had a wife in every tribe: in fact, if all this little vagabond said of himself were to be believed, he was without morals, without caste, without creed, without country, and even without language; for he spoke a jargon of mingled French, English and Osage. He was, withal, a notorious braggart and a liar of the first water. It was amusing to hear him vapour and gasconade about his terrible exploits and hair breadth escapes in war and hunting. In the midst of his volubility, he was prone to be seized by a spasmodic gasping, as if the springs of his jaws were suddenly unhinged, but I am apt to think it was caused by some falsehood that stuck in his throat, for I generally remarked that immediately afterwards there bolted forth a lie of the first magnitude. (11)

The ferocity of the language alone suggests that Irving has found his subject; it has a crude buoyancy that even the pompous count is spared, and there is good reason for that. For if the count is a posturing knight, Tonish is only a mere squire: according to the fabulous feudalism of the frontier, Tonish is reaching above his station while the Count is only distorting his own.[13] One principal element of his "inferiority," that is, is that he does not recognize it, does not acknowledge and accept the discrimination of role and discretion of imagination that the count must learn from a more privileged perspective. He is already guilty of violating his proper role by his half-breed activities, which deny the validity of such role distinctions. And he compounds that error by his tale-telling activities, which, as "lies," go beyond the count's mere misapprehensions in misleading and endangering others. As a member of the lower classes, Tonish should learn to know better, and to tell better tales.

The foundation of Tonish's bragging is his "keen eye to self interest" (12). Always self-aggrandizing, he likes to recount his "terrible exploits" (11) to others, and in so doing he not only lies about himself but misleads others about the situation around them:

I found Tonish making himself a complete oracle among some of the
raw and inexperienced recruits, who had never been in the wilderness.
He had continually a knot hanging about him and listening to his
extravagant tales about the Pawnees, with whom he pretended to have
had fearful encounters. His representations, in fact, were calculated to
inspire his hearers with an awful idea of the foe into whose lands they
were intruding. . . .

If Tonish was to be believed there was peril at every step in these
debatable grounds of the Indian tribes. (53–54)

The rangers become terrified, not without some reason but certainly
without a reasonable understanding of the true dangers. At the same
time such stories also lead them to "wild yelps of exultation at the
thoughts of having a brush with Indians" (106). The general consequence of both the fear and the exultation is that the men become
panicky and quick to the trigger. This same "gasconading" is partly
what encouraged Pourtalès to be "all agog" in his "dash into savage
life"; and this same story-telling will lead Tonish to his own tests in the
wilderness, a series of hunting expeditions.

Like Pourtalès, whose true heroism is measured not by his solitary
misadventure on the prairies but by his return to camp, Tonish manages to kill some game only when he goes out hunting with two others
from the party. Unlike Pourtalès, however, the unregenerate Tonish
fails to recognize the lesson of social dependency and community
enterprise. When he returns he not only poses once again as "the oracle
of the camp," but is "now more boastful than ever of his skill as a
marksman" (96). He attributes his earlier failures to being "out of
luck," if not "spell bound" (96); and he tells a tale about his acquaintance with the magic of the prairies. The tale, though, proves to be
another lie; what he claims happened to himself was, Irving notes,
"evidently a tale picked up among his relations, the Osages" (96). Just
as Pourtalès had been drawn to "Indian" enterprise, so Tonish is drawn
to Indian tales.

The story itself stands as a model of how tales can deceive even their
tellers. Tonish sees a white deer come out from a ravine, shoots at it a
number of times, but without success. Upset, he returns home where
he is told by an old Osage hunter that the deer had a charmed life and
could only be killed by specially cast bullets, which the Indian proceeds
to make for him. He returns to the forest, and this time fells the deer

with one charmed bullet. Here his story ends. As a defense against the charge of groundless bragging, this tale would seem an unlikely choice, implying as it does that Tonish's reputation as a hunter has depended upon the aid and wisdom of another, in particular an Indian. Yet Tonish clearly intends the story to validate his claims of marksmanship and singular cunning. In a way, it does; after all, the story never questions his marksmanship, and he is initially overcome not by any failings of his own but by forces beyond his control. Probably Tonish's main hope was to dazzle his listeners with his own authority in the mysterious Indian arts, and at this too he succeeds. But Irving places the reader outside that realm of influence, and displays the story as not only a feeble attempt at self-justification, but an ultimately self-diminishing one as well. What Tonish does not learn about his own self-interest, the readers themselves learn.

One might expect the leader of the tour to supply the balanced perspective that Pourtalès and Tonish lack. But Ellsworth is just as self-serving and deluded. In a key scene, in which he attempts to fulfill his responsibility as commissioner and diminish hostilities between tribes, Irving portrays him as a farcical figure, incapable of understanding the reality of the situation. Riding into an Osage village, the travelers are greeted by a number of old men, "while the women and children huddled together in groupes, staring at us wildly, chattering and laughing among themselves" (25). The young men of the village, they soon learn, are out on a hunting expedition. But this fact does not deter Ellsworth from engaging his role as commissioner:

> Here the Commissioner made a speech from horseback; informing his listeners of the purport of his mission to promote a general peace among the tribes of the West, and urging them to lay aside all warlike and blood-thirsty notions and not to make any wanton attacks upon the Pawnees. This speech being interpreted by Beatte [a hunter on the tour], seemed to have a most pacifying effect upon the multitude who promised faithfully that, as far as in them lay, the peace should not be disturbed; and indeed their age and sex gave some reason to trust that they would keep their word. (25–26)

Irving does not mention that there were about five hundred Indians present, for that would diminish his satirical intention of contrasting Ellsworth's inappropriate posturing with the small and squalid surroundings. Nor does he mention that Ellsworth was quite aware of that contrast, for that would diminish the power of his satire to reveal Ellsworth's blinding sense of self-importance.

In his own description of the event, Ellsworth is even more exacting about the ridiculousness of the attempt, though he chooses to locate its source not in his own stance but in the incivility of the Indians:

> They were many of them, naked—several little boys 13 years old came out before us, and when I was addressing them and urging them to peace & not to fight the Pawnees, or steal horses, and provoke revenge; these little boys made water before all the women, and even *upon* some of them, laughing, heartily to show us how they could, wet the folks around by their jet, clean [?] The squaws were more dirty than the men —both were lousy and some diseased by *vicious* indulgence[.] (18)

The commissioner may not see himself as an adventurer in Indian territory, as Pourtalès and Tonish do, but he shares with them a fundamental sense of superiority resulting from a failure of imagination, and it undermines his "mission" in the West. Further, his failure has an urgent and national resonance that the failures of the other two substitute heroes lack: he is the official representative of America.[14]

These dark implications for the nation are echoed in the troubling, inept presence of the rangers, the enforcers of the American military mission that Ellsworth has been sent to consolidate. Throughout the book the rangers are criticized for three interrelated flaws: their inexperience, their lack of discipline, and their love of adventure. Irving sums up the dangerous conjunction of these qualities in the chapter on the alarm in camp: "Still I could not but perceive, that, in case of being attacked by such a number of these well mounted and warlike savages as were said to be at hand, we should be exposed to considerable risk from the inexperience and want of discipline of our newly raised rangers, and from the very courage of many of the younger ones who seemed bent on adventure and exploit" (75). While no one in fact gets seriously hurt, the rangers are shown to be responsible for, at the least, a shameless lack of decorum and "restraint" (47, 110), and, at the most, a "reckless improvidence and wastefulness" (97). Two incidents in particular stand out as illustrations of the harmfulness of their unconsidered love of adventure.

In one particularly well-developed event—it is one of the few chapters in the book that focuses on a single happening; the false Indian alarm is another—the rangers seek out and raid a beehive. While they are quite effective in destroying the hive and scattering its inhabitants, Irving finds the act unnecessary and wasteful. But his depiction of the event expands the scope of that criticism beyond any simple attack on the mere improvidence of this one group of men. By adding an extended analogy of the bees to an "industrious" community laid to waste by a combination of its own self-involvement and the competing self-interest of its attackers, he places that wastefulness in the context of America's industrious ransacking of its own wilderness. The rangers, after all, are supposed to represent the expansion of the industrious community of America into the West. Here, though, they are shown destroying just such a community.

In setting up the analogy, Irving employs the popular notion of bees as "heralds of civilization" (29), preparing the wilderness for settlement by transforming it literally into "a land flowing with milk and honey" (30). In this positive use of the image of the bee as pre-pioneer, Irving seems to be affirming the culture's endorsement of expansionism. Much the same view can be found in Bryant's "The Prairies," published a year after Irving's tour:

> The bee,
> A more adventurous colonist than man,
> with whom he came across the eastern deep,
> Fills the savannas with his murmurings,
> And hides his sweets, as in the golden age,
> Within the hollow oak. I listen long
> To his domestic hum, and think I hear
> The sound of that advancing multitude
> Which soon shall fill these deserts.
>
> (lines 109–117)

John Frémont also used the figure in his *Report of the Exploring Expedition to the Rocky Mountains,* published a decade later:

> Here, on the summit [of the Rocky Mountains], where the stillness was absolute, unbroken by any sound, and the solitude complete, we thought ourselves beyond the region of animated life; but while we were sitting on the rock a solitary bee. . .came winging his flight from the eastern valley, and lit on the knee of one of the men.
>
> It was a strange place, the icy rock and the highest peak of the Rocky mountains, for a lover of warm sunshine and flowers; and we pleased ourselves with the idea that he was the first of his species to cross the

mountain barrier—a solitary pioneer to fortell the advance of civilization. (69–70)

At first Irving follows this convention closely. But soon he modifies it
to suggest that such an unqualified celebration of expansionism would
be not only inaccurate but dangerous as well. By shifting the perspective of the figure, he develops it into an implicit critique of that
civilization's arrival.

Specifically, he charts the bee's significance not from the expanding
Americans' point of view but from the retreating Indians' point of
view: "The Indians consider [bees] the harbinger of the white man, as
the Buffalo is of the red man; and say that, in proportion as the bee
advances, the Indian and the Buffalo retire" (29). Irving soon makes it
clear that the bees signal not only that the white man is on his way,
but that almost certain destruction will accompany him; for after the
bee comes the bee-hunter, the representative of American industrial
expansion. The critique of American industry becomes apparent in the
economic metaphors Irving uses to characterize the bees' failure to
protect their own civilization:

> Two of the Bee hunters now plied their axes vigorously at the foot of
> the tree to level it with the ground. The mere spectators and amateurs,
> in the mean time, drew off to a cautious distance, to be out of the way
> of the falling of the tree and the vengeance of its inmates. The jarring
> blows of the axe seemed to have no effect in alarming or disturbing this
> most industrious community. They continued to play at their usual
> occupations, some arriving full freighted into port, others sallying forth
> on some new expeditions, like so many merchantmen in a money making
> metropolis, little suspicious of impending bankruptcy and downfall.
> Even a loud crack which announced the disruption of the trunk failed to
> divert their attention from the intense pursuit of gain; at length down
> came the tree with a tremendous crash, bursting open from end to end,
> and displaying all the hoarded treasures of the commonwealth. (30–31)

The rangers here, who ostensibly represent American industriousness,
are merely destructive; and the bees, who also represent that industriousness, are merely self-destructive. Their two actions are interde-
pendent, two sides of the same "civilizing" process of expansion. Irving
thus identifies the rangers with another set of rival bees: "Nor was it
the bee hunters alone that profited by the downfall of this industrious
community; as if the bees would carry through the similitude of their

habits with those of laborious and gainful man, I beheld numbers from rival hives, arriving on eager wing, to enrich themselves with the ruins of their neighbors" (31). The consequence of this implosion of self-interested "industry" is the "bewilderment and confusion of the bees of the bankrupt hive" who are reduced "to buzz forth doleful lamentations over the downfall of their republic" (31–32). By the end, the adventure of the bee-hunt has become the parable of a bankrupt republic, destroying itself by its drive for profit and its blind adherence to its own adventuring. Irving's criticism focuses not so much on how industry has overrun the wilderness, but how industry itself has become overrun by greed.[15]

This republic is, of course, the America that is just then being escorted into the West by a group of its own "uncouth" rangers. In a later incident, Irving points more directly to the national implications of this journey of destruction. While "successful" in their capture of the hive, the rangers prove themselves to be generally inept at hunting until they come across a large flock of wild turkeys, an even more conventional symbol of the American pilgrimage. Like the bees, the turkeys remain basically insensible to the true danger at hand: "They flew to the trees and sat perched upon their branches stretching out their long necks and gazing in stupid astonishment until eighteen of them were shot down" (82). Irving is unimpressed by the rangers' display. As gestures of the "sport" of hunting, their shooting has achieved nothing but "carnage" (82). Later, as the tour leaves the encampment, Irving notes the arrival of an apt symbol for that carnage: "In the mean time a score or two of turkey buzzards, or vultures, were already on the wing, wheeling their magnificent flight high in the air, and preparing for a descent upon the camp as soon as it should be abandoned" (97). From turkey to turkey-buzzard, this tour has charted a line of expansion that bodes ill for the "reckless" American industry it represents.[16]

The source of the rangers' failure, as these incidents suggest, is that they went West without the "ambition to acquire a name for exactness in a profession in which they had no intention of continuing": "None of them had any idea of. . .restraint and decorum." Instead they had enlisted "for the sake of roving adventure" (34), and consequently failed as true heroic figures. Irving defines the specific heroic feature they lack, that indeed all of these characters lack, in the phrase "self dependence." In an uncharacteristically direct remark about the intentions of his book, he identifies the value of "a tour on the prairies" (including, no doubt, his book by the same name as well as the tour itself): "We send our youth abroad to grow luxurious and effeminate in Europe; it appears to me that a previous tour on the prairies would be more likely to produce that manliness, simplicity and self depen- dence most in unison with our political institutions" (32). The assump- tions behind this idea are even clearer in an entry in the 1825 notebook which Irving mined for *A Tour*:

> Independence & self dependence traits of Am: character—To be culti- vated & encouraged—have others help others look to yourself for help Our backwoodsman throwing himself into the wilderness—building a canoe—travelling on the waters
> Young Ams. to learn much by travelling in their own country—a good school of pubescence[.] (*J*5:323)

It is telling that in both passages Irving does not use the term "individ- ualism," nor the term "independence" in the published book. Both of these words contained even then a rich resonance for American readers. His intention, however, is precisely to offer a corrective to what one contemporary British visitor, James Flint, had called the "hauteur of independence," a growing emphasis on the role of individuals in Amer- ica in determining the guidelines and goals of their own behavior (Ridge 8).[17]

As mentioned earlier, for Irving independence seemed to lead inex- orably to abuse, madness, and despair, an essential abandonment of human connection. When he does celebrate it, it is qualified as an object of yearning and nostalgia incompatible with civilized life. Hence in *A Tour* he wistfully salutes "the glorious independence of man in a savage state" (21), and notes his sadness when a wild horse is caught and tamed: "The transition in his lot was such as sometimes takes place in human affairs, and in the fortunes of towering individuals.—One day a prince of the prairies—the next day a pack horse!" (70). He even seems to make a surprising nod in the direction Thoreau would take some fifteen years later:

> We are a society of slaves not so much to others, as to ourselves; our superfluities are the chains that bind us, impeding every movement of our bodies and thwarting every impulse of our souls. Such at least were my speculations at the time though I am not sure but that they took their tone from the enthusiasm of the young Count, who seemed more

enchanted than ever with the wild chivalry of the prairies, and talked of putting on the Indian dress and adopting the Indian habits during the time he hoped to pass with the Osages. (21)

But as the final qualification indicates (especially when placed in the context of what we are soon to learn about Pourtalès' "enchantment" with that "wild chivalry"), individualism was still half-savage. As such it had to be contained within the proper perimeters of social dependence.

This containment, finally, is what distinguishes the civilized man from the savage in Irving's world, and the true hero from the false. It is striking, for instance, that when considering the equivalent feature among the Indians, he calls it "self command" (92), implying that there is an extra need for self-control on the part of a people so intimately connected to nature. In one such passage, an envious and admiring description of the generic Indian hunter gradually shapes itself into an evocation of the savage spirit: "an Indian hunter on a prairie, is like a cruiser on an ocean, perfectly independent of the world, and competent to self protection and self maintenance. He can cast himself loose from every one, shape his own course, and take care of his own fortunes" (18). The anxiety implicit in these passages suggests why Irving did not substitute Indians as heroes in his own version of the tale of adventurous enterprise. This independent drive to "take care of [one's] own fortunes" was precisely what the individual in the expanding America of the early nineteenth century needed to control. That drive must remain suited to furthering the fortunes of others, of all Americans; otherwise, the hero would become the savage, and the community would lose its defender just as it would gain a far more dangerous enemy. For now the enemy would be in its own midst.

As we have seen, the imagination plays a paramount role in the cultivation of that self-dependence. If the deluded imagination can create misadventures that break down the boundaries between civilization and savagery, so the enlightened imagination can restore those boundaries and reinvigorate the true adventures of America in the West. The Americans have to learn to tell the tale properly, to recognize the falsely heroic adventuring of such figures as Pourtalès, Tonish, Ellsworth, and the rangers, who seek only independence, and substitute in its place the true adventuring of self-dependence.

Irving works out his model for success not only by undermining the popular misconceptions in the adventure tale, but by offering a critique of the role that tale-telling itself plays in the division of the men on the tour. The "author" of the Indian alarm whom Irving urges be sought out and punished may be Tonish, with his inciting tales. The author may be the rangers themselves, with their own campfire tales of Indian cunning and Indian savagery. The author may even be the half-breeds, whose tales Irving describes as "simple and artless" but which contain a remarkable power over the listeners.

Irving's examination of the power of these last tales exemplifies his strategy: "they had a wild and romantic interest heard from the lips of half savage narrators, round a hunter's fire, in a stormy night with a forest on one side and a howling waste on the other: and where peradventure savage foes might be lurking in the outer darkness" (59). The passage is a complicated one, on the one hand validating the premise that "savage foes" may indeed be lurking nearby, while on the other ridiculing the power of that premise by revealing it to be a mere artifice of the gothic literary tradition. As is evident in such books as *Tales of a Traveller,* Irving associated this artifice with self-delusion and madness. As a mode of social cohesion, the act of tale-telling here fails on two levels: as counsel on practical matters, it induces the men to go off on their own or to panic at those moments when the community most needs disciplined engagement; and as counsel on values, it leads that community away from a recognition of shared goals and actions.

Irving emphasizes these failures by contrasting the deluded white man's tales with the perceptiveness of the Indians' tale-telling. In the same passage in which he notes that Indians are not the taciturn "personifications" that the white man's tales depict them to be, he offers as proof of their humanity their own style of tale-telling:

> Half their time is taken up in talking over their adventures in war and hunting, and in telling whimsical stories. . . . They are curious observers, noting every thing in silence, but with a keen and watchful eye; occasionally exchanging a glance or a grunt with each other, when any thing particularly strikes them: but reserving all comments until they are alone. Then it is that they give full scope to criticism, satire, mimicry and mirth. (27)

In contrast to the hyperbole of the white men's tales, the Indians' stories are restrained; where theirs are pompous, the Indians' are humorous and satirical; where theirs are near-sighted, the Indians' are closely observed. Irving thus undercuts the white men's use of tales to define their position of superiority: not only do they share this supposedly civilizing activity with the Indians, but these "savages" do it better.

Irving does not, however, intend to present the Indian imagination as a model for the white man. For him the Indians remain savage insofar as their imaginations lack the particular qualities of discrimination and discipline that are required if the assimilation of the Western experience is to be profitable to both cultures. Throughout *A Tour* Irving prescribes an imaginative form for the West that adheres to the basic preservation of value represented by such social forms as hierarchy, class distinctions, and decorum. The Far West that had, since the travels of Lewis and Clark, been assimilated into American culture as a "succession of curious adventures" which "wore the impression. . .of inchantment" (Lewis in Bergon 1989, 166) needed to take on the shape of an ordered and restrained reality; otherwise America's "dreamland" would become a gothic nightmare.

As mentioned above, this fear that the Americans will lose their civilized values in the wilderness has a long history in American thought, dating as far back as the original "stranding" of the Puritans in the "Indian wilderness" after the Cromwell revolution in England had failed. Far Western expansion offered new formulations for conquering that fear. The reliance on God had been replaced with the more self-centered and secular notion of the inevitable progress of civilization; the enemies (the Indians, the self-serving individuals) who had been conceived as emissaries of the devil were now depicted as merely unregenerate impediments to that progress. But the fear itself remained. Not only the lives but the sensibilities of the Americans could be lost to the savagery of the wilderness.

We hear expressions of that fear in the opening of Dana's *Two Years Before the Mast,* in which the author explains his apprehensions about his upcoming voyage: "I could not but remember that I was separating myself from all the social and intellectual enjoyments of life. Yet strange as it may seem, I did then and afterwards take pleasure in these reflections, hoping by them to prevent my becoming insensible to the value of what I was losing" (5). When some time later the word comes that the voyage may be extended a number of years, he identifies those values with the same professional ambitions that Irving specifies in *A Tour*:

This was bad enough for the crew; but still worse was it for me, who did not mean to be a sailor for life, having intended only to be gone eighteen months or two years. Three or four years might make me a sailor in every respect, mind and habits, as well as body, *nolens volens,* and would put all my companions so far ahead of me that a college degree and a profession would be in vain to think of; and I made up my mind that, feel as I might, a sailor I might have to be, and to command a merchant vessel might be the limit of my ambition. (89)

We find that fear also in Zenas Leonard's fur trapping narrative, first published in 1839: "Although I intended to return to the mountains again, I was particularly anxious to first visit the States lest I should also forget the blessings of civilized society" (263). And we find it in Irving, when he cringes repeatedly at what he calls the "motley" nature of frontier life.

What Irving valued most, the integrity of decorum, he found missing among these supposedly heroic white men of the wilderness. This attitude is apparent in the journals he kept while on his tour, as in a passage in which he records his impressions of a gathering of Indians, half-breeds, and Whites at a frontier mission: "In These establishments the world is turned upside down[:] the Slave the master—the master the slave. The other has the idea of property[—]the latter the reality. The former owns [—] the latter enjoys it. The former has to plan & scheme and guard & economize—the latter thinks only of living[,] enjoying[—]cares nothing how it comes or how it goes" (*J*5:97). For the author who, in *A Tour,* denounces slavery, this confirmation of the dichotomy between master and slave is striking. Even in other passages in the journal, he criticizes the self-serving rationale of slave-holding as *un*civilized:

> Old father Vail addressed the Indians on the necessity of industry &c to happiness[.] An Indian replied—Father I dont understand this kind of happiness you talk of—You tell me to cut down tree—to top it—to make fence—to plough—This you call being happy—I no like such happiness. when I go to S Louis, I go to see Choteau, or Clark—He says hello—and negro comes in with great plate with cake—wine &c[.] he say eat drink If he want any thing else he say hello[—]three, four five six negros come in & do what he want[.] that I call happy—he no plough—he no work—he no cut wood—
>
> Ah, but he has negroes to do all that[.] well father[,] tell him to find

me one two three negroes to cut wood & plough for me and Ill be
willing to be happy like white man but for a man 50 years old to have to
plough &c—Im too old[.] (J5:91)

The Indian's superior reasoning undermines the logic by which the
slave-holder declares his own superiority, and it does so by revealing
the falsity in that logic's central premise: that the civilized man is
industrious.

Irving's abandonment of this perspective in *The Tour* is unfortunate
but perfectly in keeping with his sense that selfish interests must yield
to a more ordered reality. When directly confronted with the dissipation of civilized decorum in the wilderness, Irving calls upon America's
most prominent civilized values. But this is hardly surprising given
his intention to establish the foundations upon which order and
stability could be reinvested in the Western venture.

The imaginative form of *A Tour* is Irving's example. The presence
in the book of a rigid class system, both of personnel and meaning,
and of a series of narrative and compositional devices that embody this
system, is designed to point the reader to a specific code of meaning by
which the "Babylonish" language of the Western experience could be
organized. But Irving is not attempting to impose an aristocratic social
structure on the Western experience; rather he hopes to imbue the
marketplace of the West with the authority of aristocratic privilege. As
we have seen throughout the book, the essential feature of his system
of classification is the boundary-making faculty as defined by the codes
of professionalism and self-dependence, both of which are drawn from,
and apply primarily to, the marketplace.

That class system is most explicitly laid out as vehicle of interpretation in the presence of precisely that figure which most threatens these
boundaries: the half-breed. Individuals with a mixed racial background
have always been troubling and troubled figures in the American imagination. In their make-up they have been deemed threats to the integrity of the white race by defying the boundaries that separate the
civilized Whites from the savage races. This perceived threat was apparent in the word "half-breed" itself: the word "half" transformed a
mixture into a separation of the civilized from the savage, while the
word "breed" stipulated that that process essentially destroyed the
civilized half. After defining characters with mixed backgrounds as half-
breeds, many American writers then condemned them as unregenerate

and beyond redemption, or denied that they could be considered half-civilized in the first place. Francis Parkman, for instance, who had more respect for them than most writers, called them "Indian half-breeds" in *The Oregon Trail* (76). Until fairly recently, in fact, there were no half-breeds in American literature, only half-savages. In keeping with this prejudicial perspective, Irving characterized these figures as a symbol of the dangers of frontier life; specifically, a class of individuals that was finally no class at all. Because they could not be considered a race, even an inferior race, they could also not be considered a class; and because they were not a class, they were also not even individuals. In the same journal entry containing his fearful commentary about the breakdown of boundaries between master and slave, Irving sets them into a carefully composed scene as a kind of uncomposed mongrel hybrid: "Half breeds loitering about the house. dogs & cats of all kinds strolling about the Hall or sleeping among harness at one end of the piazza" (J5:97).[18]

Much time is spent in *A Tour* defining the threat of the half-breed by locating these frontier boundaries of race and class. The reader encounters the first warning at the very beginning of the book: "there was a sprinkling of trappers, hunters, half breeds, creoles, negroes of every hue; and all that other rabble rout of nondescript beings that keep about the frontiers, between civilized and savage life, as those equivocal birds the bats hover about the confines of light and darkness" (15). However "equivocal" Irving may claim the activity of these birds of the frontier, his choice of "bats" associates these "beings" with the confines of darkness. The same veiled judgment is implicit when he introduces, a few pages later, the first major half-breed character in the book, the guide and hunter Pierre Beatte. Irving tells the reader that "He had altogether more of the red than the whiteman in his composition; and, as I had been taught to look upon all half breeds with distrust, as an uncertain and faithless race, I would gladly have dispensed with [his] services" (16). The key word here is "composition," for Irving assesses Beatte's appearance both as a fractured composition in itself, and a fracturing of the principles of composition:

> I confess I did not like his looks when he was first presented to me. He was lounging about, in an old hunting frock and metasses or leggings, of deer skin, soiled and greased and almost japanned by constant use. . . . His features were not bad, being shaped not unlike those of Napoleon, but sharpened up, with high Indian cheek bones.

> Perhaps the dusky greenish hue of his complexion aided his resemblance to an old bronze bust I had seen of the Emperor. He had, however, a sullen saturnine expression, set off by a slouched woolen hat, and elf locks that hung about his ears. (16)

The passage begins as one might expect, with a pointed contrast between the savage side, here associated with the figure of the degraded white man as Indian, and the civilized side, associated with the idealized figure of Napoleon. Irving even strengthens the distinction by following a tentatively positive comparison with a reaffirmation of the contrast. But in the second section he modifies his strategy. Here the contrast is not so much between Indian and white man as between actual half-breed and idealized art object. The half-breed's exclusion from the civilized attributes of the white race is represented as an exclusion from the civilizing attributes of art. In fact, his very presence threatens those attributes. The tenor of the passage overall is precisely the opposite of achieved portraiture. Irving's own shift in focus from the face of Napoleon to bust of the Emperor appears less as a refinement of the portrait than an undermining of its coherence as a form of "composition." Just as Beatte's own composition is flawed by his half-breed existence, so too is Irving's composition of Beatte. The portrait is itself a kind of half-breed, constructed, like the figure it represents, out of negative comparisons.

The underlying criticism of the half-breed remains the same, though: of Beatte's two sides, it is obviously the "red man" that has taken precedence, effectively overpowering the felicitous shape of the white man's greatness in the images of Napoleon and the bust of the Emperor. Had Beatte been wholly Indian, then Irving would undoubtedly have lauded his features, as he does in an earlier description of the "fine Roman countenance" (20) of a young Osage. (It is worth noting in this context that the "red man" in Beatte is Osage.) But half-savagery is an affront to composition itself, the ordering and decorous balancing of materials which Irving perceived as constituting his chief activity as a professional artist.

Thus while Irving is willing to credit Beatte with great skills as a hunter and guide, he remains troubled by the frontier world to which those skills belong. The life of the frontier half-breed has taken its toll on Beatte: "He was, in fact, a living monument of the hardships of wild frontier life" (91), his left arm warped by rheumatism, his right arm broken by a fall from his horse, his left leg crushed by another fall, and his whole body scarred from hunting and Indian warfare. Maimed so by his half-breed life, he has become a monument not of a stained Roman beauty or even Napoleonic dissipation, but of the fracturing of art itself.

This use of the half-breed to represent a threat to the civilized and civilizing imagination comes across even more vividly when Irving compares Beatte to Tonish. Even though Tonish is actually not a half-breed, it suits Irving's purposes to treat him as such throughout the tour—or perhaps half-breeder would be more accurate, for Tonish's affront to composition is primarily in his marrying an Indian woman and producing "a brood of half blood children" (11). Generally posed as a comic foil to the serious and skillful Beatte, Tonish comes to represent another way in which the half-breed's self-interest can maim and distort the imagination. Throughout the book, Tonish is shown bragging that he can do what Beatte, in his taciturn independence, chooses never to discuss. Of course Tonish fails while Beatte succeeds, though that success is qualified by Irving's attitude toward Beatte himself as a half-breed. As a substitute storyteller, the mongrel Frenchman ends up not only "without morals, without caste, without creed, and without country," but "even without language" (11), turning the West into a tower of Babel and Western expansion into an uncomprehending babble of selfish tales. Not surprisingly it had been Tonish who had called out to Irving in his "Babylonish jargon." Irving uses Tonish throughout as the example of the denigration not only of the enterprise of Western expansion, but of the vehicle of meaning as well, language itself.

But Irving does not finally take Tonish himself too seriously as a threat. As a half-breed, Tonish ultimately lacks the sufficient selfhood to change the viewpoint of the touring party; he might entice them but never succeed in leading them astray, for while he may be their guide, he is in the end only a follower. According to the rigid class system that Irving defines for the tour, Tonish and Beatte are always referred to as "our" half-breeds, possessions not only of the aristocracy of the party (a unit confined to the four white "civilian" tourists) but of the class system in general. They may represent a threat to the integrity of that system but they are also its representatives.[19]

Ultimately the half-breed's role in the composition of the tour is as a mediational figure, highlighting the need for a pattern of social hierarchy based on acceptable divisions and dualities. The system of classification that he encourages, in his failures as a social figure and a tale teller, can thus be applied both to the actual organization of Western experience and to the imaginative assimilation of that experience. Irving's classed adventure tale is, in this sense, a professionalization of the Western experience, turning the West into an arena of economic and imaginative mobility that yet governs that self-interest with clearly marked advantages and disadvantages, heroism and villainy. When Irving depicts the members of both upper and lower classes to be failed heroes, and when he depicts the Indians, the perennial "others" whose function is to establish the outside perimeters of a class system, to be "failed" villains, he is also asserting the boundaries of proper adventuring in a new imaginative shape. This shape is complete with oppositions and mediations that take into account the needs for expansion and the needs for restraint. By this reformulation, the Americans, characters and readers both, can learn to assume their own proper place both in the West and in the West of their imaginations.

One principal example of this imaginative shape can be seen in Irving's presentation of the simile as a preferred practice for the adventuring imagination. Throughout the book, Irving has attacked what he perceives to be the metaphoric approach to the Western experience. Metaphors were dangerous in part because readers tended to "literalize" them, to see them as true and accurate representations of experience. Indian villains were thus "read" as representative Indians, and white heroes as representative Americans. But Irving was always careful to qualify his figurative observations. Hence the "native country" in *A Tour* is not an indigenous extension of America but a country filled with many different native groups; and the Indian "villains" and white "heroes" are not representative of their races but individual cases to be judged on the qualities they themselves exhibit rather than the ones attributed to them. Metaphor thus promotes a reductive and inaccurate view of experience, and the cultural fictions based on metaphor promote the self-interest that leads to self-destruction. By substituting the more qualified and distanced figure of the simile as the principal form of imaginative assimilation, Irving is promoting a more cautionary habit of mind. If metaphors entail unqualified endorsement, then Irving will offer similes which seek only to appreciate and ornament, providing a recognition of the boundaries separating imagination and experience, and a means for bridging that gap, an essentially civilized and civilizing act of imagination.[20]

Irving underscores this facet of the simile by "extending" the figure; that is, by underscoring the figurative process and encouraging a sense of detachment in the reader. For instance, when he describes the rangers at an encampment as looking "not unlike banditti returning with their plunder" (42), or when he evokes the "grandeur and solemnity" of Western forests by stating that he "was reminded of the effect of sunshine among the stained windows and clustering columns of a Gothic cathedral" (25), he is making the reader more conscious of the artifice involved in the simile-making process, and as a result, the reader acquires a greater sense of detachment. By thus disengaging the viewer from his or her own expectations and needs, these "extended" similes offer a way of "reading" the adventure that neither celebrates nor condemns but merely appraises.

Irving reproduces this effect of civilized detachment on a larger scale by forwarding his narrative by way of "scenes" rather than moments of action. Just as he substitutes the simile for the metaphor, he substitutes the static scene for the traditionally adventurous story (after all, he has no "story" to tell). Besides using the word "scene" itself to mark these moments (a device that emphasizes the distanced, theatrical assessment of the event), Irving makes these scenes the most frequent adventure to be had by the tourists. For example, in one chapter Irving depicts the rangers lounging in a ravine right after the party has entered the dangerous Pawnee territory. It is an oddly unadventurous moment for so charged a set-up:

> The bugle sounded the signal to mount and march. The troop filed off in irregular line down the glen and through the open forest, winding and gradually disappearing among the trees, though the clamor of voices, and the notes of the bugle could be heard for some time afterwards. The rear guard remained under the trees in the lower part of the dell, some on horseback with their rifles on their shoulders; others seated by the fire or lying on the ground gossiping in a low lazy tone of voice, their horses unsaddled, standing and dozing around: while one of the rangers profiting by this interval of leisure, was shaving himself before a pocket mirror stuck against the trunk of a tree. (46)

By appearing in place of the customary and expected adventure, this description offers a new way to "compose" the Western experience, one that goes beyond the limiting and misleading composition of the adventure tale to the spontaneous and uneventful and generally dull quality of the experience itself.

At first glance, Irving appears to be merely employing a common strategy of current travel writing derived from the eighteenth-century aesthetic of scenic tableaux. Similar passages can be found not only in his other works, but in the works of his contemporaries as well. In *The Oregon Trail,* for instance, Parkman offered this description: "In the square grassy area, surrounded by barracks and the quarters of the officers, the men were passing and repassing, or lounging among the trees; although not many weeks afterwards it presented a different scene; for here the off-scourings of the frontier were congregated for the expedition against Santa Fe" (25). Both writers carefully designed these scenes as pictorial compositions, and both saw in the forces of the frontier a threat to that genteel composition. But where Parkman's primary interest is in recreating the look and feel of the frontier as accurately as possible—note that the word "scene" has no special significance except as a frame for the focus of our attention—Irving makes the reader aware of the artifice of the effect, thereby forcing a consideration of the role the imagination has played in perceiving and evaluating the scene.

Often that role is rendered directly. In a passage in *The Alhambra,* for instance, Irving includes the artist in the scene: "The scene was a study for a painter: the picturesque group of dancers, the troopers in their half military dresses, the peasantry wrapped in their brown cloaks; nor must I omit to mention the old meagre Alguazil, in a short black cloak, who took no notice of any thing going on, but sat in a corner diligently writing by the dim light of a huge copper lamp, that might have figured in the days of Don Quixote" (11). The stance of the artist in this passage, however, differs significantly from the stance indicated in *A Tour.* Here the writer is withdrawn, and as such is perfectly suited to the quest for refuge idealized in the journey to the heart of the Alhambra. In *A Tour,* the writer may be distanced and appreciative, but he is definitively active in the expansion he records.[21]

In one such scene in *A Tour,* Irving prescribes that mixture of distance and engagement by which the "literary" imagination should approach the Western experience:

> In this rocky nook we encamped among tall trees. The rangers grad-
> ually joined us; straggling through the forest singly or in groupes; some

on horseback, some on foot driving their horses before them heavily laden with baggage some dripping wet, having fallen into the river; for they had experienced much fatigue from the length of the ford, and the depth and rapidity of the stream. They looked not unlike banditti returning with their plunder, and the wild dell was a retreat worthy to receive them. The effect was heightened after dark, when the light of the fires was cast upon rugged looking groupes of men and horses; with baggage tumbled in heaps, rifles piled against the trees and saddles, bridles and powderhorns hanging about their trunks. (42)

Though it paints a picture similar to the one described in *The Oregon Trail,* and though it underscores its artifice in a style similar to the one found in the passage from *The Alhambra,* the scene offers a more rigorous relation between picture and artifice. The extended gothic simile and the self-conscious treatment of the "effect" (like the "effect" of the analogy of Western forests to stained glass windows) not only help the readers "picture" the scene; they also keep the readers aware that the imagination is likely to transform such a moment into a literary composition. As a result, the readers come to picture more vividly the truly adventurous atmosphere of that moment. As Irving says in an earlier description of another encampment, "It was a wild bandit, or Robin Hood scene" (28), a scene, that is, with neither bandits nor Robin Hoods, but with a considerable measure of potential danger lurking in the darkness, offstage.

But if the distortions of imagination are here presented as excessively "artistic" preconceptions, Irving does not intend to associate such distortions with the work of art in general. Indeed his solution depends upon the abilities of art to align imagination with reality. In passage after passage he uses analogies to art to evoke what he feels are the actual resources of the West that the popular use of art in the adventure tale diminishes, such as the capacity for cultivation itself. For instance:

> The broad, sandy shore where we had landed was intersected by innumerable tracks of elk, deer, bears, racoons, turkeys and waterfowl. The river scenery at this place was beautifully diversified presenting long shining reaches bordered by willows and cottonwood trees; rich bottoms with lofty forests among which towered enormous plane trees, and the distance was closed in by high embowered promontories. The foliage had a yellow autumnal tint which gave to the sunny landscape the golden tone of one of the landscapes of Claude Lorraine. There was animation

given to the scene by a raft of logs and branches on which the Captain and his prime companion the Doctor were ferrying their effects across the stream, and by a long line of rangers on horseback fording the river obliquely along a series of sand bars about a mile and a half distant. (41)

The reference to Lorraine here, like the reference to the stained glass windows in the earlier quoted passage, is designed not to show how art has distanced the viewer—in this case the narrator—from the "scene," but how it allows him, in fact, to capture its essence. This is the same aesthetic strategy he advocated in his preference for the romantic history over the historical romance. That essence lies in the scene's composure, in the "beautifully diversified" yet intricately ordered arrangement of its elements, the "intersections" and "borders" by which the whole is "closed in." Such references to specific artists appear in many other passages, as do nods to art in general: "The meadow was finely diversified by groves and clumps of trees, so happily disposed that they seemed as if set out by the hand of art" (83).[22]

These references provide more than a literary device to enable the narrator a greater degree of civilized appreciation; they also provide a literary means to civilize the wilderness itself, transform it into a resource that can be cultivated by the rightly aligned imagination. In some descriptions, Irving defines the principal task of the imagination to be the taming of the wildness of the West, eliciting order from "diversity" (a frequently repeated word in these passages):

> Beyond the river the eye wandered over a beautiful champaign country, of flowery plains and sloping uplands, diversified by groves and clumps of trees, and long screens of woodland; the whole wearing the aspect of complete, and even ornamental cultivation, instead of native wilderness. (22)

> The whole scene was singularly wild; the tall grove partially illumined by the flashing fires of the camp, the horses tethered here and there among the trees; the carcasses of deer hanging around; and in the midst of all, the wild huntsman and his wild horse, with an admiring throng of rangers, almost as wild. (68)

> Casting our eyes about the surrounding waste we descried a herd of buffalo about two miles distant, scattered apart and quietly grazing near a small strip of trees and bushes. It required but little stretch of fancy to picture them so many cattle grazing on the edge of a common and that the grove might shelter some lowly farmhouse. (100–101)

If the Robin Hood scene held, in fact, no real Robin Hoods, these scenes also hold no real, or at least no really threatening, wilderness. This is not to say that Irving did not "appreciate" the presence of the wilderness itself; in fact his use of these literary conventions is largely an indication of just how threatening he found its "disorder." Rather, he is turning that appreciation into a civilizing act, a "little stretch of fancy" by which to enclothe a "singular wildness" with "the aspect of complete, and even ornamental cultivation."[23] By just such an act of imagination, the "native land" could, and should, be acquired as part of the American civilization. There would thus no longer be a conflict between the "diversity" of American mobility and the "composition" of its communal mission.

The model for this alignment of imagination is the exchange not just between the Whites and the Indians, but between writer and reader. In this sense, one might say that the author/narrator of *A Tour* does indeed become the hero of the book, a man of imagination capable of what Eudora Welty has called (in reference to the journals Irving kept on the tour) "an emotion somewhere justly between intoxication and amusement, between curiosity and pleasant objectivity." The self he projects has an "unselfconsciousness that is still elegant." As an imaginative sensibility, he offers the reader a cultivated appreciation of the West and its "natives," rather than a destructive acquisitiveness; he offers "appraisal without rapport" (178).[24]

The middle-ground required for this success is not easy to locate, however. At the beginning of *A Tour,* Irving introduces the area through which the tour is to pass as a "debatable ground of. . .warring and vindictive tribes" where "savage conflicts take place" (9–10). The reader might be expected, at this point in the book, to understand the phrase literally, a reference only to the battles among Indian tribes for possession of territory. By the end of the book, the terms of that debate have shifted. The reader has come to understand a more figurative battle taking place, in which even the definition and locus of "savagery" is in doubt. The debate is no longer among savage Indians, or between savage Indians and civilized whites, but among all the savages of the wilderness, Indians and Whites alike. Finally the debate is between, on the one side, the imaginative claims of the traditional adventure tale, and, on the other, the experiential claims of both the disordered wilderness and the Americans' unrestrained ambition to possess that wilderness. For that debate, and debatable ground, to be properly settled, the writer and reader both must constantly negotiate between their expectations and their experiences. In two of the final scenes of the book, Irving offers a model of this process in action. He also indicates the difficulties both writer and reader are likely to face.[25]

During the tour's return to "civilization," the narrator spends one night in peaceful contemplation of the stars. "The wearied rangers. . .sank to rest at an early hour," he tells us, "and I seemed to have the whole scene to myself." The "scene" evokes the most sentimental side of his sensibility, the relieved reemergence, it would at first seem, of Geoffrey Crayon from the wilderness-bound and wilderness-educated narrator. Of the specific subjects of his reveries he tells us little. He wistfully realizes that it was just such a "companionship with these beautiful luminaries which made astronomers of the eastern shepherds, as they watched their flocks at night." He humbly recalls "the exquisite text of Job," in which God challenged Job, forcing him to recognize his human limitations: " 'Canst thou bind the secret influences of the Pleiades, or loose the bands of Orion?' " The specific reference to the "exquisite" text here also humbles the narrator, whose authorial prerogatives extend not to creation or even the unlocking of mysteries, but only to a distanced contemplation. He simply feels awed: "and [I] seemed, as I lay thus under the open vault of heaven, to inhale with the pure and untainted air, an exhilarating buoyancy of spirit, and as it were, an ecstacy of mind" (114). Were Irving, as Crayon, to end the passage here, we would have merely the conventional rhapsodic finish to a piece of cultured travel writing. But he adds an interesting qualification to such endorsements of "culture."

Early the next morning, he continues, "one of the sentinels, the oldest man in the troop, came and took a seat near me; he was weary and sleepy, and impatient to be relieved." Yet before he goes to sleep, he reveals to the entranced narrator another vision of the light shed by those luminous stars: "I found he had been gazing at the heavens also, but with different feelings":

> "If the stars don't deceive me," said he, "it is near day break."
> "There can be no doubt of that," said Beatte, who lay close by. "I heard an owl just now."
> "Does the owl, then, hoot toward day break?" asked I.
> "Aye, sir, just as the cock crows."

This was a useful habitude of the bird of wisdom of which I was not aware. Neither the stars nor owl deceived their votaries. In a short time there was a faint streak of light in the east." (115)

The voice of experience, then, teaches the cultured and "literary" narrator that stars and owls are signs for more than romantic reverie; they tell that daylight is coming. This practical perspective, though, does not negate or undermine the narrator's stance. The stars "deceive" neither of their "votaries," and the owl remains the "bird of wisdom." Imagination and experience are here seen adapting to each other, a weaving of speculations that imbues a larger vision with the exigencies of real movement and limitation. It is *these* stars by which the narrator charts his new knowledge gained on the tour: the tempering of "romance" with experience through the reassertion of the stance of the professional author. If the narrator has contained within him both Crayon and Irving throughout the book, now we can say confidently that he has managed to merge the two personae, the man of letters and the man of business, the cultured Easterner and the experienced Westerner, the professional American.

Ultimately this education changes not only the way the narrator sees the new West of his nation's future, but the East of its origins as well. In the second to last paragraph of the book, the narrator describes his feelings of discomfort and unfamiliarity at being quartered back in the accommodations of a relatively civilized life: "after having been accustomed to sleep in the open air, the confinement of a chamber was, in some respects, irksome. The atmosphere seemed close, and destitute of freshness; and when I woke in the night and gazed about me upon complete darkness, I missed the glorious companionship of the stars" (122). The narrator would thus see the East anew through the adjustment of his vision in the West. He would recognize not only the cramped and sterile confines of these outposts of progress, but also the need to enlarge those confines through the "companionship" of the stars. That companionship, as we have seen, is constituted by a communion among men, and is kept alive by a merging of their imaginations, their experience, and their world.

He makes this point more directly in the other final scene depicting the men's first confrontation with civilization on their return from the tour. Tired and hungry, the party happily comes upon a frontier farmhouse. At first the dwelling hardly seems hospitable: "It was a low

tenement of logs, overshadowed by great forest trees," the narrator
notes. However, the men are soon happily surprised by the warm and
well-stocked greeting they receive from the mistress of the house, "A
fat good-humored negress. . .the spouse of a white man, who was
absent." Poor indeed she is, but she shares with them her simple supply
of beef and turnips, leading the narrator to the very heights of roman-
ticizing rhetoric that had been a focus of satire throughout the book:

> I hailed her as some swart fairy of the wild, that had suddenly conjured
> up a banquet in the desert: and a banquet was it in good sooth. In a
> twinkling she lugged from the fire a huge iron pot that might have
> rivalled one of the famous flesh pots of Egypt, or the witches' cauldron
> in Macbeth. . . . [S]he handed me [a dish of the food] with an ivory
> smile that extended from ear to ear; apologizing for her humble fare and
> the humble style in which it was served up. Humble fare! humble style!
> Boiled beef and turnips—and an earthen dish to eat them from! To
> think of apologizing for such a treat to a half starved man from the
> prairies. . . . Head of Apicius, what a banquet! (121)

This rhetoric, however, is not satirized, for it does not indicate any of
the distortions of imagination marked out by Irving as the falsely
"romantic" and adventurous vision of the West. In fact, the narrator is
quite well aware of its comic inaptness, but he uses that comedy to
underscore its authenticity of vision: so humble a fare may indeed be
adventurous to the experienced and discriminating eye.

There is both, then, a celebration and an implicit warning in the
passage. The Western experience can be a joyous and bountiful one for
the American civilization, but only if America succeeds in adjusting its
expectations to match the realities it finds there. The odd use of the
word "tenement" plays a crucial role here, for the word was already, by
Irving's time, a negative term disparaging the poverty of urban life. By
using it here in reference not only to a frontier farmhouse, but to the
very farmhouse designating the party's return to white civilized life,
Irving can only have intended to raise the spector in the reader's
imagination of a West turned to the darkest production of economic
progress.[26] But if he offers its trappings as a warning, he also finds
within it a solution: in the communal care he finds in the black woman,
in the relation between the black woman and her white husband, and
in the rhetoric that reveals the true adventure found not within the
majestic riches and dangers of the far frontiers but in the humble
poverty of the settlers. The author may have perhaps learned how to

read the stars, but the rest of the "touring party," and the rest of the nation it represented, was still awaiting its education.

The final words of the book leave the reader without any certainty that such education might occur: "and thus ended my foray into the Pawnee Hunting Grounds" (122), he says flatly in what seems to be a mere notification. Yet these words contain a hidden reiteration of the satirical perspective of the book, and thus imply a call to action on the part of the reader. As the last line, collapsing the actual Western experience with its literary representation, the tour on the prairies with *A Tour on the Prairies,* it reminds us of the parallel between experience and imagination. The "foray," that is, refers to both the tour and the book. The fact that the touring party had long before this moment actually left the Pawnee hunting grounds reminds us of the essential premise of that parallel, that this adventurous tour through the "native land" was also a tour through America itself, including both "savage" and "civilized" territory. The purpose of both the tour and the book are, as a result, directly reasserted in the term "foray," which, according to the *American Heritage Dictionary,* is a military expedition in search of "plunder." As we found in the repeated uses of the words "tour" and "excursion," this foray has become a search for American "plunder," and by extension, a plundering America. Yet just as "foray" is a more specifically military term than the others, this America is decidedly more savage than the one with which the book opened; the debatable "native land" has become the undeniably dangerous Pawnee hunting grounds, and so the "ravenous and sanguinary propensities" that the narrator had feared would overcome him had overcome America.

This parallel between experience and imagination is, of course, the book's controlling metaphor, though the book has also consistently satirized that metaphor for its failure to capture the essence of the Western experience: the story of Western expansion is precisely not the adventure tale that has come to represent it. Why then would the narrator reassert the connection in the last line? The metaphor, it would seem, may hold some truth after all. If America is indeed the Pawnee hunting grounds, then the plunder of those grounds is the plunder of America itself. That tale will indeed come true, only this time the Americans will join the villainous Indians, abundant wildlife and rich landscape as the victims of exploitation. In conquering its native land, America will conquer itself.

Perhaps, though, the disaster can yet be averted. While the phrase, as the last line in the book, places both America and the adventure tale of America in a formal closure, it suggests that the story can still be revised, can still adjust the shape of its telling to the shape of its own economic and imaginative needs. The narrator may have "ended" this foray, but the present tense that would complete the parallel (thus *ended* my foray, and thus *ends* the tale itself) is, like the education of the nation, still to come. In his next two Western books, Irving would attempt to bring this education to completion.

4

A Celebration and a Warning:
Astoria, or Anecdotes of an Enterprize Beyond the Rocky Mountains and *The Adventures of Captain Bonneville*

With the publication of *A Tour,* Irving had only partially completed his commentary on the Western adventure tale of economic expansion. He had already offered the satirical travelogue, an examination of the likely excesses of the adventuring imagination. But in *Astoria* he would add a corrective to that warning by transforming his criticism into a celebration of the original terms of the enterprise. Framed as a sober history with straightforward adventures, *Astoria* does not question the identification of economic expansion with the American mission, nor does it locate the dangers to that mission in commercialism itself. Instead it presents the enterprise as the proper course of American history, and finds the threat to that course in external factors, such as foreign influences, savage "others," incompetent insiders, and an inhospitable environment. Hence while in *A Tour* the adventuring imagination was adjusted to the conflicting demands within the culture of the marketplace, in this book it is reinvested with that culture's originating principles of self-interest, national expansion, and manifest destiny.

Irving's decision to produce this corrective was largely the result of a series of circumstances linking his own history with that of John Jacob Astor and the fur trade, and his canny sense of how those connections might profit himself as both man of letters and man of property. The contact with Mr. Astor began long before *Astoria* was conceived. The two men probably first met about 1811, the very time that the events recorded in the book were taking place, later renewed the acquaintance in Europe in 1821, and still again in 1832 when Irving returned from his long exile.[1] In fact, the welcome home dinner at which Irving declared his allegiance to the properties of American economic progressivism was held in one of Astor's buildings on Broadway. And Astor's properties provided still another contact during Irving's tour of the West. The traveling supplies that the party purchased in St. Louis were from the Astor-owned American Fur Company, and while on the steamboat ride down the Missouri River towards his starting point, Irving's boat collided with the *Yellowstone,* property of the American Fur Company and key vehicle in opening the upper Missouri to the steamboat business.

In addition to these contacts with Astor, Irving had had numerous experiences with the fur trade before the two men were introduced. During his 1803 visit to Canada he met and admired some of the partners of the Northwest Company, one of Astor's principal competitors in the Pacific fur business. This acquaintance with the trade was to be deepened during his 1832 tour. The American fur business, which had begun about 1807 and was to last only until 1843, was at its peak during Irving's visit, and he undoubtedly witnessed its presence in the trade's supply and clearing-house center, St. Louis, as well as in the variety of characters and situations he encountered along the way. He met Pierre Chouteau, Jr., whose father was one of the major figures of the early trade—one of the founders, along with William Clark and Alexander Henry, of the Missouri Fur Company—and who was himself a member of the Western division of Astor's American Fur Company. He also met William Clark, then Superintendent of Indian Affairs at St. Louis and earlier the co-leader with Meriwether Lewis of the first major government-sponsored expedition to the Far West.

Thus when Astor proposed the project of a volume on the early years of the trade, Irving was already well prepared. Within only a month of the publication of *A Tour,* Irving had moved into Astor's summer house at Hellgate, New York, to begin work on a history commemorating that businessman's failed venture into the Far Western fur trade in the early 1800s. The conditions of Astor's proposal, and of Irving's quick and certain assent, reveal the conjunction of the market-place and the literature by which that preparation was shaped into a revision of the critique of adventurous enterprise established in *A Tour.*

The terms of the deal struck between the two men were never explicitly revealed, but the very presence of a deal proved troubling for many critics at the time. Irving's response to this controversy tells us much about his attitude toward the project, especially when examined in the light of the deal itself. In a letter written fifteen years later for publication, Irving denied receiving any payment for his services. The letter, sent to the editors of the *Literary World,* and addressed to Henry R. Schoolcraft, was written in response to Schoolcraft's claim in that journal that Irving had received $5,000 to "take up the MSS." "This is the history of 'Astoria,'" Schoolcraft stated, implying a complicitous relation between the history of the book as a business deal and the history of business it portrayed. In response, Irving claimed that Astor paid only his nephew Pierre for doing much of the legwork, an unspec-ified amount to which Irving added "an additional consideration on my own account, and out of my own purse" (*MW*2:161–162). He did acknowledge, however, that Astor allowed him to purchase a share in a town he was building in Green Bay.

While Irving included no specific figures in his account, it is un-likely, given his conception of the role of the author that he had set forward in *A Tour* in particular, that he was trying to hide evidence of compromise. Instead he only wanted to reduce the likelihood of suspi-cion. As far as can now be determined, Astor paid Pierre $3,000, to which Irving added $1,000; the twenty-five shares of Green Bay land, which remained in Astor's name, amounted to about $4,000, the interests accruing to Irving totaling $2,100. As Irving seems to have refused any other payment—he had always avoided deals that might compromise his integrity as a professional while yet allowing him to profit as a professional—Astor sought other means to supplement the author for his work; specifically, he appointed Irving as the executor of his estate, for which Irving later received $10,592.66. While these fig-ures added up to no small amount of money in those days, there is no reason to conclude that Irving was thus persuaded to write a more positive account of Astor himself or the venture in general. Nor was there any coercion built into the deal itself: the only terms were that Astor agreed to pay Pierre, and Irving agreed to publish the book under the Crayon pseudonym.

Schoolcraft was not alone in suggesting collusion, however. Since the book's publication, many critics have argued that the very conception of the book as a business deal led Irving to shape its literary properties to satisfy the deal's originator; in other words, the deal was a bribe, and the book a "well paid panegyric" (Bancroft 2:568).[2] But such an argument oversimplifies the process of literary production, and fails to consider adequately the role played by the cultural and economic environment in which the deal was made. In fact, Irving was inclined to portray Astor in a favorable light long before the terms were discussed. In previous chapters we have examined some of the ideals to which Irving subscribed that helped shape his judgment, such as his commitments to a commercial culture and a professional capitalism. Astor seemed to fulfill these ideals in a manner especially pleasing to Irving: he had come to represent one of the most cherished principles of Jacksonian economics, the establishment of an entrepreneurial capitalism. As Irving perceived it, this principle not only exemplified the professionalism he had promoted in *A Tour*, but elevated it to a new level of achievement, a visionary practice: an entrepreneur is a professional who is also a man of vision, and he transforms the marketplace into a sacred arena of national mission. In short, he is just the "author" of the marketplace that Irving himself was seeking to become in his Western works.

Irving was thus drawn to Astor on a number of levels: he identified with him as a businessman and a man of imagination, admired him as a merchant who had acquired great wealth and risen to the upper classes, hoped to profit by him as a literary subject, and looked up to him as a powerful patron and man of vision. In all of these relationships, Irving had found a fellow professional. Even the patronage relation between the two men, a relation potentially threatening to the integrity of both the art and the profession, was conceived by Irving as a shared commitment to the commercialization of culture. On the one hand, if patronage threatened to reduce the production of art to a mere commercial transaction, it also supported the artist in operating independently from the pressures of the marketplace. On the other hand, if patronage seemed to call on a pre-business ethic counter-productive for the competitive professional, it also endowed capitalist competitiveness with the sureties of aristocratic hierarchy. In the end, Irving associated the relation with the imperatives of contributing to a national literature, for just as Astor was a patron of the nation in its expansion into the West, so he was a patron of Irving in his bid to make a profession of literature.

Certainly, the Irving involved in these dealings is not the Irving discussed earlier, who was so eager to condemn all business as "so sordid dusty, soul-killing a way of life"; and certainly this is not the Irving who felt that the world of business left no "quiet corner" for the artist. Early in his career, as we see in the passage surrounding one of these quotations, he had even associated Astor with this negative view of business: "By all the Martyrs of Grub Street I'd sooner live in a garret and starve into the bargain, than follow so sordid dusty, soul-killing way of life; though certain it would make me as rich as old Croesus, or John Jacob Astor himself" (*L*1:316). But nor is this the Irving one finds in much of the criticism of *Astoria,* eager to sell his artistry to the highest bidder. Irving had chosen the project for a number of reasons, some of them to do with his literary interests, some with his business interests, and all to do with what he felt were the concerns of his life as a professional.

We find these concerns displayed in his characterizations of the work at the time. As in his discussions of his earlier romantic histories, Irving frequently described the writing of *Astoria* as a professional task, involving monetary gain as well as artistic satisfaction. He wrote in many letters of "enriching" the work, of the "labor" he was bestowing upon the book which "will contribute greatly to its success," of the book as a whole as a "rich piece of mosaic" (*L*2:839, 856, 818). Pierre used the same language, perhaps picking it up from his uncle but just as likely from the culture they both inhabited. The project, he notes, was an "enterprise" in itself (*Life* 3:62).

This attention to enterprise is also evident in one of the principal reasons Irving accepted Astor's offer in the first place: to support his remodeling of the Sunnyside estate, which he had purchased shortly after the publication of *A Tour.* Astor too had the development of a property in mind: the Green Bay land speculation which he had invited Irving to join. This deal was designed ultimately to establish Astor's own, though more public, estate, a town to be called "Astor." Pierre followed the examples of both men by immediately taking his own share to Toledo, Ohio, to invest in land. The connections, then, between Astor and Irving, as well as their respective connections to the project, had already disposed Irving to an "interest" in the work, an interest strikingly congruent with the interests of the Astorian expedition itself: the merger of economic expansion, acquisition of property, and territorial possession.

This combination of literary and economic interests were shared by Astor as well. As Kenneth Porter has pointed out, Astor was "the first business man in America to attain colossal wealth." But rather than be remembered as a businessman alone, as "the Landlord of New York," Astor wanted to be seen as a "dreamer of empire,. . .[a] daring and constructive thinker on a large scale" (1:243); that is, he wanted to be recognized as an American visionary. It is a goal he sought with particular zeal because he had often been excluded, as an immigrant, from recognition by America's aristocratic social circles. He knew well that while his achievements in business alone would never elevate him in the social roster, literature might afford him the necessary endorsement of "culture." Presumably these desires account in part for his eagerness to acquire the journals kept by his explorers and trappers during the expedition.

Irving was aware of Astor's desire, and of the role it would play in the conception of the work. As he explained to Pierre after hearing the proposal for the first time, Astor "is extremely desirous of having a work written on the subject of his settlement of Astoria, . . .something that might take with the reading world, and secure to him the reputation of having originated the enterprise and founded the colony that are likely to have such important results in the history of commerce and colonization" (L2:798). If Irving's rather distanced perspective raises some doubt as to whether he approved of the goal, one has only to look at the "correction" letter he wrote about the *Astoria* payments, in which he admonished Malte Brun for describing Astor as "a merchant seeking his own profit and not a discoverer" (MW2:161–162). This phrase reveals the attraction Irving felt not only for Astor but for most powerful and wealthy men; at the same time, it indicates the formula of nationalist sentiment by which he justified what he felt was the harshness and crudity of some of their business tactics. We find the same sentiments expressed in an earlier letter in which he championed another patron, his British publisher John Murray II, as no "mere man of business" (*L2:664*). These entrepreneurial capitalists were, for Irving, the visionary professionals of economic expansion.

Yet Irving did not believe that his project was motivated or would be shaped by Astor's desire alone. Again in the *Astoria* letter he explained that

> The work was undertaken by me through a real relish of the subject. In the course of visits in early life to Canada I had seen much of the magnates of the North West Company and of the hardy trappers and fur traders in their employ, and had been excited by their stories of adventurous expeditions into the "Indian country." I was sure, therefore, that a narrative, treating of them and their doings, could not fail to be full of stirring interest, and to lay open regions and races of our country, as yet but little known. (*MW2:161*)

On the surface, these statements could as easily apply to *A Tour* as to *Astoria,* as could the gap in logic indicated by the "therefore" in the last sentence. The hidden link between his own interest, the potential interest of the reading public, and his decision to take on the project was his recognition that the subject was suitable to both his own talents and the conditions of the marketplace: like Astor, he was looking for something that would "take with the public." Unlike his position with regard to *A Tour,* however, Irving felt no self-conscious or satirical restraint about the role of these literary "interests" in the process of expansion: like Astor's expedition, his book would "lay open regions and races of our country, as yet but little known." Astoria and *Astoria* would become one.

The story that Irving had contracted to tell was of Astor's failed attempt to establish an American fur trade monopoly in the Pacific Northwest. In the tradition of Jefferson, and with his aid, Astor hoped to extend the trading arena that had been recently established in the newly purchased Louisiana territory, an extension that would ultimately include all of the "debatable" lands of the continent, and provide a link to the marketplaces of the Far East. While his plan differed, in the end, from Jefferson's—his primary interest was in trade, not settlement—his rhetoric invoked the same nationalist ideal of bringing these new territories of trade under American domination. At the same time, of course, he also hoped to bring them under his own dominion, for just as he had given the name of "Astor" to his land under speculation at Green Bay, so he was determined to give the name of "Astoria" to his outpost on the Western coast. So in 1808 he acquired a private charter for what he called the "American Fur Company" to begin moving his already lucrative trading business in the Northeast into the region of the Great Lakes. Then two years later he took another charter for the Pacific Fur Company, designed to bring the trade the rest of the way to the coast. A number of men were hired to travel to the mouth of the Columbia River by land and by boat and there establish a fort and trading post, a foundation for a fur trading empire. After enduring many hardships along the way, some of the men did indeed reach the coast, and did build a significant, if small, fort. Within a few years, however, the project failed. By 1812 many of the original "Astorians" were dead, the fort had been seized by the British, and the British had erected their own fur trade monopoly in the territory.

Despite the general distrust of commercialism expressed in *A Tour,* Irving found little in this story for concern, and much for commemoration. Astor's original vision was noble because it represented not simply his own interests but the interests of the nation. Its failure, in turn, could easily be construed as a sign both of its own integrity, and of the dangers to the community from traitorous forces within and foreign forces without. If the satire of *A Tour* had demonstrated the need for the professionalization of economic expansion, the West, and the literature that represented their conjunction, *Astoria* could integrate that process into the process of American history, into the national enterprise of commerce and colonization. American history itself would thus become redefined as a history of marketplace expansion; that is, a tale of adventurous enterprise.

The history of the fur trade was an ideal subject for that integration, for it provided a narrative framework by which Irving could examine the course the nation had taken in its expansion into the West, and into the Jacksonian era. According to the popular imagery, the trade was set in the wilderness, like the nation itself; peopled by adventurers and profit-seekers only loosely tied to the obligations of communal or company life; and threatened by rival competitors, themselves lacking the restraints of an enterprise dictated by the idealism of market expansion. In short, the history of the fur trade was the archetypal form of American narrative history, an adventure tale of explorers, pioneers, Indians, and businessmen set in the context of Western expansion. A seeming embodiment of the typological history later articulated by Frederick Jackson Turner, the history of the fur trade looked back to the origins of America itself, and forward to the fulfillment of its mission.

Two years after writing *Astoria,* Irving explained in a lengthy letter to his friend Gouverneur Kemble the logic of this prophetic history. Strikingly, his reasoning justifies the same excesses of capitalism that, in *A Tour,* called forth his satirical criticism. The passage needs to be quoted in full to capture the complex narrative perspective by which Irving, in *Astoria,* modified his approach to adventurous enterprise:

> As to the excessive expansions of commerce and the extravagant land speculations, which excited such vehement censure, I look upon them as incident to that spirit of enterprize natural to a young country in a state of rapid and prosperous development; a spirit, which, with all its occasional excesses, has given our nation an immense impulse in its onward career, and promises to carry it ahead of all the nations of the globe. There are moral as well as physical phenomena incident to every state of things, which may at first appear evils, but which are devised by an all-seeing providence for some beneficent purpose. Such is the spirit of speculative enterprise which now and then rises to an extravagant height and sweeps throughout the land. It grows out of the very state of our country and its institutions, and, though sometimes productive of temporary mischief, yet leaves behind it lasting benefits. The late land speculations, so much deprecated, though ruinous to many engaged in them, have forced agriculture and civilization into the depths of the wilderness; have laid open the recesses of primeval forests; made us acquainted with the most available points of our immense interior; have cast the germs of future towns and cities and busy marts in the heart of savage solitudes, and studded our vast rivers and internal seas with ports that will soon give activity to a vast internal commerce. Millions of acres which might otherwise have remained idle and impracticable wastes have been brought under the dominion of the plow and hundreds of thousands of industrious yeomen have to multiply and spread out in every direction, and give solidity and strength to our great confederacy. (*L*2:919–920)

These comments may at first seem to constitute a complete reversal of the attack on excessive self-interest in *A Tour,* and a repudiation of the critique of speculation he would publish only a year and a half later in "A Time of Unexampled Prosperity." But the operative terms here remain the same, as does, finally, the endorsement of commercialism in the name of empire. While capitalism may cause damage, for instance, the "spirit" of enterprise allows it to prevail, and even justifies the damage. And America's "providential" purpose is embodied within the order of both nature and the marketplace: the "spirit of enterprize natural to a young country" impels the nation on its "onward career." (Irving had even begun writing "prof" but crossed it out for the more concrete "busy marts.") The damage done is deemed unsystemic and merely temporal, subsumed in the vast sacred and national narrative of economic expansion.

This careful endorsement of speculation was not strictly a departure for Irving. Its foundations can be found in a similar passage from an early journal, in which he identified speculation as a "natural" response to America itself and American expansionism:

> the impatience of restraint, the neglect and almost contempt for minor observances, the restless spirit[,] speculative turn and proneness to hyperbole, with which Americans are charged, may be traced to the unsettled mode of their life—the rapid changes that are continually taking place in the state of society and the face of the country around them—to the frequent shiftings of place and occupation—the vast migrations they undertake—the wild scenes through which they pass and the grand and indefinite scale on which they are accustomed to see natural objects. He who is brought up among forests whose shades extends, he knows not whither—whose eye roves over plains of boundless extent—who looks forth upon inland seas, where no opposing shore is visible; who sees vast rivers flowing down from he knows not whence, and rolling a world of waters to the far distant ocean of which he has only heard. Who beholds every thing around him changing as if by enchantment— what was once a wilderness becoming a busy hive of population—what in childhood he saw a village grown into a city before he arrives at manhood—every where reality outstripping imagination—surely it is no wonder that such a one should be speculative and hyperbolical. (*J*2:64–65)

While Irving's anxiety about speculation is evident in such phrases as "impatience of restraint" and "reality outstripping imagination," the basic tenor of the passage is an acceptance of that anxiety as a necessary condition of a natural process, and a vindication of the criticisms with which Americans have been "charged." The "bankrupt" hive of *A Tour* is here just a "busy" hive; the pastoral innocence of "The Creole Village" is here compatible with the transformations of expansion and development; the crossing of boundaries is here embraced by the "boundless extent" of the American landscape. The "enchantment" of speculation, which Irving was often to condemn as a threat to both nation and nature, becomes an extension of both, and an affirmation of the national character. Reality may outstrip imagination, but both are ultimately linked in the furtherance of American progress.

The narrative logic implicit in these passages was well-suited to the telling of the story of Astoria, and also well-suited to Irving's revision of his satirical stance toward commercialism. Unlike *A Tour, Astoria* is presented simply as an objective history, reliable and impartial, the very form Irving had undermined in *A Tour* and *A History of New York*. Not only is there now a "story to tell," but there are moral and political messages to convey.

These messages work on a number of levels. On the most general, Irving is attempting to commemorate the "spirit of enterprize" itself as it is embodied in Astor and the bravest and most loyal of his workers; on the more concrete, to focus attention on the boundary dispute with England that had begun with the founding of Astoria and its capture in the War of 1812. This latter concern was perhaps an even more controversial issue in the 1830s when Irving began writing the book. As Andrew Myers has pointed out, the slogan "54 40 or fight" was coined in 1836, the year *Astoria* was published (1964, 58). By writing a history of the origins of the dispute, Irving hoped to identify what he called, in an article published a few years later, "this great territorial right, which involves empire" (*MW*2:136).[3]

By their embodiment in this tale of adventurous enterprise, though, these two messages do not so much dispute as revise the earlier critiques in *A History of New York* and *A Tour* about both the nature of American historiography and the rights of a marketplace empire. There are still the villains of expansion to be overcome, and still the tensions within free enterprise to be eased. There is still the need to endow the West, Western expansion, and Western literature, with the culture of professionalism, through such formal elements as class and character, narrative form and figurative language. The only difference is that the dangers are no longer seen as residing within the very ideals and social construction of American society. The only individuals truly "native" to America are the Americans, and the only individuals who threaten America are either foreigners, Indians (who are now classified as foreigners), or inept government officials (who inadvertently aid the foreigners).

While these changes do not essentially alter the ideological configurations of the adventure tale form, they do substantially limit the writer's capacity for critical range and depth. For instance, in eliminating his satirical perspective, Irving has also eliminated its complex symbolic structure as well. Indians are now only savages of one sort of another, not free enterprisers in disguise; likewise, the trappers are simply employees in the fur business, not savages disguised as free enterprisers. But if Irving thus weakens the potency of criticism embodied in the motifs he had employed in *A Tour,* such as the mistaken identity, he has not entirely eliminated his critical perspective. Indeed he chooses to exhume the very reductive symbolism of the adventure tale of which he had earlier been wary—Indians and trappers as either villains or allies of the American quest—in order to apply it with the same cautionary message: the enterprise of economic expansion does have its enemies, if not from within then from without.

This reduction of the ambiguities of figurative representation to the literalization of history, the internal contradictions into external conflicts, the expansion of economic enterprise into the adventure of the American mission, places Irving's Western histories within the dominant tradition of American romantic historiography of the period. The vision of history one finds in the works of such contemporary writers as Francis Parkman, George Bancroft and William Prescott, follows three basic premises: that there is, in Diedrich Knickerbocker's words, a "requisite unity [to] history" (*HNY* 379), that that unity is best represented in narrative form, and that the most suitable narrative form for the discovery and expression of that unity is the romantic history, or history of great exploit and enterprise. As Hayden White has explained, these "standards of coherence," such as lay behind any piece of historical writing, amount to nothing less than a "philosophy of history" itself (1978, 122, 127), and in these works, that philosophy takes its operative language, assumptions, and ideals from the narrative prescriptions of American history, specifically the American endeavor of adventurous enterprise. The American history that we find in *Astoria* is the romance of economic idealism.

A look at Irving's use of the basic formal elements of narrative form —the causal relations between events and their placement within the larger movement through time—will reveal the ways that this romance, and the economic idealism behind it, affected the shape of Irving's American history. The cause-effect relations found in Irving's two histories of the fur trade are precisely those of the ideology of enterprise: the heroes pursue a goal of economic expansion against villains who obstruct that goal; and each event realizes the causes of self-interest and the common good, and the effects of mobility and hierarchy, the joining of the self to the community and the severing of ties between them. These adventures are then placed within the context of sacred time that had been a fundamental construct of American historiography since the Puritans. *Astoria*'s American trappers and their foreign competitors, for instance, play out the drama of enterprise in a period of the past that is emblematic of both the sacred origins of the nation and its potential future.

One of the peculiarities of this historical vision is its ability to fuse ideology and narrative, no simple task since the dramatic form dictated by the former in this case essentially violates narrative's two basic elements, causality and the chronological passage of time. In the place of an analysis of how commerce leads to colonization, profit-making to empire, industry to exploration to expansion, one finds only the assertion that the activities are identical, each an expression of the other. In the place of an analysis of how contemporary social and economic activities might have affected the timely decisions of Astor and the others, one finds only the evocation of the transcendent principles of sacred time. Yet the overall effect of the form is the transformation of ideology into history, and vice versa. The mission of enterprise and expansion becomes the basis of historical process, and is preserved from the considerations of causal reasoning because it contains the rightness of history itself.

This denial of causal relation is, however, never revealed. The expansion of American enterprise depended upon its ability to transcend both its internal contradictions and the practical excesses to which they gave rise, an ability secured through the claims of the sacred mission. This ideological effect on the narrative is perhaps most notable in the framing of the conflict as a confrontation between the forces of the sacred and the secular. Astor is depicted as the beacon of the sacred ideals and his enemies as the vulgarizers, men who replace the visionary reach of expansion with the grasp of mere acquisitiveness. American history is thus represented as a drama of secularization, in which the sacred ideals are under siege by, on the American side, the substitution of profit for principle, as one finds in many of Astor's trappers and in the disappointing government officials, and, on the un-American side, the acquisitive and anti-competitive activities of Indians and foreigners.

As a result, the ideals are preserved from any direct scrutiny that would reveal them to have caused any of the system's failings and consequent failures; conceivable connections between industry and catastrophe, exploit and exploitation, have become inconceivable in the context of the narrative.

But if Irving is often critical of individual trappers in Astor's employ, his portrayal of Astor himself, and his venture in general, is generally restricted to the positive terms of justification and celebration. He mentions nothing of the characteristic treachery of the American Fur Company, nor of the extent of Astor's business interests in creating the company in the first place. Irving's representation of the loyal trappers in Astor's employ as courageous profit seekers stands in stark contrast to the depiction offered by the contemporary military man Zachary Taylor of the same men as "the greatest scoundrels the world ever knew" (Riegel 314); Irving's description of Astor's company as small and consequently vulnerable to its fierce foreign competitors is at some remove from DeVoto's portrayal of a company so much larger and more ruthless that it could make more effective use of such corrupt manipulations as bribery (1947, 120); and Irving's presentation of Astor's chartering of the company as a gesture of national expansion is strikingly different from the description by fur trade historian Hiram Chittenden of the act as "a fiction intended to broaden and facilitate [Astor's] operations" (1:167).[4] While Irving was sure to have come across such negative portrayals in his researches, he would wait until his next book, *The Adventures of Captain Bonneville,* to acknowledge this more "sanguinary" side of the trade (to use one of his own words from *A Tour*); trappers, he writes there, are prone to a particularly "savage" form of competition: "next to his own advantage, the study of the Indian trader is the disadvantage of his competitor" (*B* 9). But in the narrative context of *Astoria,* these impulses are generally assigned not to the loyal representatives of the Astor's American Fur Company but to the disloyal trappers, as well as to the foreigners.

Astoria's failure is depicted as a consequence mainly of secular, and secularizing, forces from without, such as the English and the Indians. These villains seek to impose a false vision of history on the land. In this sense, the stories in *Astoria* can be read as struggles between two different visions of history; and in the end, the secular story of the defeat can itself be defeated by the sacred tale. The book transforms the catastrophic events of history into a sacred narrative, a defeat into a promise of success, a logic of causal relation into a promotion of ideological goals, an examination of a moment in time into a transcendence of time altogether. Like the history of capitalism it is chronicling, *Astoria* thus becomes a competition designed to end competition, to give American history the monopoly over history itself.

The choice of "sacred" and "secular" as the operative terms of the narrative opposition is not an invention of Irving's. As noted in the discussion of the origins of adventurous enterprise, from the earliest colonial literature, economic motivations were justified through a rhetoric of sanctification, and by the nineteenth century, that rhetoric had simply been shifted away from its explicitly religious context to the realm of economic ideals. What concerned Irving and other American historians was not that economic idealism was itself a denigration of religious and communal faith, but rather that individual enterprisers often forgot those sacred ideals, had "secularized" them and thus disturbed the balance of self-interest and communal obligation upon which the American mission depended.[5] Irving's desire in *Astoria* was to use the grand theme of entrepreneurial capitalism to redress that balance, by sanctifying the professional arena within the marketplace, and endowing it with the prerogatives of national mission.

Astoria thus shares with the earlier European writings in this tradition a narrative consolidation of the interests of self, nation, and God into a representation of human history as manifest destiny. What distinguishes this book from the others are those distinctly American terms and literary formulations by which those connections are made. In his book on the art of American romantic historiography, David Levin has described a number of the specific narrative strategies common to the tradition in which *Astoria* is situated. First, writes Levin,

> the subject had to be an interesting narrative, on a "grand theme," in which a varied group of remarkable, vigorous characters acted heroically on the largest possible stage. The grand theme involved the origins of a nation (preferably, in some way, America), the progress of Liberty in her battle against Absolutism, the conquest of a continent, or all of these. (11)

This approach to subject and theme precisely describes the larger conception with which Irving approached *Astoria*, an "enterprise" "originated" and a "colony" "founded" by Astor "that are likely to have such important results in the history of commerce and colonization." In another letter Irving echoed the sentiment, adding the dramatic flourish that would turn the historical events into the stuff of history itself:

> My present idea is to call the work by the general name of *Astoria*. . .[and] under this head to give not merely a history of his great colonial and commercial enterprise, and of the fortunes of his colony, but a body of information concerning the whole region beyond the Rocky Mountains. . .comprising the adventures, by sea and land, of traders, trappers, Indians warriors, hunters, &c[.] (*L*2:802)

The history and the information would be joined by the "adventures" of the individual participants; and the adventurous enterprise would thus become the history.

The terms of these adventures will, in turn, be dictated by two other formulations of romantic historiography, that "History was the unfolding of a vast Providential plan" (Levin 25–26), and that the dramatic arena of that plan was the inevitability of "human progress" (27–28). The adventurers themselves will represent the qualities associated with the dictates of that progress, a progress defined in American thought as consisting of the activities of both commerce and colonization; in short, economic expansion. The corresponding heroic virtues, according to Levin, were "courage, self-reliance, candor, and vigorous activity" (39), and were "merged with bourgeois admiration for industry" (40), while the villains of this essentially "chivalric" formulation were characterized by "the lie" and "the sacrifice of honor" (39), precisely the qualities that would most threaten a society run by the marketplace axiom of self-interest. Irving ascribes just these attributes to the businessmen, trappers and Indians in his Western works.

Not all romantic histories were tales of adventurous enterprise, of course. But in Irving's histories, we find the two forms identified with each other. By connecting their general assumptions and narrative devices, he was also associating American history with the progress of economic expansion. Irving's "grand theme" was precisely the expansion of the marketplace into the West, and in that theme he found a recapitulation of American history from its visionary past to its economic present. A closer examination of the way these literary and economic elements fit together reveal the conjunction of history and adventurous enterprise that was to become the normative nineteenth-century view of the westward movement.

One of the basic structural devices in *Astoria* is the frame. In the opening and closing chapters and in brief reiterations in chapters 42 and 55, Irving establishes the terms of his "theme." As we have seen, he had used the device many times before, usually to undermine the reliability of the narrator and thus magnify the satirical edge of his social and psychological portraits. But in *Astoria,* the frame is offered to strengthen, rather than undermine, his homage to Astor and the enterprise of commercial colonization.

Irving is not without critical intentions, however. His purpose in telling the story of this man and his "grand scheme," he explains, is not simply to commemorate its intrinsic grandness as a part of the national history, but to address the real and present political problems revealed by the failure of the expedition. Out of this failure should come a greater understanding of the threats to economic expansion, and a recognition that Astoria should be reestablished so as to provide a claim on the Northwest as American territory. The villains, according to this theme, are primarily the British, whose successful fur trade had led to their own claims to the area, but these villains have also acquired inadvertent support from the American government, which had continued to maintain its distance from the project. The failure of Astor's project is thus redeemed, reconstituted as a warning to Irving's readers, the present and future Americans, that their adventurous enterprise might soon follow the fate of Astoria itself.

Two fundamental assumptions underlay this transformation. First, Astor's vision was itself great in both its national and providential, its secular and religious, elements; and second, the responsibility for its failure lay not in the vision at all but in its betrayal. So Irving proclaims throughout the book that Astor was the "master spirit of the enter-prize" (253), the author and unifying agent of a "great scheme of commerce and colonization" (27): "The facts. . .will prove to be linked and banded together by one grand scheme, devised and conducted by a master spirit" (4). This last phrase is a striking presence in an "Author's Introduction," for it essentially announces Irving's abdication of his own authorship in the account to come. Yet this is precisely Irving's point: he is retelling a history, not inventing a romance, and the true author of that history is the "master spirit of the enterprize." From the heroic American visionary radiates the global expansion of American progress.

In the opening chapters Irving gives a brief biography of Astor that underscores this connection between Astor as profit-seeking individual and Astor as American visionary, between Astor's history and the history of the nation. He is, we learn, "a man whose name and character are worthy of being enrolled in the history of Commerce, as illustrating its noblest aims and soundest maxims" (15). In the language of American Puritanism, Astor's genius for business is a quality of character, and that character embodies the whole of American commercialism in microcosm:

> He began his career, of course, on the narrowest scale, but he brought to the task a persevering industry, rigid economy and strict integrity. To these were added an aspiring spirit that always looked upward, a genius bold, fertile and expansive, a sagacity quick to grasp and convert every circumstance to its advantage, and a singular and never wavering confidence of signal success. (15–16)

The "genius," or spirit of place, of America is precisely represented in Astor: "bold, fertile, and expansive." And its "noblest aims and soundest maxims" are also his own:

> Indeed it is due to him to say that he was not actuated by mere motives of individual profit. He was already wealthy beyond the ordinary desires of man, but he now aspired to that honorable fame which is awarded to men of similar scope of mind, who by their great commercial enterprizes have enriched nations, peopled wildernesses, and extended the bounds of empire. He considered his projected establishment at the mouth of the Columbia as the emporium to an immense commerce; as a colony that would form the germ of a wide civilization; that would, in fact, carry the American population across the Rocky Mountains and spread it along the shores of the Pacific, as it already animated the shores of the Atlantic. (23)

In keeping with the American historical vision, the resolute character of Astor's conviction is presented as most grand when that enterprise is most threatened, and the adventures are most dangerous. Irving then brings historical immediacy to bear by quoting from a letter by Astor himself: "*Our enterprize is grand, and deserves success, and I hope in God it will meet it*. If my object was merely gain of money I should say think whether it is best to save what we can and abandon the place, *but the very idea is like a dagger to my heart*.'" "This extract," Irving concludes, "is sufficient to shew the spirit and the views which actuated Mr. Astor in this great undertaking" (309).

To put it simply, Astor is an American Columbus. To trace the lineage, one need only go back so far as Irving's own biography of Columbus, *The Life and Voyages of Christopher Columbus,* published a few years earlier. Like Astor, Columbus is represented as a man of "enterprizing spirit and lively imagination" (12) with a "devout and enthusiastic spirit" (56). And like Astor's scheme, Columbus' plan serves the interests of both commerce and culture, both the secular and the sacred. While "not the least recommendation of [his] enterprize" might be, in the opinion of Ferdinand, to "open a direct course to India across the ocean, to bear off from the monopoly of oriental commerce" (47), in Columbus' mind the project was essentially religious: "he would devote the profits arising from his anticipated discoveries, to a crusade for the rescue of the holy sepulchre from the power of the infidels" (56). "It is essential to a full comprehension of the character and motives of Columbus," Irving tells us,

> that this visionary project should be borne in recollection. It will be found to have entwined itself in his mind with his enterprize of discovery, and that a holy crusade was to be the consummation of those divine purposes for which he considered himself selected by heaven as an agent. It shews how much his mind was elevated above selfish and mercenary views—how it was filled with those devout and heroic schemes, which in the time of the crusades had inflamed the thoughts, and directed the enterprizes of the bravest warriors and the most illustrious princes. (162)

Were one to transcribe the religious terms into economic ideals, then the description would apply equally well to Astor. Even the narrative language is essentially the same: "visionary," "schemes," "enterprize." Like Columbus, Astor is finally not "actuated by mere motives of individual profit" but by a sacred mission. The American Columbus simply has a different Jerusalem to liberate, the promised land of the Far West.[6]

If this typology places Astor as the quintessential American visionary, it also locates him in a lineage of American founding fathers, figures who translated the vision into practice. Irving explicitly associates Astor with Jefferson and his plan for opening the West to trade and settlement. Implicit in this connection, though, is a more general evocation of Astor as the first of America's indigenous patriarchs,

George Washington. There is much similarity, for instance, between Irving's Astor and the Washington that appears in Irving's five volume biography, published twenty years later. Where Columbus was the type for the American as man of imagination, Washington was the type for the American as man of the practical. A "self-disciplinarian in physical as well as mental matters" (1:17) with "an eye to the profitable rather than the poetical" (1:24), Washington succeeded because of "his own scrupulous principle of always living within compass" (1:40). His experiences in the wilderness made him a knowledgeable military commander; his "business habits" (1:176) made him an efficient leader; his "adventurous spirit" (1:246), "mingled with practical purposes" (1:206), and his "propensities as a sportsman" (1:204), made him a shrewd adversary; and his "justice and impartiality" (2:292) made him a model of selflessness: "For he knew no divided fidelity, no separate obligation; his most sacred duty to himself was his highest duty to his country and his God" (5:475). His visionary capacities, that is, are the capacities of the practical man, the translator of principal into practice.

The attributes associated with Columbus and Washington are just those Irving had associated with professionalism in *A Tour*: Columbus' imagination is met by Washington's practicality, and together they attend to grand scheme that secures the interests of the self to the interests of the community. Of particular relevance to the history of Astoria is that both pursue that scheme amidst dangers from the outside, such as Indians and a harsh environment, and dangers from within, such as incompetent superiors and treacherous subordinates. Like Columbus and Washington, Irving's Astor would be ennobled by adventures of frustration and failure. In the end, all three would become members of that fraternity of the natural aristocrats of spirit and commerce, adventurers in the enterprise of American expansion.

But Irving faced some difficulties in representing Astor as the heroic American and founding father. For one thing, unlike Columbus and Washington, Astor was not a man of action, and so was not especially suitable for the role of hero; he had to rely on others to venture forth, to enact his vision in the wilderness. In fact, central to Irving's conception of the book is that this very rift between vision and practice was partly responsible for the failure of the expedition. Irving's solution to this problem is well in keeping with his vision of a professionalized culture. He divided the attributes of heroism along the lines of a division of labor: the heroic vision was associated with Astor's entrepreneurial position, the heroic actions with the loyal and efficient labor of certain of his employees, and the villainous anti-vision with the incompetence or betrayal of other employees, or the competitive or anti-competitive efforts of Indians and foreigners.

For another thing, like Columbus Astor was foreign born, and so was potentially unsuitable for the designation of founding father. Irving's solution to this problem was not, as one might expect, a call to the shared heritage of Americans in the immigrant community. Such a perspective would diminish the purity of the conception of Astor as American visionary. Also, it would violate the adventure form of the book as a whole, in which the villains are defined precisely by their "foreignness," their un-American spirit. Instead, he deflects the issue altogether by describing Astor as an "adopted citizen" (15), chosen by the chosen people to pursue American ideals. Astor is thus freed from the distractions of his own history and recast in the historical mold of the American merchant.

But he is more than just the typical merchant. He is the "master spirit," the patriarch of the enterprise; that is, he is the founding father of American commerce. In his introduction to *Bonneville,* Irving refers to Astor as "the patriarch of the Fur Trade in the United States" (3), a conception that is in evidence throughout *Astoria.* Irving calls him "the father of the enterprize" (*Ast* 33) and "the venerable projector" (356), and repeatedly describes the Astorian settlement itself as an "infant" or "embryo" colony. By this language, Astor not only becomes another founding father, but the father of the nation as marketplace. At the same time, his enterprise is identified as one of the young America's first steps toward adulthood.

This language of maturation takes on a special significance in the context of the venture's failure, charging it with a grief that is both personal and national: the diminished promise is now part of the history of American lineage and threatens the happiness and prosperity of the survivors. The pervasiveness and power of this narrative perspective at the time can be seen in its presence even in the contemporary reviews of the book. Everett Emerson, for example, explained the failure of Astoria in these terms: "As a commercial adventure, it resulted in the almost total loss of the vast capital which had been embarked in it; and as a commencement of the settlement of the country, it was equally abortive" (1837, 200). By thus merging the popular metaphor of maturation with the equally popular metaphor of

commercial expansion as adventure, Emerson has revealed the premise
of prophetic narrative at work in the book's vision of history. For
America to succeed in its current expansion into the West, it must
remember the losses it had incurred in its youth. In this sense, Irving's
maturational history of the Astorian expedition is a narrative model of
how the culture should "read" its current economic expansion in the
context of all American history.

According to the traditional use of this figure of maturation, this
abortion was definitively not the fault of the father, the "venerable
projector," but of the environment into which the child was thrust, a
wilderness of mobility that offered as little guidance as it did security.
This wilderness is only metaphorically located in the natural world; in
fact, it is located in the marketplace, and its elements are those features
of the marketplace—self-interest, competitiveness, and acquisitiveness
—that that wilderness had come to represent in American culture.
Irving first identifies those elements in the opening chapters of the
frame and then repeatedly refers to them throughout the book, but it
is at the end that his formulation is most direct and most urgent:

> That Mr. Astor battled resolutely against every difficulty and pursued
> his course in defiance of every loss, has been sufficiently shewn. Had he
> been seconded by suitable agents and properly protected by government,
> the ultimate failure of his plan might yet have been averted. It was his
> great misfortune that his agents were not imbued with his own spirit.
> Some had not capacity sufficient to comprehend the real nature and
> extent of his scheme; others were alien in feeling and interest, and had
> been brought up in the service of a rival company. (355)

The father may be the spirit of the enterprise, but it is the children who
must bring the enterprise to fruition; they must adventure into the
wilderness and implant that vision into the American land. In *Astoria,*
those children fail, an inheritance that Irving sees as a warning to the
Jacksonian generation set to occupy the position of father, of authority,
left vacant by the previous generation. Uncertain of its own ideals, and
thus inadequate to defend them against "alien" forces from without,
the culture remains a child in the wilderness.[7]

The failure, then, has two related causes: the initial vision has been
diminished in the wilderness, and the forces dedicated to its defeat
have been strengthened, capable of reformulating that vision to their
own ends. In this scheme, the heroes and villains of adventurous

enterprise are more collaborators than opponents. But the narrative does not leave the reader in despair over this loss of differentiation. Irving creates a narrative form of doublings and reversals that reveals the dangers to the American identity and mission in the wilderness. Just as the sacred history of Astoria must transcend its perverted representation in the secular history of self-interest, so Astor and his loyal trappers must overcome the savage "otherness" of their own dark doubles. If the goal of Astor's vision was the establishment of a "foothold of American commerce and empire on the shores of the Pacific" (326), then the failure will leave that territory in the hands of the British; and yet the two will mirror each other in the competition. If the creator of that vision was an "adopted citizen" of America, then the betrayers will be those excluded from the roster, the foreigners whose allegiances lie still across the ocean; and yet the two will compete in their loyalty. If the father of the enterprise was a man of vision, then the children will be without vision, self-interested individuals who see nothing but short-term profit; and yet the success of the former will depend on the avidity of the latter. If the project showed its promise in its qualities of youth and "infancy," then its destruction will be seen as an "abortion"; and yet the abortion will provide a passageway for the birth of a new generation to come. If that vision of enterprise was the adventure of the American mission, then its failure will be a "tissue of misadventures" (355). Here is the quintessential economy of American romantic historiography: the ideology of enterprise combines with the tale of adventure to distinguish heroic self from villainous other, and to contain them in an endless narrative of competition, a competition that can issue only in monopoly.

In many ways, this motif of doubling serves the same purpose as the class system in *A Tour*: by distinguishing entrepreneur from leader from trapper, original from copy from counterfeit, the reader will learn to read the history of the fur trade through an organizing template of fixed meanings based on the values of professionalism. At the same time, however, the purpose which this particular template serves is very different, as becomes evident when we compare the doubling with another motif in *A Tour*, the mistaken identity. In the earlier book, the perspective was satirical and self-reflexive. Irving had explored the values and actions of the self as the source of the invented other, a paradigmatic view of the marketplace as the author of its own self-justifying drama. In *Astoria*, however, the perspective is serious and promotional, positing self and other as opposing forces in a struggle between absolute right and wrong. Economic enterprise here plays its proper role in the drama written in, and by, sacred history itself. It is largely because the former view frustrates the claims of history that Irving found it necessary to return to history in the next two books. If, as he suggested in *A Tour*, the savage strains of economic expansion threatened to bring the historical mission of adventurous enterprise to a halt, then the delineation of savagery into a discreet other would place the enterprise back within its proper dramatic form, the prophetic history of the American mission.

The narrative form one finds in *Astoria* follows these assumptions. With each celebration of Astor comes a chastisement of the British and their cruel competitiveness, the foreigners within Astor's own company and their disloyal self-interest, the Indians and their savage acquisitiveness, the government and its narrowness of national vision. Even the readers are implicated in this criticism, insofar as their reading endorses the pursuit of the secular bounties of marketplace expansion without engaging its sacred principles. This mirroring pattern within the frame is also duplicated in the construction of the rest of the book. On the one hand, the relation between vision and failure in the frame is recapitulated in the relation between the frame and the narrative. The frame's sacred mission is illustrated through a series of decidedly secular narratives, and in this secularization can be read the collapse of the enterprise. On the other hand, the narratives themselves contain characters and events that represent both the democratic nobility of Astor's plan and the selfish ignobility of its betrayal.

These narratives fall into four separate sections. First there is the story of the voyage of the *Tonquin* (chapters 4–12), in which the first group of Astorians travel to the mouth of the Columbia River to build the fort; instead, they meet with disaster at the hands of the Indians. The second section concerns the expedition by land of Wilson Hunt and a party of trappers (chapters 13–41); like the group aboard the *Tonquin*, these men too pass through a series of deprivations and disasters that diminishes them along the way. Next comes the tale of the return land expedition led by Robert Stuart (chapters 43–50), which follows the same path of hardship and destitution. And finally, the fourth section draws together the series of events that led up to the fall of Astoria to the British (chapters 51–60). The further these adventures get from Astor and the "grand scheme," from "civilization" itself, the more secular the context of motivations and characters and events. The communal enterprise becomes embodied in the individual exploits, the sacred enterprise in the gestures of profit-seeking and Indian fighting and trading. Even the word "enterprise," which is so frequently repeated in the frame, is replaced by less inclusive terms like "hardihood," "diligence," and "aspiration."

On one level, this translation of sacred scheme into secular adventure fulfills the narrative requirements of adventurous enterprise. Astor has the vision, and his loyal employees the adventure. But in this case, that translation is also deemed a failure. The fall of Astoria is characterized as a "fall" of enterprise into mere self-interest, of adventure into loose adventuring. In each of these narrative sections, Irving strives to identify the reasons for this degradation of both enterprise and adventure, and to reacquaint his readers with the proper course of American narrative history.

As the first of these sections, the *Tonquin* story sets the pattern for the others. The cast of characters is headed by Captain Thorn, the pilot of the ship who stands as Astor's representative in the wilderness, his diminished reflection. It is his faulty leadership that precipitates the disaster. While he respects Astor's values, such as the "value of property," he takes those values "to a dangerous length" (39), applying them literally and without the largeness and flexibility of true vision: "He evidently had but a narrow idea of the scope and nature of the enterprize, limiting his views merely to his part of it; everything beyond the concerns of his ship was out of his sphere; and any thing that interfered with the routine of his nautical duties put him in a passion" (33). While basically "honest" (34), he is yet "deficient in patience and pliancy and totally wanting in the chicanery of traffic" (73). Worst of all, he assumes his own vision of the world is an adequate grounding for the pursuit of the enterprise: from the beginning he dismisses Astor's warnings about the fickleness of the Indians. The fault, then, lies not with Astor but his representative. While the original vision of the enterprise remains pure and accurate, encompassing the world in its dangers as well as its promise, it cannot protect itself against the savagery of the wilderness. Thorn's flaws are described in precisely these terms of the wilderness: a "Savage pride" (78) that is a diminished version of Astor's ambition, and a narrowness of insight that is a diminished version of Astor's business sense. Like the reckless enterprisers in *A Tour,* he lacks the "necessary self command" (78) to bring success to the venture. In other words, his failure is the secularization of the master spirit of enterprise, the selfish application of the communal plan. He is the unprofessional, the American as bad businessman.

The disaster follows precisely upon Thorn's repudiation of Astor's main instruction: "to be courteous and kind in his dealings with the Savages, but by no means to confide in their apparent friendship, *nor to admit more than a few on board of his ship at a time*" (78). While anchored in a harbor just north of the final destination, Thorn allows the local natives to come aboard in great numbers, and then throws one of the chiefs overboard because he feels insulted by an offer the chief has made for some otter skins. A slaughter quickly follows, with the ship finally blown apart by an explosion set by one of the last survivors of the crew. The apocalyptic nature of the denouement, described in much horrific detail, signals to the reader that the entire series of events, including the faulty leadership and clashes with both crew and Indians, is prophetic. In this case, the apocalypse presages the fall of Astoria. But the prophecy is also figurative; insofar as the Astorian expedition is a model of American history, so the fall of Astoria might presage the fall of America itself in its marketplace expansion into the wilderness.

Thorn's failure is not depicted as the sole cause of the disaster. According to the narrative scheme, his faulty leadership must be matched by the failings of faulty followers and compounded by the treachery of foreign competitors. Just as Thorn represents the diminished double of Astor, so the betraying trappers, Indians, and foreigners represent the dark doubles of Astor, the savage "others" whose perfidious presence is required to complete the sacred narrative, to turn history into ideology, and ideology into history. The readers first encounter these others in the partners and clerks of the crew. If Thorn is an overly rigid commander, it is in part because he has a reckless crew. Their chief traits—an overreaching sense of importance on the part of the partners, and unprofessionalism on the part of the crew members—work together to trigger his "harshness and imprudence" (78) and vice versa, and so the American union of self-interest and common good is threatened on the very ship of state that is designed to transport it to the West.

Significantly, no individual characters are singled out from among this crew as particularly villainous; at this point all the participants together create the disaster. But there is some foreshadowing of a narrative development in the book in which the villains are gradually individuated, the British siphoned off from the Americans, the agent of savagery from the agent of civilization. First we find the vanity of the partners ascribed to a corrupting British influence:

> The partners . . . had been brought up in the service of the North West Company, and in a profound idea of the importance, dignity and authority of a partner. They already began to consider themselves on a par with the M'Tavishes, the MacGillivrays, the Frobishers and the other magnates of the North West, whom they had been accustomed to look up to as the Great ones of the Earth, and they were a little disposed, perhaps, to wear their suddenly acquired honors with some air of pretension. . . .
>
> Thus prepared to regard each other with no very cordial eye, it is not to be wondered at that the parties soon came into collision. (33–34)

Astor, it seems, has been displaced by the idols of his foreign competitors, which in turn has led to the displacement of the American democratic spirit.

Not surprisingly, then, there concurrently arises an individual figure who is described as "the champion of their cause" (34), Duncan M'Dougall, one of the partners and another of Astor's doubles in the book. M'Dougall, who will later betray Astor by selling Astoria to the British, is here described as "an active, irritable, fuming, vain glorious little man, and elevated in his own opinion, by being the proxy of Mr. Astor" (34). Here we see the embodiment of savage individualism itself, removing the process of mobility from its validating social context and placing it within his own acquisitive valuations: "elevat[ing] himself in his own opinion." While in *A Tour* this danger was associated with the Americans, in *Astoria* it is identified with the foreign influence, the British.

But M'Dougall is not strictly the villain here; he may threaten Thorn's authority, but it is Thorn himself who throws the chief overboard. Instead, as with the apocalypse itself, M'Dougall's presence is part of the prophecy of the later fall of Astoria in which he will play a central role. His portrayal also prophesies how the treatment of character, and particularly villainy, will itself change in the course of the book. By the time of the final disaster, villainy will emerge as a feature of particular self-interested characters: villainous individualism as embodied in individuated villainy. At this point, though, the role of villain is dispersed among the crew members and the captain. The Indians are included as well, for like the crew they have been reckless and are at least partly responsible for raising Thorn's ire; their harsh treatment at the captain's hand is presented as both appropriate and extreme, as is, in turn, their response. Thorn's "savage pride" is matched by everyone else's savagery. As much as all of these characters are enemies, they are also partners in this disaster, paying both in the lives they lose now and the lives they will forfeit in the future. Thus they follow the model of prophetic history, fulfilling each other's fate even as they destroy each other in the process.

The source of this villainy, then, is in the savagery of self-interest that destroys the community. But this is not the self-interest of economic expansion that Irving identified as the villain in *A Tour*. While the British and the Indians who here come to represent this savagery are an essential part of this narrative, they are also its resident outsiders, closed off from the privileges of the marketplace that are finally available only to the American white man. Irving may tell us that the Indian chief who made Thorn angry was only following the style of competitiveness introduced to the Indians by the Americans; as Robert Stuart, one of Astor's leaders, reports, "The habits of trade and avidity of gain have their corrupting effects even in the wilderness" (70). But this view of savagery as produced by the evils of competition is decidedly different from the view of savagery as competition itself. The Indians here are already savage and merely made more so by the corruption. Their villainy may be roused into action by Thorn's rage, but they are always potential villains, as Astor's instructions had indicated. The source of villainy itself, though, remains a constant: savagery, the vulgarization of the enterprising spirit in the wilderness.

Irving ends this opening narrative with a reminder of Astor's enterprise, and thus the larger framework of vision and sacred history by which these events acquire their meaning as American history: "It is a catastrophe that shows the importance, in all enterprizes of moment, to keep in mind the general instructions of the sagacious heads which devise them" (78). He returns us to the East where we find Astor hearing of the news while out for an evening at the theater. He laments the blow to this "great scheme of his ambition," but manages to maintain a valiant front appropriate to his surroundings. As Irving sets the scene,

> A friend who knew the disastrous intelligence he had received expressed
> his astonishment that he could have calmness of spirit sufficient for such
> a scene of light amusement. "What would you have me do?" was his
> characteristic reply; "Would you have me stay at home and weep for
> what I cannot help?" (78–79)

The spirit of enterprise, forever blameless, must also remain forever
vigilant, despite all the setbacks and dangers. Astor must continue to
rely on those adventurers he had sent out to implement the sacred
scheme.

The next two narratives repeat this basic pattern, journeys of deprivation and hardship bound on the one hand by failures of vision and
on the other by attacks of savagery. But Irving does expand the range
of details relevant within the pattern. The movement of characters
becomes more loosely defined: a journey West is followed by a journey
East, but without specific significations applied to the directions. The
adventures are more loosely connected: various confrontations occur
between Indians and trappers, both friendly and hostile, and between
the trappers and the landscape. The information about the West is now
barely integrated into the narratives: frequently and without warning,
the reader is presented with descriptions of Indian customs, varieties
of landscape and indigenous plant and animal life. Yet this apparent
weakness of dramatic structure does not undermine the narrative intention already established in the book. Whatever the causes—a sloppi-
ness of conceptual design on Irving's part, an inability or unwillingness
to digest the material gathered in Pierre's researches, or an attempt to
realize, in narrative form, the experience of aimlessness and danger
peculiar to the Western experience—the general effects remain constant
throughout all the sections. Particular patterns of conflict and resolution recur, such as the gradual distillation of particular heroes and
villains, usually paralleled in their individual confrontations with each
other and with Indians. These patterns are, in turn, embedded within
larger rhythms of hardship and relief, isolation and convergence, movement and stasis. Taken as a whole, these "standards of coherence"
establish the proper guidelines for economic expansion, the prescription for "professional" conduct, that Irving had identified in *A Tour*.

We come first to the trappers. If Astor is the "master spirit of the
enterprise," then the trappers must be the chosen children. And indeed
while Astor is said to have "covenanted to bear all the losses that might
be incurred" (26) in the venture, the trappers are fittingly designated

the "Israelites" in this covenant. Regarding the moment when Hunt's party, after a long and difficult journey across the continent to reach Astoria, sights what looks at first to be the end of their hardships, Irving writes, "They hailed it as the poor Israelites hailed the first glimpse of the promised land, for they flattered themselves that this might be the great plain of the Columbia, and that their painful pilgrimage might be drawing to a close" (223). But if they are the Israelites as chosen people, they are also the Israelites as wanderers in the desert, for, as Irving points out, the journey is not yet over. When they do arrive at the Columbia, they find not a promised land but an already dilapidated outpost. As the chosen people, the trappers must also remember that they are only beginning their pilgrimage, that they still live in a fallen world, and are themselves fallen. At this time in history, they are only "like" the Israelites, a reminder in keeping with Irving's trepidations about the acquisitiveness of metaphor in *A Tour*. They must remember above all that an infidelity to the spirit of their quest may keep them forever from finding the promised land.

This representation of the trappers as exemplifying both the diminished spirit of enterprise and its vulgarized practice is in evidence throughout the book, particularly in the descriptions which arise from the narrative scheme of adventurous enterprise. They are called "fellow adventurers" (81, 227, 252) when they abide by the regulations of communal conduct, "this forlorn fraternity of adventurers" (314) when that community faces hardships, and "loose adventurers" (7, 99) when the ties that bind them to the community are severed altogether. They are sometimes vigilant in their loyalty to the company, the community and the nation, with "a share in the general enterprize" (192–193), and sometimes too free in this "land of perfect freedom" and "lawless depths": "strange and fearless wanderers of the wilderness" (119) who are always dangerously close to becoming "freebooting vagabonds" (246). A "life of this unsettled and precarious kind," Irving tells us, "is apt to render man selfish" (52). Generally they exhibit both qualities in nervous balance, the impulses to serve self-interest and the common good:

> A Western trapper is like a sailor; past hazards only stimulate him to further risques. The vast prairie is to the one what the ocean is to the other, a boundless field of enterprize and exploit; however he may have suffered in his last cruize he is always ready to join a new expedition,

and the more adventurous its nature, the more attractive is it to his vagrant spirit. (104)

From this company of adventurers Irving gradually singles out two figures to represent its opposing sides, the principal hero of the narratives, Robert Hunt, and the principal villain, Duncan M'Dougall. Hunt is specifically designated Astor's double in the book: he is "the only real representative of Mr. Astor" (355), which means that he not only embodies Mr. Astor's positive traits, but does so in diminished form. He may be valiant in his adventures, but he is not Mr. Astor himself. Mr. M'Dougall is the less decorous "Astor's proxy" (34), a denomination emphasizing the purely economic relationship between the two men and thus the source of M'Dougall's villainy, his divorce of the profit motive from the enterprise as a whole. Indeed, M'Dougall is even described as being "a little puffed up with the idea of being Mr. Astor's proxy" (37), essentially denying his obligations to the company by asserting in their place his personal pride. With Astor as the author of the vision, and Hunt and M'Dougall as his projected alter egos, the story of failed adventurous enterprise can be brought to its conclusion.

As the positive Astor, Hunt's characteristics are evident throughout. He is adventurous: "he arrived. . .after a year's seafaring that might have furnished a chapter in the wanderings of Sinbad" (336); he is enterprising: "He knew the pride and interest taken by [Astor] in his great enterprize, and that he would not be deterred by dangers and difficulties from prosecuting it; much less would he leave the infant establishment without succor in the time of trouble. In this, we have seen, he did but justice to Mr. Astor" (338); and most of all, he is loyal: "he was a conscientious man that seems ever to have aimed at a faithful discharge of his duties, and to have had the interests of his employers earnestly at heart" (335). As Irving sums it up, "His first thoughts were for the welfare of Astoria" (336). He is the chief fellow adventurer of the enterprise.

Yet he is not able to save Astoria from failure. The other men in the company, beset with dangers from without (Indians) and within (traitorous trappers), undermined by their own insufficient sense of adventurous enterprise, abandon Astoria to the British. As an explanation of their action—and, for Irving, a legacy for the Americans that will follow them into the wilderness—the four major partners on the scene leave a "manifesto" behind, detailing the circumstances of deprivation and uncertainty which they claim to be "unequal to the expenses incurred" (325). They then declare their intentions to "abandon this undertaking, and dissolve this concern" according to the original terms of the agreement whereby the scheme could be discontinued anytime within the first five years if it proved "unprofitable" (325). Hence the "grand scheme," here reduced to a simple economy of profit and loss, is abandoned, and the manifesto becomes a Declaration of Independence in reverse, commemorating the retreat of American enterprise from its own first principles.

But even the partners as a group are not wholly responsible for the abandonment. That role is reserved for one particular partner in their midst, Duncan M'Dougall, and the foreign forces he represents and marshals in his betrayal of the enterprise. M'Dougall is the most harshly criticized character in the book. As Hunt's, and Astor's, dark double, he is the precise repudiation of the values they represent. Where Hunt is adventurous, M'Dougall is merely thrill-seeking; where Hunt is enterprising, M'Dougall is merely selfish; where Hunt is loyal, M'Dougall is unfaithful, a betrayer of adventure, enterprise, and loyalty itself. His ties to the American Fur Company and the "civilized" world are, in the end, only superficial; his true loyalties are to the Northwest Company and the Indian wife he acquires in his travels. Hunt calls him "hollow and collusive" (350), and Irving, "vain glorious" (34).

M'Dougall's crimes are many, but there is one in particular that most vividly conveys the threat he represents to Astor's, and America's, mission. At the time when Astoria was most vulnerable, cut off from supplies, under imminent attack by the British, M'Dougall, in his guise as "Astor's proxy," goes to negotiate with the members of the Northwest Company then surrounding the fort. There he sells Astor out for his own profit. As Irving puts it, and as the overall dramatic structure of the book confirms, "He has been accused of availing himself of a wrong construction of powers vested in him at his own request, and of sacrificing the interests of Mr. Astor to the North West Company, under the promise or hope of advantage to himself" (344). In support of the accusation, Irving offers the damning evidence: "shortly after concluding this agreement, [M'Dougall] became a member of the North West Company, and received a share productive of a handsome income" (345). Hardly one of the "fellow adventurers" who take a "share in the general enterprise," M'Dougall represents the dangers of a profit motive wholly devoted to individual gain: he has "bargained away" the "property" (350) upon which the American enterprise rests.

Significantly, his betrayal is depicted not as an extension of market-place behavior but rather as a defeat of the marketplace in the service of a foreign power. But that should not be surprising. From the beginning of the book he has been singled out as a foreigner by birth, another dark doubling, perhaps, of Astor, this time of his foreign background, his "adopted citizenship" in America. The symbolic moment comes when, just before the negotiations, M'Dougall prevents the "young men" in the fort, whom Irving repeatedly describes as "natives of the United States" (343), from raising the American flag. Even before the negotiations, his disloyalty was certain.

This disloyalty leads us to the corporate villain in the drama, the Northwest Company that seeks the monopoly of the territory in the name of its own scheme of commerce and colonization. In keeping with the narrative pattern of doubling, this company is very much the dark double of Astor's American Fur Company. Where his company seeks the expansion of a competitive marketplace, theirs seeks only monopoly; where his brings mobility within a fixed social structure, theirs brings only stasis and hierarchy. Generally, the British commercial system is described as feudal, essentially antithetical to the marketplace envisioned by the Americans. They form "a kind of commercial aristocracy" (11), and "considered themselves" to be "lords of the ascendant" (12, 343) who hold a "feudal sway" (13) over the wilderness: they "held themselves up as the chivalry of the Fur trade" (88). Their fusion of commerce and colonization is precisely not the aristocratic capitalism represented by Astor and his company, but rather an anti-capitalist aristocracy in the guise of capitalism.

With the sale of Astoria, the adventure tale is essentially completed, but Irving still needs to reiterate the sacred scheme that dictated the terms of the adventure in the first place. In the book's final chapter and an appendix, he returns us to the master spirit and his last valiant attempts to rescue his venture. "Having given the catastrophe at the Fort of Astoria," Irving begins, "it remains now but to gather up a few loose ends of this widely excursive narrative and conclude" (350), which is to say end the adventure tale as well as draw conclusions about it. He notes that the return parties from Astoria "experienced on the way as many adventures, vicissitudes and mishaps as the far famed heroes of the Odyssey" (353); these mishaps are in turn described as a "succession of adverse circumstances and cross purposes." As in the other narratives, these adventures are no more than a "tissue of misadventures" (354), a recapitulation of the conditions under which the true adventure of enterprise had been defeated. He then reminds the reader that that defeat involved not just Astor's business venture but American expansion in general:

> It is painful. . .to see a grand and beneficial stroke of genius fail of its aim: but we regret the failure of this enterprize in a national point of view; for, had it been crowned with success it would have redounded greatly to the advantage and extension of our commerce. . . . In our hands, beside the roving bands of trappers and traders, the country would have been explored and settled by industrious husbandmen; and the fertile valleys bordering its rivers, and shut up among its mountains, would have been made to pour forth their agricultural treasures to contribute to the general wealth. (355)

"In a word," he concludes, "Astoria might have realized the anticipations of Mr. Astor, so well understood and appreciated by Mr. Jefferson, in gradually becoming a commercial empire beyond the mountains, peopled by 'free and independent Americans, and linked with us by ties of blood and interest' " (356).

While this formulation seems to contain a contradiction between the formation of an independent state and the expansion of the American "empire," the narrative conception of adventurous enterprise serves to eliminate the contradiction: just as the adventure of the individual needed to be wedded to the enterprise of the nation, so the enterprise of the individual needed to be wedded to the adventure of the nation, the individual profiteers to the westward movement. Significantly, though, while the contradiction has been eliminated, the tension remains: the individual still poses a threat to the communal mission, and the community to individual integrity and courage; and the British and the Indians still pose a threat to both Americans and America. So Irving adds a final warning. He chastises the government for neglecting the "overture" (356) of Mr. Astor (and presumably the overture of America itself), and notes that the territorial issue will be raised again a few years hence, in 1838. We should all be prepared to return to the question of Astoria, the "watchword in a contest for dominion on the shores of the Pacific" (356).[8]

Finally, Irving includes a few documents in an appendix: a letter from Astor to the government asking for assistance, a later letter from Albert Gallatin recalling the circumstances under which the assistance was turned down, some notes on the current state of the fur trade, and a section from the Captain Bonneville manuscript which Irving was soon to use as a basis for his next, and last, Western work. While adding little to the narrative dimensions of the work, the appendix maintains the posture of a legitimate history while imbuing that history with the cultural imperatives of the present moment. As such, it also opens the way for an update of the history of the fur trade. Irving may, in fact, have already planned the Bonneville volume, and so the mention of Bonneville could be calculated to groom his readers' expectations. In any case, his conclusion leads directly into the next book, bringing the reader up to the present and still relevant issues of empire and mission. By alerting the reader to the need for a further look at the circumstances of the fur trade, Irving is suggesting that his history of the past is only half told. His tale of adventurous enterprise will attain the "requisite unity" of history only after he has applied its narrative scheme to the current drive into the Western territories, only after he has measured the validity of its prophecies.

The Adventures of Captain Bonneville

In the opening to *The Adventures of Captain Bonneville,* Irving explains the origins of the book, and he does so by forging the connection to *Astoria* that had been intimated in that book's appendix:

> While engaged in writing an account of the grand enterprise of ASTO-RIA, it was my practice to seek all kinds of oral information connected with the subject. Nowhere did I pick up more interesting particulars than at the table of Mr. John Jacob Astor; who, being the patriarch of the Fur Trade in the United States, was accustomed to have at his board various persons of adventurous turn. . . .
>
> Among these personages, one who peculiarly took my fancy was Captain BONNEVILLE, of the United States' army; who, in a rambling kind of enterprise, had strangely engrafted the trapper and hunter on the soldier. . . . [H]is expeditions and adventures will form the leading theme of the following pages[.] (3)

Irving's decision to write a history of those adventures came at a later meeting, at which Irving found the military man at work on just such a history. As Irving tells it, Bonneville put the manuscript at his disposal "to fit it for publication and bring it before the world" (6). Presumably the decision was made quickly. In its essential structure and its underlying themes, Bonneville's story must have seemed an ideal resource for continuing the work on the West he had begun in *A Tour*.

The basic outline of that story, at least as Irving tells it, offers much material for a consideration of the contemporary conditions of adventurous enterprise. A military officer, Bonneville had spent most of his assignments in the West, where he grew acquainted with both the wilderness and the fur trade. In 1832 he requested a leave from the army so that he could lead a fur trade expedition into the Far West; along the way he would also monitor Indian and British strength and positions, and map the territories for military information. The army agreed. For the next three years he and his company of 110 men traveled across the continent. Like the Astorian expedition, Bonneville's expedition thus merged commerce and colonization, private interest and public duty. He even built a fort and named it after himself. The scheme was embodied in the customary adventures: deprivations, battles, achievements in exploration and the mapping of much new terrain. And, in the end, Bonneville's entry into the trade also failed, mired in incompetence, disputes among the parties, and a hostile environment.[9]

Irving was certain enough of the story's appropriateness to his own interests to pay Bonneville $1000 for the manuscript. He makes no reference to this arrangement in his own book, though not, as in the case of *Astoria*, to deny that the writing of the book was compromised by its prospects as a marketplace transaction. Rather, he simply wanted to save himself money and time later on in research, as well as to protect himself from any conflict of authorship. Just as in the cases of *A Tour* and *Astoria*, he perceived in the project a property of professional value: "I cannot but think," he wrote his friend Aspinwall, "that the work will command attention and circulation, and ought to be paid for accordingly" (L2:902). Irving was prepared to approach this project as he did *Astoria*: a property in itself that examined the nature of property, the fur trade as pathfinder for economic expansion.

On the whole, Irving treated the material from the familiar perspective of adventurous enterprise: Captain Bonneville's adventures in the Western fur trade are also the adventures of the marketplace in the wilderness of Jacksonian America. In this sense, the book functions much like *Astoria*. It offers the same endorsements of enterprise and the same critiques of loose adventuring, while attempting the same fusion of business and imagination; in brief, the professionalization of Western expansion. But it is also a continuation of that project, an update of the story to account for the changes in the conditions of Western expansion, and in the marketplace in general, that have taken place since the fall of Astoria.

Irving establishes the narrative continuity between the two works in the book's frame. The opening chapter begins with a reference to Astoria, rehearsing once again the fall of the "grand enterprise of Mr. John Jacob Astor, to establish an American emporium for the fur trade" (7). The British are blamed, as is the "unfortunate supineness of the American government" (7). At the end, as at the end of the earlier work, Irving reminds the reader of the need to reestablish our dominance in the Far West:

> The facts disclosed in the present work, clearly manifest the policy of establishing military posts and a mounted force to protect our traders in their journeys across the great western wilds, and of pushing the outposts into the very heart of the singular wilderness we have laid open, so as to maintain some degree of sway over the country, and to put an end to the kind of "black mail," levied on all occasions by the savage "chivalry of the mountains." (270)

He puts it more directly still in the appendix:

> The resources of the country,. . .while in the hands of a company restricted in its trade, can be but partially called forth: but in the hands of Americans, enjoying a direct trade with the East Indies, would be brought into quickening activity; and might soon realize the dream of Mr. Astor, in giving rise to a flourishing commercial empire. (275–276)

He even repeats the attack on the "supineness of the American government" (274). This context of Astor's vision is then reinforced throughout the book, much as it was in *Astoria*. Along the way one encounters not only direct references to Astor, but indirect reminders conveyed through descriptions of meetings between Bonneville's party and members of the American Fur Company. The stage is set, then, for *Bonneville* to continue where *Astoria* left off.[10]

Irving begins by offering a brief history of the fur trade since the fall of Astoria. During the twenty years since the British had first established their monopoly in the Northwest, American trappers returned to compete again in the trade. As Irving describes it, the basic terms of the adventurous enterprise have remained the same: through adventures with the British, Indians, landscape, through conflicts among themselves and within themselves, the Americans still enact the enterprise of expanding the boundaries of the marketplace to the Far Western wilderness. But if the basic terms have continued, the drama has become modified to accommodate those changes in the West and in the marketplace that had occurred since Astor's time. Expansion into the West has brought more territory within the borders claimed to be part of America; and the economic expansionism of the Jacksonian period has made the economic opportunities of the West seem more tangible and more available.

On the most basic level, these changes have made the drama more intense: the stakes are now higher and more immediate, and the competition is fiercer. The need to control the trade in the Northwest, and thus conquer the territory itself, is no longer just a "grand scheme" but a political necessity. The trade also has a broader popular appeal; as the adducements to profit and adventure seem to increase, the number of participants rises. In keeping with these new conditions, a new class of trappers and traders has emerged, more self-interested but also more efficient in extending the boundaries of American commerce. Among this "wild and warlike school" (9), a number of leaders have established themselves, such as Jedediah Smith, Thomas Fitzpatrick, Jim Bridger, and Robert Campbell. They have organized networks of trappers across the West into companies and competed not only with the British but with each other. Even the American Fur Company, no longer managed by Astor, has been brought "once more into the field of their ancient enterprise" (9). The result of the renewed competition is not only the entrenchment, once again, of the American fur trade, but the discovery and mapping of new routes across the Rockies, routes that will ultimately enable settlers to follow.

In this familiar context of commerce and colonization, the trappers in *Bonneville* appear as representative Jacksonian businessmen, and their regressive primitivism a representation of Jacksonian acquisitiveness. Such a view is not necessarily a criticism; for many members of the fur trade at the time and many historians since, the adventures of the fur trade were an essential part of its business. For instance, Warren Ferris, one of the trappers of the American Fur Company, wrote of the reasons that had enticed him, in 1830, to join his first expedition to the Rockies: "Curiosity, a love of wild adventure, and perhaps also a hope of profit,—for times *are* hard, and my best coat has a sort of sheepish hang-dog hesitation to encounter fashionable folk—combined to make me look upon the project with an eye of favor" (Goetzmann 1963, 406). Later historians such as Bernard DeVoto (1947), Robert Glass Cleland (1963) and William H. Goetzmann (1963) delineated the mixture of profit-seeking, mobility, and adventurousness that drew the fur trade personnel westward. "Such is the mountaineer," Irving concludes his update, "the hardy trapper of the West; and such, as we have slightly sketched it, is the wild, Robin Hood kind of life" (*B* 12).

But with these achievements have also come new dangers. If increased competition has led to increased exploration, it has also led to greater divisiveness among members of the trade, dispersing the trappers and traders not only across the continent but away from each other; and in this way too these trappers and traders are representative Jacksonian businessmen. The fur trade that we read about in *Bonneville* is not only more generally motivated by self-interest than the trade depicted in *Astoria,* but also more inclined to lead to the destruction of self, company, nation, and mission. But these new conditions are less an indictment of economic expansion than of those forces in the marketplace that might lead to ruin. As we have seen in the other Western writings, what bothered Irving was not the fur trade or even business per se, but the increasing vulgarization of competition in the wilderness of Western expansion, and by Bonneville's time that competition had come to bear little resemblance to the honorable trade envisioned by Astor. Had Astoria not fallen in the first place, Irving explains, these ill effects of competition might have been avoided; the marketplace of the American wilderness would have remained a peaceable and profitable monopoly. But the wilderness has ultimately proven to be too powerful, the temptations to self-interest too seductive. Irving had warned against these very dangers of marketplace expansion in *A Tour* and *Astoria*. The world that Captain Bonneville has entered, then, is still the world of adventurous enterprise, but the adventures are more perilous, and the enterprise more imperilled.

These developments provide the foundation for Irving's sequel to *Astoria*. He extends his warnings about the marketplace to the very Jacksonians who had come to occupy the West in the interim. The terms of the warning remain the same as well: if Jacksonian America is to avoid the tragic fate of Astoria, it must imbue its adventurous imagination with the proper spirit of professionalism, the equilibrium of self-interest and the common good. But the warning is also more urgent, for, as the very premise of a updated sequel suggests, America is already dangerously close to ruin.

This prophetic model of self-destructive expansionism had always been at the center of Irving's vision of the West: all three Western books focused on economic expeditions that failed. Bonneville, Astor, Ellsworth, all end up in the East, empty-handed, a grim presentiment for the future of the westward mission. But the basic tenor of the books is finally not one of failure at all; nor are the books designed to discredit the marketplace or disavow the claims of the adventuring imagination. In his cautiously optimistic frames and his careful criticisms of the excesses of both business and imagination, Irving was seeking to transform the prophecy into a warning, and thereby redeem America's adventurous enterprise.

Such, at least, was the case in *A Tour* and *Astoria,* and the intention in *Bonneville*. But while Irving continues to support this basic narrative program, he seems less certain in this third book about the likelihood of its promised redemption. Something goes awry in the execution; the certainties of the prophetic history become muddled in contradictions and inconsistencies. It is as if the closer Irving came to the present, the less faith he had in the very prescription for renewal that he had outlined in his previous two books.

This ambivalence becomes evident early in the book, as the reader begins to encounter an uneasy mixture of providential history and aimless adventure. While *Bonneville* continues the basic structure of *Astoria,* with the frame establishing the context of enterprise and a series of adventures illustrating that enterprise, the enterprise itself appears considerably diminished in scope, and the adventures lack even the synchronicity of movement found in *Astoria* that would allow for their narrative transformation into the spirit of the enterprise. As a tale of adventure it is meandering and uncompelling; as a tale of enterprise, it is unfocused and unconvincing; as a tale of adventurous enterprise, it is unsuccessful. Irving failed to bring to Bonneville's adventures the coherence or strength of conception that had made his two earlier books successes as works of both the imagination and the marketplace.

One might argue that this failure was precisely Irving's conception in the first place: that, in the end, he had come to see Jacksonian America as a place where imagination and the marketplace were incompatible, where failed adventures and failed enterprise had come to characterize both Western expansion and the tale of adventurous enterprise. His warnings in *A Tour* and *Astoria* had finally come true. But while there is much evidence in the book to support this reading, especially in Irving's portrayal of Bonneville's relation to the fur trade, there is also much evidence to the contrary. Throughout the book, Irving tries valiantly to fit the Bonneville story into the scheme of adventurous enterprise. That these efforts remain unconvincing may have less to do with any disapproval of Bonneville, the fur trade, or the conditions of the marketplace, than with the simple fact that he was faced with an adventure tale and adventure hero that were themselves not very compelling. While the literary properties of Astoria were already rich with national implications, Bonneville's story would not be so easily transformed.

The most obvious signs of these difficulties can be found in the construction of the adventure tale. Despite the dictates of the historical frame, it is no easy task to locate, much less follow, the plot. While the book is decidedly more linear than *Astoria,* mainly pursuing only the single track of Bonneville's journey, it is also a more "rambling kind of enterprise" (3). Bonneville moves West, meets Indians and trappers, explores the landscape, and returns, and nothing in these adventures provides them with a context by which the reader can discover a larger meaning. There are no narrative patterns, such as mistaken identities and doublings, no models of social structure, such as a class system or fraternity of professional sensibilities, no consistent depiction of event, such as contests between self-interest and communal obligation. The failure here is not so much that the characters have crossed over the bounds of respectful decorum—that at least would entail a considered literary judgment—as that the boundaries seem to have been eliminated altogether as signposts of meaning. Even the rare interjections that Irving offers as explanatory notes about the dangers and enticements of wilderness life lack the consistency that would allow one to perceive a totality of imaginative conception.

Irving does not exactly abandon the adventure tale; in fact, he attempts to maintain the semblance of adventure. But he does so without a discernable or consistent form, and often even undercuts the very narrative premises upon which adventure rests. From chapter to chapter the book shifts its orientation from compendium of information on the West to fur trade history to adventure tale to critique of adventure tale.[11]

Often Irving establishes the requisite environment of peril only to abandon or undermine it. For instance, he takes care to note the precariousness of Bonneville's military plan with regard to the Indians: "The Captain. . .calculated to strike [the Indians'] minds, and impress them with such an idea of the might of his nation, as would induce them to treat with kindness and respect all stragglers that might fall in their path" (186). But the Indians that Bonneville encounters are only occasionally dangerous. It is difficult, indeed, to find any consistency in the Indian portraits or any indication of a consistent intent on Irving's part. In chapter 9, for instance, Indians are characterized as meta-Christians, half-Christians, savages in need of Christian humanization, and gamblers. Neither the villains of *Astoria* nor the non-villains of *A Tour,* they are also hardly even characters.

The same absence of characterization can be found in Irving's treatment of the British. He notes the threats posed by the British presence in the West, the Hudson's Bay Company who "are adroitly proceeding to fortify themselves in their usurpation, by securing all the strong points of the country" (274). But he as often describes the men of the company in a positive light: "however hostile the members of the British Company may be to the enterprises of American traders, they have always manifested great courtesy and hospitality to the traders themselves" (189).

Some critics have attributed these infelicities of literary form to a slackening of Irving's integrity as a writer. Simply put, Irving did not give the project his fullest attention as a literary task because he was treating it brusquely as a mere commercial transaction. In completing his trilogy on the dangerous rift between business and imagination in the Western venture, he simply embraced that rift himself, capitulated to what he saw as the demands of the marketplace to abandon the restraint, taste, and respect for decorum that he had so championed in the figure of the professional writer. Certainly writers such as Cooper and Hubert Howe Bancroft saw it so. But while there is evidence to support this interpretation, such as the speed with which he produced the book from Bonneville's manuscript and a few other sources, it is too harsh an assessment of Irving's inclinations as a professional, and limited in its vision of the creative process. Most importantly, it does not account for the particular pattern of confusions that appear throughout the book.

In fact, a close look at a few of the book's central elements, such as plot and character, reveals that Irving's faith in the redemptive possibilities of adventurous enterprise has become tenuous. Business and imagination appear incompatible: as business has become increasingly oriented to self-interest, the imagination has become increasingly incapable of imbuing that self-interest with a respect for the bounds of decorum. In other words, the very mission of professionalism that had been the basis of Irving's other two Western works, providing them with a form and a meaningful relation between that form and the book's thematic content, is in jeopardy. The confusions and inconsistencies of *Bonneville* thus reflect a deeper despair over both the urgencies of the marketplace and the efficacies of literature.

This despair is evident in the portrayal of the contemporary fur trade as more impervious to the refinements offered by the directives of civilized decorum. The new "order" (10) of trappers and traders, explains Irving, consists of men who are more singularly intoxicated with the life of the trade than their predecessors: "No toil, no danger, no privation can turn the trapper from his pursuit. His passionate excitement at times resembles a mania" (12). To use Robert Cleland's phrase, these new trappers are a "reckless breed of men" who pursue their trade not by transforming the wilderness but by becoming part of it. Most representative of this group, for Irving, are the "free trappers," members of a more "independent class" who, according to Bonneville, " 'come and go when and where they please; provide their own horses, arms, and other equipments; trap and trade on their own account, and dispose of their skins and peltries to the highest bidder' " (47). The days of strict dedication to the company had passed.

For Irving, this method of trade provided a frightening example of the atomizing effects of economic expansion upon Jacksonian society. Rather than conquering the wilderness in the name of civilization, these new trappers and traders succumb to the wilderness in the name of adventure: "You cannot pay a free trapper a greater compliment," Irving explains, "than to persuade him you have mistaken him for an Indian brave; and, in truth, the counterfeit is complete" (47). The economic language in this remark is especially apt. For Irving, the flaw in American expansionism lay in its economy, the primary mode of exchange between its claims to civilization and the savage wilderness it sought to acquire. In the substitution of the counterfeit for the truth, that economy will suffer in the end. In *Bonneville*, we find that what the Americans had really come to acquire was savagery itself.

If this shift in the tenor of the marketplace threatens the nation, it also threatens one of the central premises of adventurous enterprise, the embodiment of the enterprise in the adventures of particular individuals. In *Bonneville,* it is not finally the self-interested individuals who are the source of the threat. Where in *Astoria* Irving had made heroes of the valiant trappers and traders, and villains of the self-interested, here he makes the trade itself the villain, and offers no heroes to supply the defence. The trappers themselves are sometimes portrayed as "savage" and sometimes as hardy and adventurous, but are never made the primary actors in the drama. The battle is now between the trade and the wilderness, or more properly, between the values of the marketplace and the conditions of expansion. And the trade is losing, as the spirit of capitalism is reduced to the "savagery" of the wilderness.

While this view of the trade provides an interesting critique of economic expansion, Irving has some difficulty in making it succeed as an adventure tale. The problem is that this undermining of adventurous enterprise is also an undermining of its essential narrative form. With the trading system as villain, all the individuals involved, including not only the trappers but the Indians and even Bonneville as well, are reduced to mere participants. Acts of individual villainy and heroism disappear within the "savagery" of experience itself. The literary devices of structure, plot, setting, characterization, even language itself, become mired in inconsistency and lassitude.

This weakening of plot and character is especially evident in the portrayal of Bonneville. Irving has a particularly difficult time trying to present Bonneville as the hero of the book, and his adventures as heroic. The case for Bonneville as an heroic or even competent figure was not very strong at the time, and has never really improved. Historians have, on the whole, dismissed him and his expedition as a failure, and an insignificant one at that. Hiram Chittenden, for instance, who had energetically defended both Astor and Irving's *Astoria,* proclaimed that "The adventures of Captain Bonneville in the Rocky Mountains from 1832 to 1835 have attained a prominence in the history of the West to which they are not entitled." He even quoted Irving himself in explanation: "They and their hero are an apt illustration of Diedrich Knickerbocker's profound idea of the power of history to rescue men and events from the 'wide-spread, insatiable maw of oblivion' " (1:396). Recently, William Goetzmann has echoed the charge, noting that while

Bonneville had succeeded in supplying useful maps, his expeditions "added little to the history of exploration" (1966, 156–157).

While Bonneville's limitations did not completely discourage Irving from pursuing his commitment to the tenets of adventurous enterprise, they did make his task as a writer more difficult. In order to reconcile his model of adventurous enterprise with the history of Bonneville and his expedition, he would have to transform Bonneville into an adventurous enterpriser, and his failure into a parable of American prophetic history, as he did Astor's. But such a task would require adjustments in the form of the tale. He would have to alter the context of mission so as to accommodate both Bonneville's diminished stature and the diminished adventures over which he presided.

Irving is diligent in the attempt, and the effects of these modifications can be felt in many different forms. The sacred scheme of *Astoria* becomes a more modest enterprise. Even the fervent nationalism of *Astoria* is reduced to a mere effort at maintaining "some degree of sway over the country" (270). Bonneville's expedition emerges not as a "great scheme" but as a profit-making venture with marginal ties to the national interest, and Bonneville himself appears not as a "master spirit of enterprise" but as a man of modest ambitions and modest talents for leadership, a minor-league Astor with limited vision but earnest commitment.

In this context, Bonneville does indeed fulfill some of the requisite elements of adventurous enterprise, albeit in a limited fashion. He is presented to the reader as a military man who, after having been stationed in the Far West among "Indian traders, mountain trappers, and other pioneers of the wilderness," became "so excited by their tales of wild scenes and wild adventures, and their accounts of vast and magnificent regions as yet unexplored, that an expedition to the Rocky Mountains became the ardent desire of his heart, and an enterprise to explore untrodden tracts, the leading object of his ambition" (4). Not wholly self-interested, however, Bonneville balances his request to take a leave from the service with his offer to maintain his national allegiance by collecting information for the War Department about the Indians and the landscape. Thus he combines "public utility with his private objects" (4). While he is not quite the grand entrepreneur or the valiant adventurer, he is still the "type of the military aristocrat" (Slotkin 1985, 120), a figure long admired in American culture and well-suited to bringing professionalism to the adventures of Western economic expansion.

But Irving's diligence is not always sufficient to accommodate either Bonneville or the story of his adventures. Another Bonneville appears in the book as well, a figure who fails to demonstrate the spirit of the adventurous hero. As soon becomes evident, Bonneville never manages to master the shrewdness required for success in the fur trade; and overcome by the savage competitiveness of wilderness life, he returns at the end in poverty. While he did indeed return with the information he had promised, including a number of valuable maps, the discoveries associated with his expedition were either incidental or accomplished independent of his own efforts. The major achievements are effected by his men while off on their own, or by members of rival companies. The "Adventures of Captain Bonneville" are not finally Bonneville's adventures at all.

On one level, this shifting between the different perceptions of Bonneville, and the consequent diminishing of Bonneville as credible hero of the book, affirm Irving's concern about the increasing savagery of economic expansion. In this sense, *Bonneville* becomes just the warning against the excesses of Jacksonian expansionism that Irving had intended. Insofar as Astor has here been replaced by Bonneville as the representative authority of the enterprise, his failure of both the spirit and the adventure proposes an even bleaker view of America's future than was indicated in the story of the fall of Astoria. But if this was indeed Irving's intention, it is never sufficiently realized in the book itself. Bonneville's failure is never quite transformed by these adjustments. He remains a figure neither wholly elevated by imagination nor defeated by the marketplace; neither a hero of adventurous enterprise nor a villain of Jacksonian expansionism. His adventures become as aimless as his enterprise; inevitably, the book of those adventures follows suit. *Bonneville* fails to bring adventure and enterprise into any meaningful relation, and adventurous enterprise itself becomes lost in the wilderness.

Irving's description of the nature of Bonneville's failure is telling in this context: he fails precisely by blocking the very merger of imagination and experience, of culture and the marketplace, that was the foundation of hope in *A Tour* and *Astoria*. In those earlier books, Irving assumed that Americans were capable of shaping their cultural imagination to contain the potentially divisive aggressions of marketplace expansion; the narrator of the first book and the reader of the second come to distinguish between the false adventures of self-aggrandizement and the true adventures of professionalism. But in the character of Captain Bonneville, we find the impossibility of such literary reparation.

In the book's "Introductory Notice," Irving includes a brief biography of the captain that establishes an irreconcilable oppostion between economic realities and the very faculty of imagination. Bonneville's father is described as "a man not much calculated for the sordid struggle of a money-making world, but possessed of a happy temperament, a festivity of imagination, a simplicity of heart, that made him proof against its rubs and trials" (3), and his son, we are told, had "inherited too much of his father's temperament to make a scheming trapper, or a thrifty bargainer" (5). Bonneville was, though, compensated by that very inheritance of a delicate and "excitable imagination" (3), a "susceptibility to the grand and beautiful" (6).

On one level, this compensation merely places Bonneville in a long tradition of heroes of sensibility. From Filson's to Bryan's to Flint's Daniel Boone we find figures whose heroism as adventurers is inseparable from their ability to appreciate the sublime in nature. In a characteristic conjunction of scenes, Filson's Boone views "the beautiful level of Kentucke" from the "top of an eminence" (51), then is attacked by Indians in that level below, only to effect a brave escape. According to Irving's formulation of the professional imagination in *A Tour* and *Astoria,* Bonneville's receptivity, his preference for appreciation over domination, should provide an adequate tool for mastering the savagery of self-interest in the wilderness.

But in fact that sensibility is presented as decisively separated from his abilities as an adventurer; in fact, as a sign of passive resignation in the face of the "rubs and trials" of the world, it is precisely set in opposition to the adventures he is likely to encounter in the wilderness. Because he is *only* a appreciator, and because that appreciation is now presented as a means of escaping from, rather than entering into, the marketplace, he can succeed neither as a participant nor as an observer. He fails, that is, as a professional, and so fails both as a man of the marketplace and as a man of the imagination. He is just the opposite of the natural aristocrat of imagination and marketplace Irving had established in his portrayals of Columbus, Washington, Astor, and the educated narrator of *A Tour*. While his men are busy expending themselves in competition, Bonneville is off enjoying the view. "Here a scene burst upon the view of Captain Bonneville," Irving tells us in a typical instance, "that for a time astonished and overwhelmed him with its immensity" (135). The passive voice is inseparably linked with the capacity of imagination. His "susceptibility to the grand and the beautiful" has rendered him incapable of mastering the forces of the wilderness.

In the end, the only "grand scheme" Bonneville can offer his men is "to establish a trading post somewhere on the lower part of the [Columbia] river, so as to participate in the trade lost to the United States by the capture of Astoria" (159). But in the context of Irving's critique of that trade, such a scheme can only lead to further ruin. Indeed, that post, which Bonneville named Fort Bonneville in the tradition of Astor and his empire building, had no impact on the trade at all. Even its failure lacked the apocalyptic certainty of its predecessor.[12]

We have seen this rift between business and culture before: in the misguided expansionism of the tourists and rangers of *A Tour,* and in the unprofessional excesses of the trappers, Indians, and foreigners of *Astoria.* In this book, though, the leader is himself thus afflicted. As the representative of the new generation of Jacksonian Americans seeking to inhabit the role of authority in the nation's dramatic development, Bonneville's failure is especially disturbing. He may be attempting to follow in Astor's footsteps, to realize his and Jefferson's vision, but he is incapable of producing the vision that could *originate* a world anew. His receptive imagination is antithetic to the aggressive sense of acquisitiveness that has become a requisite skill of survival in the Jacksonian marketplace. He is a writer who cannot complete his own manuscript, a "history made man," as Chittenden called him (1:433). In Bonneville's very lineage, we find the motif of maturation itself perverted, a father who gives his son only the tools for failure. By those tools, Bonneville is not only doomed to fail at defeating the competition intrinsic to the wilderness experience, but he is also doomed to fail at failure. Unlike Astor's apocalypse, Bonneville's defeat fails to provide a model for the transformation of loss into profit. According to Irving's own scheme of prophetic history, redemption depends upon the proper exercise of imagination; in this case, the imagination seems fatally obstructed.

Underlying this critique of the receptive imagination is a doubt about the efficacy of literature in the Jacksonian marketplace. Irving seems particularly concerned the effectiveness of his own style of writing, the very stance of distanced appreciation that he had offered as a model for the Western adventure. While he never says so directly, Irving seems throughout the book to identify with Bonneville as both an author and an actor in the marketplace: where Bonneville fails to publish his own manuscript and to compete successfully in the fur trade, Irving fails to produce a successful book from the former and about the latter. If Astor had displaced Irving as author of the history of a failed Astoria, Bonneville and Irving stand together as authors of a failed adventure tale. Where in the two earlier books Irving had put forth the professional writer as the cultured redeemer of the market-place, here he offers a portrait of the writer as both failed appreciator and failed businessman. In terms of the metaphor of maturation, the writer's potency as a force of culture has become increasingly diminished in Jacksonian America.

Ironically, one cause of this failure of imagination lies in the very workings of the metaphor. In the figure of Bonneville, as well as Astor, the patriarchal role is possessed by men too old to engage directly in any real romance or procreation. Astor gives birth only to a vision, and Bonneville not even to that. At age fifty, Irving must have felt himself part of that weakening generation. Perhaps he had begun to associate his cultured style with a literature doomed to fall before the growth of the marketplace.

Not surprisingly, Irving never really addresses these fundamental sources of disruption and denial in the book. After all, were he to accept the implication that according to his own formulation the virtues of the imagination and the demands of the marketplace were finally incompatible, he would need to reconsider the entire belief system of adventurous enterprise that he had so far cultivated. Such an adjustment of imagination would entail nothing less than a radical reconstruction of narrative itself and of his own identity as a writer. Instead he attempts to evade the problem. He maintains the formal structure of prophetic history, and handles the "problem" of Bonneville by simply leaving him out of the book as often as possible. But neither of these choices helped him solve the larger problem of locating an informing narrative structure.

In the end, the book is without those elements of composition that had unified the two earlier books. The class system in which Irving had put so much faith in *A Tour* is virtually absent in *Bonneville,* as is its imaginative foundation, the sensibility of decorum and restraint that

Irving had associated with the narrator of *A Tour* and Astor. From the portrayal of Bonneville as the failed representative of adventurous enterprise, to the depiction of the fur trade as failed representative of American commercialism, Irving's narrative undermines the very quest it purports to illustrate. No longer mediated by the qualities of professionalism or the efforts of the professional, the imagination and the marketplace become once more at odds.

Irving's uncertainty about the relation between adventure and enterprise had led him to attempt an adventure tale without a discernable enterprise; consequently, he ended up without discernable adventures. At the end of the book he offers what are essentially the remnants of the context of sacred history with which he had opened. He writes of the need to overcome "the savage 'chivalry of the mountains' " (270). Yet this is an oddly unemphatic and incomplete exhortation. There is no mention of America, of its glorious past and promissory future. Only the troubled present remains.

And troubled it was. When Irving published the book in 1837, his concern over the atrophied imagination of his contemporary Americans might have found an equally concerned and attentive readership. Speculation had reached a peak of intensity, resulting in one of the nation's first major financial depressions. Ironically, however, that very depression slowed down the sales of the book. If Irving's warnings lacked the persuasiveness of his own imaginative conviction, they lacked also just the audience that most needed convincing.

When the book finally did find its audience, though, it quickly became a popular success, an indication that those warnings would likely have been missed anyway. For most of the contemporary reviewers, *Bonneville* was finally indistinguishable from *Astoria,* both books considered as straightforward adventurous histories of American commerce and colonization. Hardly anyone distinguished between the literary merits of the books and the merits of their subject, and so the issue of the work of the imagination with which Irving himself was so concerned was generally lost on his audience. Like Irving himself in *Bonneville,* readers and critics pulled back from confronting any recognition of the failure of imagination that dominated their claims to that history, and embraced, instead, the adventurous enterprise that Irving had criticized in *A Tour.* Everett Emerson noted in his familiar language that he had read *Astoria* "with interest and profit" (1837, 205), while an unnamed critic of the *London and Westminster Review* described the book as an "extremely skillful description of a mercantile speculation—a speculation indeed which conducted those who were to carry it into execution amidst the wildest scenes of western America, and which had rather the air of a daring and wild expedition of a hunting tribe than the calculating proceeding of a cool and thrifty merchant" (1837, 143). Even those writers critical of the books focused their discussion on the issue of economic expansion rather than the literary qualities of the works. Hubert Howe Bancroft, for instance, attacked Irving not so much for writing a bad book as for idealizing Astor: "Had [Astor's] scheme been based on self-sacrifice, on pecuniary loss for the public good, or the promulgation of some great principle, the current of unqualified sycophancy, sentimentality, and maudlin praise which runs through *Astoria* might be more bearable" (Chittenden 1:432).

But these criticisms were also met with ardent defenses of Irving in the name of adventurous enterprise. After quoting Bancroft's review, for instance, Chittenden offered his own support for Irving (and Astor) by reminding the reader of the place that enterprise played in all such adventures:

> Since when has Mr. Bancroft known of a commercial enterprise being organized on the basis of "pecuniary loss for the public good"? Commercial undertakings are not conducted in that way. It is no criticism of Mr. Astor's projects to say that their sole purpose and aim were money-making. All great projects of discovery of colonization have been founded in commerce. . . . It may, however, be truly said of the Astorian enterprise that it *did* involve the "promulgation of a great principle"—the cause of American empire on the Pacific coast—and it did involve enormous pecuniary loss in an enterprise that was fraught with the highest possibility for the public good. (1:245)

Chittenden defended *Bonneville* with the same reasoning, even while he dismissed Bonneville himself as a participant in these "great projects of discovery and colonization."

Perhaps the only writer to note Irving's underlying concern for the role of the imagination in that commercialism was Edgar Allan Poe. While not much can be gathered from his favorable review of *Astoria* —typically, he does little more than quote from the book—two of his other works published soon thereafter reveal, through an ingenious parody of Irving's structure and style, the extent to which he had recognized Irving's subject. In *The Narrative of Arthur Gordon Pym* (1838), the first installment of which appeared in the same issue of the *Southern Literary Messenger* as the *Astoria* review, and in *The Journal of Julius Rodman* (1840), Poe characterized the expansionist imagination as irrational, patricidal and hypochondriacal.[13] *Pym,* for instance, contains a retelling of the Tonquin disaster in which the motivations of savage self-interest are exaggerated beyond the comforting confines of adventurous enterprise. The Indians who overwhelm the ship are here rabid cannibals, and the explosion is caused not by a lone white civilized survivor but by the cannibals themselves who foolishly set the ship on fire. No agents of reason remain.

Poe's retelling does not so much reject Irving's version as revise it, forging an even more sinister merger between imagination and adventure. The model of literary production he offers in "The Philosophy of Composition" (1846) is just the anti-professionalism Irving had warned against in *A Tour*. The writer is characterized as an agent of the irrational and violent appetite of the unconscious, and the marketplace as an arena of irrational and violent consumption. The more the writer claims he is rational, the more the appetite grows; the more of these adventures the marketplace accepts, the more it expands. The narrator's dark adventures may take place only in the wilderness of his own psyche, but the terms are the same: the adventurous enterprise of American expansionism is becoming as dangerous as it is inevitable.[14]

While Irving was disinclined in his Western works to pursue Poe's pathway to unconscious motivation—he preferred the formulation of savagery as conscious self-interest—he did share the view that the imagination, as an integral part of the marketplace, was the ultimate source of redemption or destruction for Jacksonian America. In *Astoria* he sought in the history of American business a model for the merger of marketplace and imagination that would allow both to flourish in the wilderness. If properly restrained and yet sufficiently enlarged to suit the vision of the American mission, the imagination could indeed conquer and cultivate that wilderness, both within the West and within American culture. But as the confusions of his last Western work reveal, the history of the nation as he conceived it did not quite fit the model. The adventure had become separated from the enterprise, and a new adventure threatened to take its place, an adventure tale of the marketplace alone, devoid of the guidance of the professional imagination, and under the spell of an imagination already distorted by self-interest. The cultural commerce he had envisioned was fast becoming a commercial culture. Still, in the end, he maintained his allegiance to the form. The adventurous enterprise would remain the story of American economic expansion, and of the history of the nation in its pursuit through the wilderness to the land of promises.

Afterword

Irving had made a shrewd professional judgment when he embodied his return to America in these Western tales of adventurous enterprise. He found a subject and a literary form that proved to be of great interest to both his readers and himself, and through his skills had turned that interest to account. In *A Tour* and *Astoria,* he had identified the spirit of American enterprise that gave the adventure of economic expansion its form, as well as its remarkable potency as a cultural fiction. And in *The Adventures of Captain Bonneville,* he had brought that adventure up to date. He had found a meeting place between business and culture, producing within it both an imagination of the marketplace and a marketplace of the imagination.

From the very beginnings of the nation, that narrative design had been an integral part of the way Americans perceived themselves and their efforts to "succeed" in the world. It had begun framed in the rhetoric of a religious passion, a sacred narrative of the manifest destiny to acquire the New Jerusalem. By Irving's day it had become identified with the ideals of economic endeavor. The impassioned rhetoric of religious mission remained, however, as did the central tenets of the drama: the world was to be drawn into the American adventure and transformed into an American marketplace. The tourists, rangers, Indians, entrepreneurs, trappers, businessmen and foreigners, even the land itself and all it produced, were to become part of a literary form that protected the enterprise at, and for, all costs.

Irving was not the first to connect adventure and enterprise, but his works were formative in articulating those connections. They also established the form's significance as an American literature of expansion for the remainder of the century and into the next. Indeed, the tale not only persisted but expanded the range of materials and ideological tensions it entertained. With each development in Western expansion, and with each change in the nature of the marketplace, came new stories to tell: new patterns of trade, immigration and settlement that followed upon the Comstock lode and silver mine strikes that began in the 1850s, the rapid evolution of businesses in farming and land and cattle, the introduction of the railroads that were to change the operation of all the industries that had preceded them. A new cast of characters evolved, including miners, cowboys, outlaws, barmaids, schoolmarms, and immigrants, and a new variety of adventures, including mining strikes and labor strikes and showdowns. The nature of those adventures also changed. With the advent of corporate capitalism at the end of the century, for instance, the drama acquired a populist and tragic configuration: the role of corporate villain that Irving had ascribed to the British would now be played by American monopolies run by brutally wealthy capitalists eager to exploit the less fortunate; and the role of hero that Irving had ascribed to the community-minded American would now be played by an alienated individualist, poor, isolated, and all the more American for his rejection of the marketplace. In these tales, the hero might defeat the monopoly but never the marketplace; he must return to his lonely vigil in the wilderness. But despite such changes, the underlying tale remained the same: the adventurings of the professional American in the enterprise of America itself. The virtues of the hero were still drawn from the marketplace, and his adventures were still designed to redeem its basic precepts. The spirit of commerce remained intact.

Representative examples of the tradition make up a strikingly varied list of forms and concerns. There are the travel accounts and historical narratives such as Francis Parkman's *The Oregon Trail* (1849), J. Ross Browne's *Adventures in the Apache Country* (1869), Clarence King's *Mountaineering in the Sierra Nevada* (1871), Mark Twain's *Roughing It* (1872), Dan De Quille's (William Wright's) *The Big Bonanza* (1876), and Theodore Roosevelt's *The Winning of the West* (1889–1896); the romantic histories, such as Parkman's *La Salle and the Discovery of the Great West* (1869) and *Montcalme and Wolfe* (1884); the dime novels featuring Deadwood Dick, Calamity Jane and Buffalo Bill; the mining camp and cowboy narratives, such as Bret Harte's *The Luck of Roaring Camp and Other Sketches* (1870), Stephen Crane's Western stories and journalism, Owen Wister's *The Virginian* (1902), and Andy Adams' *The Log of a Cowboy* (1903); the tall tales included in such works as Augustus Baldwin Longstreet's *Georgia Scenes, Characters, and Incidents* (1835), Johnson Jones Hooper's *Some Adventures of Captain Simon Suggs, Late of the Tallapoosa Volunteers* (1845), and Joseph Glover Baldwin's *The Flush Times of Alabama and Mississippi* (1853); and the protest fiction, such as Hamlin Garland's *Main-Travelled Roads* (1891) and Frank Norris' *McTeague* (1899). More recently, some of the elements of the tale found their way into the Western films of the 1940s and 1950s, such as *Red River* (1948) and *Winchester '73* (1950).

These works differ from each other in many ways, of course, and one runs the risk of denying those differences by grouping them together under the rubric of adventurous enterprise. Yet I hope that this rubric will also reveal the interplay of imagination and marketplace that lies at the heart of so much Western fiction, and America's sense of its own adventurings. Throughout all its variations, the tale of adventurous enterprise has proven to be a primary means by which Americans both pursued and criticized their economic ideals, a profit-making tool and a critique of profiteering. From *Astoria* to *Roughing It* to *The Virginian,* from the tales of fur trapping to mining, railroading to cattle herding, from the satire to the sober history to the tall tale, the tale maintained its "sway over the country." In Irving's works we see the beginning of this process whereby the enterprise became the adventure, and the marketplace became an integral part of the American cultural imagination.

Notes

Preface

1. For a comparison of the ways in which male and female writers represented the Western experience, see Annette Kolodny's *The Lay of the Land: Metaphor as Experience and History in American Life and Letters* and *The Land Before Her: Fantasy and Experience of the American Frontiers, 1630–1860*.

2. For a representative sampling of these works, see William L. Hedges, *Washington Irving: An American Study, 1802–1832* and Jeffrey Rubin-Dorsky, *Adrift in the Old World: The Psychological Pilgrimage of Washington Irving*. While these two books do not include an examination of the Western writings, they do provide, along with Stanley Williams' *The Life of Washington Irving*, the best available introduction to Irving's career. Regrettably, Rubin-Dorsky's book appeared too late for me to avail myself of its insights and observations.

1. The Tale of Adventurous Enterprise

1. This image of Boone as an man of adventure preparing the way for commerce had been common for some time. In the appendix to John Filson's *The Discovery, Settlement and Present State of Kentucke* (1784), entitled "The Adventures of Col. Daniel Boon," Boone himself, as the narrator, tells of

having been solicited by the Governor of Virginia "to go to the Falls of the Ohio, to conduct into the settlement a number of surveyors that had been sent thither by him some months before; this country having about this time drawn the attention of many adventurers" (58). Following the man of adventure were the "adventurers," the investors in the enterprise.

2. "*A spirit of adventurous enterprise*" was the first of three Western qualities specified by Baird. The other two were "*Independence of thought and action*" and "*An apparent roughness,* which some would deem *rudeness of manners*" (102). My exclusion of them does not imply that they are incidental to the study of Western literature; indeed, in much of the criticism they provide the primary focus. Rather, I am placing the emphasis on a trait that has not as yet received critical consideration.

3. In my discussion here, I am much indebted to John Cawelti's seminal discussion of these tales and related forms in *Adventure, Mystery, and Romance: Formula Stories as Art and Popular Culture.*

4. The idea to compare these two Boones comes originally from Henry Nash Smith. As Smith also points out, Daniel Boone's own reason for moving West was neither to escape from, nor to spread, civilization, but to acquire more land. See his discussion of the evolution of the Boone figure in *Virgin Land,* 53–58.

5. Ribault's narrative was later included in Hakluyt's *Divers Voyages Touching the Discovery or America and the Islands Adjacent* (1582).

6. For a useful discussion of the intersections between Smith's careers as explorer and writer, see Everett H. Emerson's critical biography, *Captain John Smith.*

7. Annette Kolodny has offered other useful paradigms by which to interpret Smith's adaptation of the romance form to the values of expansionism. In *The Lay of the Land* (19–21), she discusses the connections in Smith's work between the pastoral ideal and the work ethic, while in *The Land Before Her* (3) she notes how his use of the trope of the land as female reveals the connections between sexism and expansionism.

8. Because I am placing the term "West" in this broad typological tradition, I should indicate what I am including in the category of "Western" literature. Some twentieth-century critics have argued that any analysis of Western American literature must begin with a definition of the boundaries of the West, but that task becomes irrelevant when one approaches the literature from the typological perspective I have outlined, in which America itself is identified as the West. It is irrelevant as well, at least for my purposes here, when one considers the West even as a discrete territory within the continent. Not only did the boundary change throughout the nineteenth century, but so did the claims as to what within that boundary might be designated as the "real" West. The tales of adventurous enterprise were set in a variety of locations, from the

"wilderness" of Kentucky to the shores of the Pacific, but all of those locations were considered at the time to be contained within the general area of the "West." This West of the imagination marks the boundaries of my category of Western literature. For a representative example of the more recent attempts at defining the "West" in Western literature as a geographical area with determinable boundaries, and "Western" as a determinable relation between that area and the people inhabiting it, see John Milton, *The Novel of the American West,* xi-xiv.

9. As Richard Slotkin has shown (1973, 94–115), the early captivity narratives emerged with just these animating narrative principles: the individual trial that represented the national and religious mission, the anxiety of captivity that indicated guidelines for perseverance and humility. As in John Smith's works, these tales associated the hardiness of the adventure with the dedication to the enterprise.

10. The passage from Gregg is also included in Smith (179). For a fuller discussion of the relation between the desert and garden imagery in American literature during this period, see the rest of the chapter in Smith, 174–183.

11. This merger of nature and commerce as a representation of the properties of the West can be found in earlier writings as well. For instance, John Filson notes in *The Discovery, Settlement and Present State of Kentucke* (1784) that "There are four natural qualities necessary to promote the happiness of a country, viz. A good soil, air, water and trade" (107), all of which are plentiful in Filson's West, i.e., Kentucky. With the substitution of trade for fire as one of the "four elements," the commercial domination of the landscape is established as a feature of nature itself.

12. This address to Congress was dated January 18, 1803, and has been published as "Confidential Message on Expedition to the Pacific." For the full text see *The Writings of Thomas Jefferson* 8:192–202.

13. In "Thoreau's Enterprise of Self-Culture in a Culture of Enterprise," Leonard N. Neufeldt argues that by the 1840s these terms had "shed[] much of [their] moral meaning" (238). My readings suggest otherwise. Neufeldt's article does contain, though, the most useful overview of the changing meanings of "enterprise" during this period now available, and an especially interesting analysis of Thoreau's use of the term.

14. For Pocock's basic position, see his *The Machiavellian Moment: Florentine Republican Thought and the Atlantic Republican Tradition* and *Virtue, Commerce, and History: Essays on Political Thought and History, Chiefly in the Eighteenth Century*. An introduction to Appleby's position and the debate in general can be found in her "Introduction: Republicanism and Ideology"; for the more elaborated argument, see her *Capitalism and a New Social Order: The Republican Vision of the 1790s*. Diggins' contribution can be found in his *The Lost Soul of American Politics*.

15. The popularity of this merger of class and capitalism can be confirmed by the presence of no fewer than six of Horatio Alger's heroes in the West. As in the most famous of these novels, *Digging for Gold: A Story of California* (1892), Alger produced a hero who, like the Virginian, was both natural aristocrat and upwardly mobile businessman. The merger is also evident in a related form, the success manual, which began to appear in the 1840s and 1850s, about the same time as the tale of adventurous enterprise. For a discussion of the Alger books, see John Seelye's introduction to the Collier edition of *Digging for Gold*; and for an examination of the success manuals, see John G. Cawelti's *Apostles of the Self-Made Man*.

16. Nicholas Biddle, *History of the Expedition Under the Command of Captains Lewis and Clark, to the Sources of the Missouri, Thence Across the Rocky Mountains and Down the River Columbia to the Pacific Ocean* (1814).

17. Irving also generously directed Hoffman to send the sheets of the book to his friend Colonel Aspinwall, "in the hopes that [he] might be able to make a bargain with some bookseller for the republication of it." "Hoffman is a most particular friend," he wrote Aspinwall, "in whose success I take great interest" (*L*4:735). As the wording suggests, Irving likely had business as well as friendship on his mind, perhaps hoping that Hoffman's book might create a broader market for his own forthcoming work.

18. John T. Flanagan, *James Hall: Literary Pioneer of the Ohio Valley,* and Randolph C. Randall, *James Hall: Spokesman of the New West*.

19. The journal had originally been named the *Illinois Monthly Magazine,* but Hall changed the title in 1832, presumably to broaden its claims as a journal of national quality and interest.

20. For a discussion of the contemporary measurements of, and attitudes toward, best sellers, see Frank Luther Mott, *Golden Multitudes: The Story of the Best Sellers in the United States*. According to Mott's figures, for the years between 1819, when Irving had his success with *The Sketch Book,* and 1832, when he left for his Western tour, Cooper had five top selling books while Irving had only three good selling books, what Mott calls "better sellers." Hardly a disreputable sales record, but one which Irving found worrisome.

21. For much of my discussion here I have relied on Ray Allen Billington's *Land of Savagery, Land of Promise: The European Image of the American Frontier*.

22. Such positive images could be found in a variety of other forms as well, both literary and non-literary. Among contemporary trapper journals, for instance, we find Englishman George Frederick Ruxton's *Life in the Far West* (1848), a popular account of the adventurous life to be had in the fur trade. Also widely disseminated in Europe were the enticing portraits of the West provided by such folkloric materials as songs and folk tales, collections of Indian artifacts, and the paintings and sketches of such artists as Karl Bodmer, whose exhibits were much more popular in Europe than in the United States.

23. Both Charles Fenno Hoffman and Timothy Flint visited the museum, though with predictably different responses. Hoffman, who saw artifacts as objects to be used rather than displayed, was offended by the "gross and impious humbug" of the museum's theatricality (2:135); and Flint, who saw the West as a theater of nature in itself, was pleased with its exhibitions as a field of "rich study for the naturalist." For the source of Flint's quotation and a useful description of the history of the museum, see M. H. Dunlop, "Curiosities Too Numerous to Mention: Early Regionalism and Cincinnati's Western Museum."

24. An investment of $20,000 in Ohio land was grandly unsuccessful. Irving also invested and lost money in a steamboat company and a South African copper mine. Like Mark Twain, the next major American author to fail so profoundly in speculative investments, Irving continued to invest money despite his losses and his frequent criticism of commercial ventures.

2. *Irving, the West, and the Work of the Imagination*

1. Irving had made use of this stance many times before, and the same phrasing as well, which he had borrowed from the Bible. In Genesis 23:4, Abraham pleads with the Hittites for the land to bury his wife: "I am a stranger and a sojourner among you; give me property among you for a burying place, that I may bury my dead out of sight." Journal entries regarding *A Tour* and *The Sketch Book* indicate not only Irving's knowledge of the passage but the appeal it held for him as a description of his own sense of alienation: "For the greater part of the time that I have resided in [England]," he wrote of the period 1815 to 1817, "I have lived almost unknowing and unknown; seeking no favours, and receiving none; 'a Stranger and Sojourner in the land,' and Subject to all the chills and neglects that are the lot of the Stranger" (*J*5:403). But if the underlying meaning remained the same, the use of the allusion differed from text to text. In *A History of New York,* for instance, Irving's phrasing was close enough to the original to remind the reader of the Biblical passage, and so establish a context for reading Knickerbocker's history: Knickerbocker's reference to himself as "a stranger and a weary pilgrim in [my] native land" (454) not only reveals his slightly self-mocking sense of himself as a prophet and of his task as a sacred quest, but also underscores Irving's satire of that pose. But in both the dinner speech and *A Tour,* Irving chose to shy away from the implications of direct allusion. The "property" he wanted to cultivate in these cases was not Abraham's final resting place, but the property of his own potential as an author and a citizen.

2. Despite the implications of Philip Hone's comment, Irving's warmth toward Jackson was ultimately more personal than political, and not directly tied to any project of self-interest. As he described the visit in a letter to his brother Peter, "I have been most kindly received by the old general, with

whom I am much pleased as well as amused. . . . I took care to put myself promptly on a fair and independent footing with him; for, in expressing warmly and sincerely how much I had been gratified by the unsought, but most seasonable mark of confidence he had shown me, when he hinted something about a disposition to place me elsewhere, I let him know emphatically that I wished for nothing more—that my whole desire was to live among my countrymen, and to follow my usual pursuits. In fact, I am persuaded that my true course is to be master of myself and of my time. Official station cannot add to my happiness or respectability, and certainly would stand in the way of my literary career" (*L2*:705).

3. See especially Cass' *Inquiries, Respecting the History, Traditions, Languages, Manners, Customs, Religion, &c. of the Indians, Living within the United States* (1823), "Policy and Practice of the United States and Great Britain in their Treatment of Indians" (1827), and "Removal of the Indians" (1830).

4. The letter was eventually published as *Washington Irving on the Prairie, or A Narrative of a Tour in the Southwest in the Year 1832*.

5. While Latrobe's book included not only his account of the Western tour but of other travels as well, Irving was still worried that the book posed a threat to his own project. In the same letter in which he offered the sheets of Hoffman's book to his friend Colonel Aspinwall, he also urged that his own book be put "*instantly* to press" without allowing for inspection by booksellers: "I am a little more cautious than usual, because I learn that my fellow traveller Mr Latrobe is about publishing his travels in the U. S. in which he accompanied me. The Bookseller to whom my work was offered might have his in hand at the very time. Be on your guard, therefore, in this respect—but say nothing on the subject. I shall put the work to press here almost immediately—barely leaving time to give the publication in London a fair chance—So I entreat you not to procrastinate. If there is no other way to effect this promptness, have the work printed at my expense, and dispose of the edition" (*L4*:735). Here we see Irving's shrewdness as a professional, and the sense of urgency that accompanied his efforts to protect his "investment." The edition of Latrobe's book I will be using throughout, *The Rambler in Oklahoma: Latrobe's Tour with Washington Irving*, is a twentieth-century edition including the Western section alone.

6. Pourtalès never did revise his journals and letters for publication. They were discovered 136 years later in a trunk, and in 1968 were published under the title *On the Western Tour with Washington Irving*.

7. *Indian Sketches*, xxi. The younger Irving goes on to clarify the identities of these adventurers in the very economic terms that his uncle would explore in his Western works: "adventurers, who intended to cut adrift from civilization, and to seek their fortunes upon the prairies and in the mountains beyond them." As in the case of Timothy Flint's Daniel Boone, this seeking for fortune

was not really an escape from civilization at all, but an expansion of its fundamental principles. The complete quotation can be found in John Mc-Dermott's introduction to his edition of the work, and comes not from the original 1835 edition which McDermott used as the basis for his text, but from the later 1888 edition of the book.

8. The article was first published in the journal *The Magnolia* in 1837, then later in book form in *Wolfert's Roost* (1855). It also found its way into the Author's Revised Edition of *The Adventures of Captain Bonneville* (1849). Such recycling was a common strategy of Irving's. Presumably, he felt the sketch close enough in subject matter and approach to complement the concerns of his last major Western work; possibly, he also felt it was a way to make the new edition appear as "new" as its name, and so more appealing and more profitable.

9. Irving accurately credits himself with the coining of this phrase, but it should be noted that he was simply offering an epithet for a long tradition of concern in America. As early as 1808, Benjamin Rush described Americans as "idolators" who "worshipped one god. . .but that god was GOD DOLLARS" (Takaki 69).

10. As Andrew Myers has pointed out (1976, xxiii), it is especially ironic given Irving's feelings on the subject that at one point a bank was established that not only used his name but his picture as well on the in-house currency.

11. Irving expressed much the same disappointment when he returned, in 1853, to the town of Ogdensburg on the Oswegatchie River, which he had visited in 1803 on his first tour into the wilderness. What he remembered as a place of "perfect romance" like the early Sleepy Hollow was now a "bustling" place of "trade" (*L*4:431–433, 435–437). Significantly the revelations expressed in these articles and letters were acquired, in part, by means of the very vehicle of commercial expansion that had brought "civilization" to these areas: the steamboat. In fact, the subtitle of "The Creole Village" is "A Sketch from a Steamboat," a further indication that Irving was well aware of the inevitable complicity of literature in the process.

12. The review was of *The Works, in Verse and Prose, of the Late Robert Treat Paine,* and was first published in the *Analectic Magazine* 1 (March 1813): 249–266.

13. For a discussion of this attitude toward imagination, and Irving's own struggles with its dictates, see Michael Bell, *The Development of the American Romance,* esp. 7–22 and 63–85.

14. As in the case of "The Creole Village," I am using the version of "A Time of Unexampled Prosperity" included in the Twayne edition of *Wolfert's Roost*. The article was originally published in *Knickerbocker Magazine* 15 (1840): 303–324.

15. While Irving preferred in such early works to dwell on these villains of

speculation, he also offered the occasional hero of business. For instance, in *Bracebridge Hall* (1822) Geoffrey Crayon praises the character of Jack Tibbets, generally known as Ready Money Jack Tibbets, for his dedication to work and his determination to pay for everything "in cash down" (37). He is not averse to spending money, however: "Notwithstanding his thrift," Crayon notes, "he has never denied himself the amusements of life, but has taken a share in every passing pleasure. It is his maxim, that 'he that works hard can afford to play' " (37). Jack's genial heroism lies precisely in his sound, if somewhat unimaginative, business sense, and his rejection of any speculative impulse.

16. One source of Irving's particularly aggressive rhetoric here is perhaps the same sense of disappointment that afflicted Frances Trollope: a failure of his own "golden dreams." In a letter written a few years earlier regarding those investments he even uses the same imagery of light and dark, and storms, to describe his hopes: "My confidence in quick returns from land speculations slackened early last summer, or rather in the spring, when I saw how wildly everybody was rushing into them; and I have ever since made my calculations to "weather along," as the sailors say, for some time to come, without any of the funds I have invested. It takes down some of my towering plans, and may induce me to burn the candle only at one end; but I will make up for it by a perfect illumination, should things really turn out rightly, and I come to a great fortune!" (*L*2:883–884). The imagery is so similar, in fact, that Irving might have consciously drawn upon it for the article.

17. For a discussion of this aspect of speculation later in the century, see Walter Benn Michaels, *The Gold Standard and the Logic of Naturalism*, 64–68.

18. Another perspective one might take toward these contradictions is that they are finally not contradictions at all, and that Irving's concept of professionalism was drawn exclusively from the marketplace. What Carolyn Porter (1981) characterized as the stance of the "participant observer" in American literature may apply to Irving's own position in this commercialization of culture: when the process of capitalistic production has sufficiently mystified the relation between producer and product, the individual simultaneously becomes embedded in that world, a passive and objectified participant, and alienated from it, a passive and objective observer; that is, a participant as observer. Thus the stance of objective detachment from the marketplace that Irving associated, in part, with the artistic sensibility was, in fact, a feature and consequence of the marketplace. This view may also explain, to some extent, the ideological convergence of competing economic ideals during this period, the celebration of both Federalism and Jacksonianism, both hierarchy and mobility, in the marketplace. While the debate appeared to concern itself with the value of the marketplace, the perspectives of the two parties were both germinated in the marketplace. Irving proved to be an exemplary participant in this debate, often taking both sides. Yet these two interpretations of Irving's professionalism—as

an adaptation to, or reflection of, the marketplace—need not be mutually exclusive. Insofar as the marketplace was in an early transitional period at this time, his professionalism also reflected an adaptation of eighteenth-century values to a nineteenth-century marketplace.

19. At this early point in the profession, there was little organized advertising and promotion. Irving was not only one of the first writers to become a celebrity, but also one of the first to recognize the promotional advantages in using his status as a celebrity as a form of advertising.

20. Of the many books and articles on the rise and ethics of professionalism, a few have been especially useful to my discussion here: Thomas Haskell, "Professionalism *versus* Capitalism: R. H. Tawney, Emile Durkheim, and C. S. Peirce on the Disinterestedness of Professional Communities," in *The Authority of Experts: Studies in History and Theory,* 180–225; Magali Sarfatti Larson, *The Rise of Professionalism: A Sociological Analysis*; and Bernard Barber, "Some Problems in the Sociology of the Professions," in Kenneth Lynn, ed., *The Professions in America,* 15–34. On the development of the American literary profession in particular, see William Charvat, *The Profession of Authorship in America, 1800–1870.*

21. Emerson had his own formula for this integration of imagination and marketplace. While he criticized Irving for seeking to expand his "merchantable stock" in the West, he also described his own primary resource, his journal, as his "Savings Bank" (*Journals* 4:250). While Emerson seems to be contradicting himself, an examination of his metaphors reveals a well-considered distinction. Irving's professionalism is mercenary, according to Emerson, because he treats his talent and fame like a "stock," which is to say a speculative venture, an ultimately illusory process based on the meanest exercise of self-interest. His own professionalism, however, is morally superior because he treats the products of his self-interest like a savings bank, a resource for further growth and development. His "savings bank" thus equates fiscal restraint with moral resource by opposing fiscal to moral speculation. Seen from this perspective, though, Emerson's assumptions are not as different from Irving's as he suggests in his criticism.

22. This concern with the "diseased" imagination was common not only in Western literature but in other forms of American romantic literature, particularly the gothic. As Michael Bell has explained (7–22), a principal subject of these genres is the individual imagination that has lost the capacity for "relation."

23. Later in the century Stephen Crane made the same point in "The Blue Hotel" when Johnnie responds to the Swede's baffling performance as a character in a Western adventure tale by asking "[W]hy don't he wait till he gits *out West?*" (*Prose* 809).

24. Of course, Carson himself was just as surprised. As an expectant reader himself, he shared the rangers', and his culture's, "guilt": early in the autobiog-

raphy he admits he had gone West in the first place because he "heard so many tales of life in the mountains of the West" (9).

25. As discussed above, Herman Melville attached Hall in *The Confidence Man* (1857) as a racist for just such descriptions as these. According to Melville, while Hall claimed to be offering a criticism of the cruelty of "backwoodsmen" like Moredock, he finally defended them, and even shared in their self-justifying "metaphysics of Indian hating." In Melville's novel, a character sardonically called "the judge" (in reference to Hall) declaims what he believes to be a learned discourse on Indian hating, assuming all the while to be himself above the predatory strains of such savagery. But he employs his "reasoning" to much the same effect. In the end, Hall and Moredock are revealed as one and the same, "Indian hater[s] *par excellence*" (Melville 130).

3. A Satire of Western Economic Expansion

1. I use the terms "white man" and "white men" advisedly, not to confirm the implicit exclusion of such people as women and Blacks, of course, but only to identify the culture's predominant mode of discourse at the time.

2. Irving achieves the same effect even in those cases when he notifies the reader that he does indeed have a "tale" to tell. *Tales of a Traveller* (1824) is one of his most successful works in this mold. A collection of tales in the German gothic style, *Tales* opens with Geoffrey Crayon's seemingly relaxed criticism of the ease with which people produce books in this "story telling and. . .story reading age": "Thanks to the improvements in all kind of manufactures, the art of book making has been made familiar to the meanest capacity" (3). In much the same vein, he tells us, he too will write a book, though he will endeavor to introduce, with appropriate modesty, a "sound moral" in each tale. Far from relaxing our critical faculties, however, this admonition of moral intent focuses our attention on the very nature of those "explanations" that literature offers us: the book we are about to read is a maze of deluded storytellers, and we should be wary of the tales they tell, however coherent, intricate, or entertaining we might find them. We should also be wary, it follows, of Crayon's own claims to moral certitude.

3. The source of the phrase "Indian wilderness" suggests its nationalistic origins: it comes from the first paragraph of Cotton Mather's *Magnalia Christie Americana* (1702), the title of which literally translates as "the life of Christ in America" but more generally refers to the American mission to follow "His Divine Providence" who "hath *Irradiated* an *Indian Wilderness*" (*Selections* 1) for the founding of the New Jerusalem.

4. Frederick Merk noted the same economic impetus to early Western expansion, though he reversed the order of events in the process: "Here was the course of empire taking a familiar pattern," he wrote, "economic penetra-

tion, followed by territorial possession" (1978, 258). Whichever the order, however, the basic connection between land acquisition, the growth of the economy, and the spread of the civilized empire remains primary.

5. For an indication of the range, and rage, of the early American attitudes toward Philip, see Richard Slotkin and James K. Folsom, eds., *So Dreadfull a Judgment: Puritan Responses to King Philip's War, 1676–1677*.

6. This quotation is representative enough to have found its way into both Rogin (115) and Pearce (1967, 165).

7. For a detailed investigation of the range of images in this and other contexts, see Roy Harvey Pearce, *Savagism and Civilization: A Study of the Indian and the American Mind*, Michael Paul Rogin, *Fathers and Children: Andrew Jackson and the Subjugation of the American Indian*, Richard Slotkin, *Regeneration through Violence: The Mythology of the American Frontier, 1600–1860* and *The Fatal Environment: The Myth of the Frontier in the Age of Industrialization, 1800–1890*, Tzvetan Todorov, *The Conquest of America: The Question of the Other*, trans. Richard Howard, and Charles Segal and David C. Stineback, *Puritans, Indians, and Manifest Destiny*.

8. The description of Sublette's meeting comes from Bernard DeVoto (1947, 86).

9. Here as in other places in his work Irving uses "Babylonish" to refer not only to the city of Babylon but to the Tower of Babel as well. For example, see also his reference to the "babylonish jargon" of the citizens Rip Van Winkle finds upon his return (*SB* 37).

10. This predication of an outraged sense of justice on Indian duplicity was indeed general on the frontier. For instance, fur trapper Osborne Russell note in his journal that "the best way to negotiate and settle disputes with hostile Indians is with the rifle: for that is the only pen that can write a treaty which they will not forget" (60). As Russell's metaphor of the pen suggests, this use of the rifle was a direct extension of the words, specifically the treaties and tales, that legitimized it.

11. Some critics have seen this choice as a failure of literary nerve or sophistication that ultimately limited the range of the book's concerns. William Spengemann, for example, notes that while Irving's book contained all the "raw materials of a truly Romantic narrative," namely "the wildly expectant youth destined for disillusionment, a sense of the discrepancy between literary representation of the primitive life and the brutal facts, a belief in the power of the wilderness to transform the traveler's character, and an awareness of the difference between immediate sensation and later reflection," his narrator's role as a "comparatively aloof, inactive observer" fails to bring those materials to their richest literary form, specifically the examination of a growing sensibility in intimate contact with its environment, an accounting of unique experience in an "original and significant form" (52, 55). Carl Woodring anticipated Spen-

gemann's judgment on a more general level, especially with regard to the Crayon persona: "Irving's style never reveals the self within, the self struggling toward growth. Crayon never makes himself more interesting than his subjects" (Myers 1972, 40). But while these criticisms do indeed apply to many of Irving's other books, they are largely inappropriate with regard to *A Tour,* a book in which the satire depends upon this characteristic deflation of the romantic notion of selfhood.

12. Ellsworth, like Irving, was deeply critical of Pourtalès' self-indulgence, but for different reasons. It was not the adventuring per se he minded, but its sexual component: "[Pourtalès] has a curious compound of character, brilliancy & fun mixed with frivolity and base sensuality—his age (19 nearing 20) is some apology, and his transatlantic indulgencies, may be added in charity—still his conduct cannot be justified, & he will later in life, look back upon his western follies (to say the least) with shame—I have ventured through a friend, to mention the deep mortification which may be inflicted upon his future domestic felicity (arrangement for which are making for him on his return at 21) by the appearance of red progeny, who will rise up to call him father!" (67) In his own book, Irving evaded this issue entirely, partly, I assume, because of his own prudishness, but also because it had little to do with the focus of his critique of the adventure tale.

13. Irving had always been fond of this feudal imagery, and generally employed it as he does here, to establish the definitive "bounds of respectful decorum." In *The Alhambra,* for instance, he described another of his guides as "my valet, cicerone, guide, guard, and historiographic squire" (*A* 37). The comedy of this figure, though, is largely an exercise in local color; unlike the comic depiction of Tonish, it has no greater pretensions as a critique of social posturing or self-proclaimed heroism.

14. While Irving repeatedly underscores the non-American background of Pourtalès and Tonish—Pourtalès is described as an effete European, and Tonish as a "mongrel Frenchman" (105)—he does not intend to imply that American adventurers are somehow superior. Indeed, there are no such American characters in the book. Rather, their foreignness serves as a reminder that such false adventuring ultimately threatens the "mission," the community enterprise which Ellsworth represents.

15. Frémont sensed the same ominous signs in the figure of the bee as American pioneer in the wilderness: "I believe that a moment's thought would have made us let him continue his way unharmed; but we carried out the law of this country, where all animated nature seems at war; and, seizing him immediately, put him in at least a fit place—in the leaves of a large book, among the flowers we had collected on our way" (70). Significantly, the destruction is imaged through its confinement in a product of the literary imagination.

16. The use of animal imagery, and particularly the imagery of animal communities, as a strategy of social criticism has a long tradition outside of American literature as well, of which Irving was likely aware. A notable example is Bernard de Mandeville's *The Fable of the Bees; or, Private Vices, Publick Benefits* (1729). In a later chapter in *A Tour,* Irving gives the approach a distinctly Western slant: the discovery of a community of prairie dogs gives rise to a meditation on the politics of communal life in the West. (The chapter is appropriately titled "A Republic of Prairie Dogs.") Not surprisingly, while these animals manage to create a "domestic economy" that accommodates even their natural predators, the rangers shoot a few and throw "the whole sensitive community in confusion" (109). In this case, though, Irving also adds a word of caution about his own imaginative strategy: "The dusk of the evening put an end to our observations, but the train of whimsical comparison produced in my brain by the moral attributes which I had heard given to these little politic animals, still continued after my return to camp; and late in the night. . .I could not help picturing to myself the inhabitants gathered together in noisy assemblage, and windy debate, to devise plans for the public safety, and to vindicate the invaded rights and insulted dignity of the republic" (110). As in the rest of *A Tour,* Irving finds the imaginative conception seductive, but is reluctant to accept it as the truth of the matter; thus he reminds us that while the imagination is the foundation of our moral sense, it must be employed with caution.

17. In many ways, Irving's "self-dependence" is similar to Emerson's "self-reliance," a concept that found its way into print only a few years later in his essay of the same name. Both men sought to contain the selfishness implicit in self-interest, and enlist those gestures in the larger aims of the community. Emerson's "reliance," however, was based on a far more profound faith in the individual as the source of that unity; for him, the interests of the self, once properly recognized, sufficiently encouraged, and actively expressed, were identical with the interests of the community. Irving's "dependence," on the other hand, implied that the individual needed to develop a larger frame of social reference from the beginning.

18. Jefferson had his own use of the term "half-breed" that throws some light on Irving's belief that issues of race were also issues of class. For Jefferson, half-breeds were not figures of mixed race but rather of mixed wealth. In William Taylor's description, "Directly below the aristocrats were their descendants and relatives—'half-breeds,' Jefferson called them—who aspired to aristocratic status without possessing the necessary wealth to bring it off" (33). For Irving, as for Jefferson, the boundaries of class were as present in the "nature" of society as the boundaries of race were in nature itself.

19. Understandably, neither Deshetres nor Beatte was especially pleased with the way Irving portrayed them in *A Tour*. They felt particularly insulted

by their representation as half-breeds, a reaction that reveals the pervasiveness of the racist class system endorsed by the book. A few years after the book's publication, George Catlin met up with Beatte and found him upset by the characterization: "Beatte had complained of this to me often while out on the prairies; and when I entered his hospitable cabin, he said he was glad to see me, and almost instantly continued, 'Now you shall see, Monsieur Catline, I am not "*half breed,*" here I shall introduce you to my father and my mother, who you see are two very nice and good old French people' " (2:93). But it was "Tonish," with his storytelling powers intact, who cut to the heart of the offense. In a letter from Evert Duyckinck, who met up with him in 1837, we learn that he "threatened to make his own book of the journey" and even to hurt Irving physically: "*Let me meet Irving on one of the Prairies and one or other of us shall lose his scalp!*" But then he launches his shrewdest attack: "And by way of reply to the Indian wife story he cautiously cast his eye around on the stoop & whispered something very dark concerning Wash. Irving and a 'yellow woman' at Fort Gibson" (McDermott 1944, 61).

20. Similes were, of course, a staple of Irving's style throughout his career, and often signified the same general posture of civilized detachment. In the context of *A Tour,* though, with its intent focus on the relation between the literary and the social, the use of the simile takes on a special significance.

21. These differences are even more apparent in the first edition of *The Alhambra,* in which the passage about the artist is followed by Irving's customary narrative disclaimer, discussed earlier in this chapter: "I am not writing a regular narrative, and do not pretend to give the varied events of several days' rambling over hill and dale, and moor and mountain" (*Al* 26). In this case, the attention drawn to the "old meager Alguazil" in the previous paragraph only reinforces Irving's stance of passivity and withdrawal.

22. Such references have led many critics to see *A Tour* as "excessively literary," and, as such, a failure as a "realistic" portrayal of the West. Robert Edson Lee, for instance, criticized Irving for an "inability to see in the West anything as existent in itself, without a romantic glow" (67), and Kathryn Whitford claimed that Irving's preference for "romantic" words, which she characterizes as "European terms and metaphors," is evidence that Irving was "unsuited for the enterprise both by temperament and training" (31–36). The foundation of such criticism is the assumption that Irving's romantic perspective was only an affectation, and not a conscious strategy. A persuasive argument to the contrary was offered by Wayne Kime, who demonstrated that the basic design of the book is that of a "carefully articulated narrative of a single initiatory action" in which the narrator abandons his "naively conventional preconceptions about Western life and gradually achiev[es] a clearer awareness of the West as reality" (65, 55). Using Lee's discussion as a rallying point, Kime

counters that Irving's "literary" references are, in fact, largely confined to the first third of the book, and that their gradual winnowing is an expression of the narrator's increasingly able and accurate perception of the West "for what it was" (65). My own reading puts less emphasis on the narrator as focal point of the book's thematic development, and also differs on the extent to which a "real" West emerges with determinable attributes. As I see it, Irving only goes so far as to indicate that such a reality exists, but stops short of identifying its features; his book is chiefly designed to demonstrate that that reality has thus far resisted representation in the adventure tale. Still, I have found Kime's discussion as useful as it is convincing. Another stimulating examination of *A Tour* as decisively anti-romantic is William Bedford Clark's essay "How the West Won: Irving's Comic Inversion of the Westering Myth in *A Tour on the Prairies.*"

23. Irving repeats this metaphoric connection between cultivation and clothing throughout the book, often to make the same point from the opposite perspective. For instance, he uses the phrase "uncouth garb" (30, 36) to characterize the rangers' "forlorn appearance" (36) as a representation of American moral and imaginative disorder.

24. It should be noted that Welty distinguishes *A Tour* from the Western journals—specifically from the edition of the journals edited by John Francis McDermott—in just these terms, suggesting that in the former Irving abandoned the spontaneity of this style of engagement, preferring the more "finished" product. But I disagree, and find her comments equally applicable to both books. If there is any difference between the stances taken by the two narrators, it is only in the degree to which each stance becomes a focus of concern in the work.

25. At the end of *The Prairie* (1927), Cooper offered his own version of the West as a "debatable ground." As the book closes, the conflicting claims of the good and bad white men, the white and red men, and everybody and the intermediary figure of Natty Bumppo, are left finally unresolved in the image of the unsettled prairie.

26. Dana used a similar term in *Two Years Before the Mast* to imply much the same warning about an excessively avid commercialization of vision. Upon his return visit to a still relatively barren stretch of California coast in 1859 he noted the striking presence of "an enterprising Yankee," who had erected, in an area with "no other human habitations," a "shanty of rough boards, where he carried on a very small retail trade between the hide ships and the Indians." The Yankee, he concludes grimly, was "years in advance of his time" (462–463).

4. A Celebration and a Warning

1. The 1811 date is the conjecture of Andrew Myers (1964, 11).

2. For the rest of Hubert Howe Bancroft's criticism on this score, see his *History of the Northwest Coast* 2:568–570; see also Vernon Louis Parrington, *Main Currents in American Thought* 2:165–168. Cooper, of course, presumed the worst and claimed upon Astor's death that Irving received $50,000 for his work as executor, certain evidence that Irving had no professional integrity (*Letters* 5:330). It is particularly ironic in this context that Irving was also on the memorial committee established in Cooper's name.

3. The article, entitled "The 'Empire of the West'," was a review of an article in the *North American Review*. It first appeared in the *Knickerbocker Magazine* in 1840.

4. While all three men were writing of the company in the 1820s, their criticisms represent the general attitude among fur trade participants toward the American Fur Company from the beginning.

5. For representative works of American romantic historiography that engage these same concerns, see especially Francis Parkman's *La Salle and the Discovery of the Great West* (1869) and *Montcalme and Wolfe* (1884).

6. Characteristically, Cooper not only recognized the figurative relation between Astor and Columbus but decried it as evidence of the likelihood that Irving had sold out to Astor: "Columbus and John Jacob Astor. I dare say Irving will make the last the greatest man" (*Letters* 5:330). For an analysis of Irving's Columbus as an American figure in more general terms, see John D. Hazlett, "Literary Nationalism and Ambivalence in Washington Irving's *The Life and Voyages of Christopher Columbus*."

7. The figure of Henry Ellsworth in *A Tour,* for instance, can be read as just such a failed patriarch, still a child with a misguided perception of his authority.

8. Once the territorial issue had been settled in 1846, Irving's original ending became inadequate as the conclusion of a "history," and so, for the Author's Revised Edition of 1849, Irving added a final paragraph. He noted the agreement reached with the British, now described as "our transatlantic kindred," and the response of Astor, the "venerable projector" who can now have "the satisfaction of knowing, ere his eyes closed upon the world, that the flag of his country again waved over 'ASTORIA' " (356). This addendum does not so much resolve the conflicts raised by the history as remind the reader of the need to maintain the perspective of expansion and enterprise.

9. Since the book was first published, objections have been raised as to the accuracy of this account, and corresponding charges have been made that Irving somehow "altered" the "facts" to suit his own purposes. According to some historians, for instance, Bonneville's leave from the army was only a ruse

to allow him to roam freely in the Western territories and gain access to information that might have been unavailable to people outside the trade. And the apparent denial of this ruse in the book reveals Irving to be not only an inaccurate historian but a dishonest one: he keeps Bonneville's secret so as to make him seem more genuinely the free-spirited adventurer, more definitively a man of the Western wilderness, and thus make his own book more adventurous as well. But the available materials do not confirm either the historical claim or the criticism with any certainty. The various contemporary accounts, such as military records and trapper journals, often conflict and so remain inconclusive; both Bonneville's and Irving's manuscripts have disappeared, so it is difficult to determine which portions in the book to ascribe solely to Irving; and Irving himself revealed nothing about this matter in his letters and journals. It is safe to assume, in any case, that *The Adventures of Captain Bonneville* is, in its published state, ultimately a product of Irving's imagination, and reflects his concerns over the role of that imagination in the expanding marketplace of Jacksonian America.

10. One of the connections between Bonneville and Astor not discussed in the book is the financial relationship between the two men. Slight evidence exists that Astor may have funded Bonneville's expedition. Bonneville himself claimed to have received backing from a syndicate of wealthy New York businessmen, but identified only one by name: Alfred Seton, one of Astor's employees on the Astorian expedition. Irving himself is not much more specific. In the "Introductory Notice" to *Bonneville,* he also mentions Seton, but declines to name the organizer of the syndicate; he describes him only as "a gentleman of high respectability and influence" (4). There are a number of reasons to assume this gentleman to be Astor. First, upon Bonneville's return from the West, he visited Astor even before reporting to the military (Hafen 275–276). Second, his acquaintance with Astor, as Irving describes it at the beginning of *Bonneville,* suggests that Bonneville had had earlier dealings with Astor relating to the fur trade. These dealings, though, while leading to Irving's acquaintance with Bonneville, probably had little effect on the shape Irving forged for his book about Bonneville. For Irving, it was sufficient to claim that the relationship among Astor, Bonneville, and himself was a fortunate convergence of adventurous enterprise.

11. Even the history of the book's title reveals its "rambling" form. In the first American edition, the title was *The Rocky Mountains: or, Scenes, Incidents, and Adventures in the Far West; Digested from the Journal of Captain B. L. E. Bonneville, of the Army of the United States, and Illustrated from Various Other Sources,* while in the first British edition, published only months later from the same page proofs, the title became *Adventures of Captain Bonneville, or Scenes Beyond the Rocky Mountains of the Far West.* As the different emphases suggest, the account of the fur trade and the adventure tale are never sufficiently

merged. (It should be noted, though, that the change in title was first suggested not by Irving but his English publisher. Still, while Irving required
some persuasion at first, he later came to prefer the new title, and decided to
use it for his Revised Edition of 1849.) Perhaps the most precise title was the
one of the second English edition (1837): *Captain Bonneville, or Enterprise
Beyond the Rocky Mountains. A Sequel to "Astoria."*.

12. The fiasco of Fort Bonneville has been the attention of much debate
among historians. Some have claimed that its uselessness was evidence of
Bonneville's inadequacies as a leader, as a participant in the fur trade, and as a
man of the West. Others have claimed that while its placement and construction made the fort ineffective for the fur trade, the fort was well-designed for
the needs of the military, an unremarkable result given that Bonneville was
trained not as a trader but as a military man. Whatever the reasons for its
failure, though, the significance of that failure, in the context of my argument,
lies in its essential insignificance as an event in both the development of the fur
trade and Irving's account of that trade.

13. *Astoria* and *Bonneville* were not Poe's only sources of information and
parody. He also used the Lewis and Clark journals, among other works. For
an indication of the range of these sources, see the detailed notes for both
books included in *Edgar Allen Poe: The Imaginary Voyages*.

14. Like Irving, Poe saw speculation as the representative "reckless adventure" of the imagination of the marketplace. In "A Descent into the Mael-
strom" (1841), for instance, he described the decision of some fishermen to seek
their quarry in dangerous waters as a bad "venture": "In fact, we made it a
matter of desperate speculation—the risk of life standing instead of labor, and
courage answering for capital" (*Poetry* 438). The absurdity of the decision is
conveyed by the inappropriate abstractness of the analogy; the marketplace has
dulled the narrator's capacity to recognize the true recklessness of the adventure.

Works Consulted

Editions of Irving's Works

Irving, Washington. *The Alhambra: A Series of Tales and Sketches of the Moors and Spaniards*. 2 vols. Philadelphia: Carey & Lea, 1832.

———. *A History of New York, from the Beginning of the World to the End of the Dutch Dynasty*. 1809 edition. In *Washington Irving: Tales and Sketches*. New York: The Library of America, 1983.

Pochmann, Henry A., Herbert L. Kleinfield, and Richard Dilworth Rust, eds. *The Complete Works of Washington Irving*. Madison: University of Wisconsin Press; Boston: Twayne, 1969–19—.

   I. *Journals and Notebooks,* vol. 1, 1803–1806 (Nathalia Wright, ed.).

   II. *Journals and Notebooks,* vol. 2, 1807–1822 (Walter A. Reichart and Lillian Schlissel, eds.).

   III. *Journals and Notebooks,* vol. 3, 1819–1827 (Walter A. Reichart, ed.).

   IV. *Journals and Notebooks,* vol. 4, 1826–1829 (Wayne R. Kime and Andrew B. Myers, eds.).

   V. *Journals and Notebooks,* vol. 5, 1832–1859 (Sue Fields Ross, ed.).

VI. *Letters of Jonathan Oldstyle* and *Salmagundi; or The Whim-whams and Opinions of Launcelot Langstaff, Esq. & Others* (Bruce I Granger and Martha Hertzog, eds.).

VIII. *The Sketch Book of Geoffrey Crayon, Gent.* (Haskell Springer, ed.).

IX. *Bracebridge Hall; or, The Humourists; A Medley by Geoffrey Crayon, Gent.* (Herbert F. Smith, ed.).

X. *Tales of a Traveller by Geoffrey Crayon, Gent.* (Judith Giblin Haig, ed.).

XI. *The Life and Voyages of Christopher Columbus* (John Harmon McElroy, ed.).

XII. *Voyages and Discoveries of the Companions of Columbus* (James W. Tuttleton, ed.).

XIII. *A Chronicle of the Conquest of Granada* (Earl N. Harbert and Miriam Shillingsburg, eds.).

XIV. *The Alhambra* (William T. Lenehan and Andrew B. Myers, eds.).

XV. *Astoria, or Anecdotes of an Enterprize Beyond the Rocky Mountains* (Richard Dilworth Rust, ed.).

XVI. *The Adventures of Captain Bonneville* (Robert A. Rees and Alan Sandy, eds.).

XVII. *Oliver Goldsmith: A Biography* and *Biography of the Late Margaret Miller Davidson* (Elsie Lee West, ed.).

XVIII. *Mahomet and His Successors* (Henry A. Pochmann and E. N. Feltskog, eds.).

XIX. *Life of George Washington,* vols. 1 and 2;

XX. *Life of George Washington,* vol. 3;

XXI. *Life of George Washington,* vols. 4 and 5 (all three vols. Allen Guttman and James A. Sappenfield, eds.).

XXII. *The Crayon Miscellany* (includes *A Tour on the Prairies; Abbotsford* and *Newstead Abbey;* and *Legends of the Conquest of Spain*) (Dahlia Kirby Terrell, ed.).

XXIII. *Letters,* vol. 1, 1802–1823;

XXIV. *Letters,* vol. 2, 1823–1838;

XXV. *Letters,* vol. 3, 1839–1845;

XXVI. *Letters,* vol. 4, 1846–1859 (all four vols. Ralph M. Aderman, Herbert L. Kleinfield, and Jenifer S. Banks, eds.).

XXVII. *Wolfert's Roost* (Roberta Rosenberg, ed.).

XXVIII. *Miscellaneous Writings: 1803–1859,* vol. 1;

XXIX. *Miscellaneous Writings: 1803–1859,* vol. 2 (both vols. Wayne R. Kime, ed.).

XXX. *Washington Irving: Bibliography* (Edwin T. Bowden, comp.).

Critical Works and Other Sources

Agnew, Jean-Christophe. *Worlds Apart: The Market and the Theater in Anglo-American Thought, 1550–1750*. Cambridge: Cambridge University Press, 1986.

Alger, Horatio, Jr. *Digging for Gold: A Story of California*. With introduction by John Seelye. New York: Collier, 1968.

Appleby, Joyce. *Capitalism and a New Social Order: The Republican Wisdom of the 1790s*. New York and London: New York University Press, 1984.

——. "Introduction: Republicanism and Ideology." *American Quarterly* 37 (Fall 1985): 461–473.

Astoria, or Anecdotes of an Enterprise Beyond the Rocky Mountains, by Washington Irving. Review in *The London and Westminster Review* 27 (1837): 173.

Baird, Robert. *View of the Valley of the Mississippi, or The Emigrant's and Traveller's Guide to the West*. 2d ed. Philadelphia: H. S. Tanner, 1834.

Bancroft, Hubert Howe. *History of the Northwest Coast*. 2 vols. Vols. 27–28 of *Works of Hubert Howe Bancroft*. San Francisco: The History Company, 1886.

Bell, Michael Davitt. *The Development of the American Romance: The Sacrifice of Relation*. Chicago and London: University of Chicago Press, 1980.

Benson, Lee. *The Concept of Jacksonian Democracy: New York as a Test Case*. Princeton: Princeton University Press, 1961.

Bercovitch, Sacvan. *The American Jeremiad*. Madison: University of Wisconsin Press, 1978.

Bergon, Frank, ed. *The Journals of Lewis and Clark*. Penguin Nature Library. New York and London: Penguin, 1989.

Bergon, Frank and Zeese Papanikolas, eds. *Looking Far West: The Search for the American West in History, Myth, and Literature*. New York: New American Library, 1978.

Berkhofer, Robert F., Jr. *The White Man's Indian: Images of the American Indian from Columbus to the Present*. New York: Knopf, 1979.

Biddle, Nicholas. *History of the Expedition Under the Command of Captains Lewis and Clark, to the Sources of the Missouri, Thence Across the Rocky Mounains and Down the River Columbia to the Pacific Ocean*. Philadelphia: Bradford & Inskeep; New York: A. H. Inskeep, J. Maxwell, 1814.

Billington, Ray Allen. *America's Frontier Heritage*. New York: Holt, Rinehart and Winston, 1966.

——. *The Far Western Frontier, 1830–1860*. New York: Harper & Row, 1956.

——. *Land of Savagery, Land of Promise: The European Image of the American Frontier*. New York and London: Norton, 1981.

Bird, Robert Montgomery. *Nick of the Woods; or, The Jibbenainosay: A Tale of Kentucky*. Cecil B. Williams, ed. New York: American Book Company, 1939.

Black Hawk. *Black Hawk: An Autobiography*. Donald Jackson, ed. Urbana: University of Illinois Press, 1955.

Blau, Joseph L., ed. *Social Theories of Jacksonian Democracy: Representative Writings of the Period 1825–1850*. The American Heritage Series. Indianapolis and New York: Bobbs-Merrill, 1954.

Bold, Christine. *Selling the Wild West: Popular Fiction, 1860–1960*. Bloomington and Indianapolis: Indiana University Press, 1987.

Bowden, Mary Weatherspoon. *Washington Irving*. Twayne's United States Authors Series, 379. Boston: Twayne, 1981.

Bradford, William. *Of Plymouth Plantation, 1620–1647*. Samuel Eliot Morison, ed. New York: Knopf, 1952.

Brodwin, Stanley, ed. *The Old and New World Romanticism of Washington Irving*. With introduction by William L. Hedges. New York: Greenwood Press, 1986.

Brooks, Van Wyck. *The World of Washington Irving*. New York: Dutton, 1944.

Brown, Charles Brockden. *Edgar Huntly; or, Memoirs of a Sleepwalker*. Sydney J. Krause and S. W. Reid, eds. Kent and London: Kent State University Press, 1984.

Bryan, Daniel. *The Mountain Muse, Comprising the Adventures of Daniel Boone; and the Power of Virtuous and Refined Beauty*. Harrisonburg: Davidson & Bourne, 1813.

Bryant, William Cullen. *Representative Selections*. Tremaine McDowell, ed. New York: American Book Company, 1935.

Byrd, William. *William Byrd's Histories of the Dividing Line Betwixt Virginia and North Carolina*. With introduction by William K. Boyd. Raleigh: North Carolina Historical Commission, 1929.

Cabeza de Vaca, Álvar Núñez. *Adventures in the Unknown Interior of America*. Cyclone Covey, trans. and ed. Albuquerque: University of New Mexico Press, 1983.

Calhoun, Daniel H. *Professional Lives in America: Structure and Aspiration, 1750–1850*. Cambridge: Harvard University Press, 1965.

Canby, Henry Seidel. *Classic Americans*. New York: Harcourt, Brace, 1931.

Carson, Kit. *Kit Carson's Own Story of His Life*. Blanche C. Grant, ed. Taos, New Mexico: Kit Carson Memorial Foundation, Inc., 1926.

Cass, Lewis. *Inquiries, Respecting the History, Traditions, Languages, Manners, Customs, Religion, &c. of the Indians, Living within the United States*. Detroit: Sheldon and Reed, 1823.

——. "Policy and Practice of the United States and Great Britain in their Treatment of Indians." *North American Review* 24 (April 1827): 365–442.

——. "Removal of the Indians." *North American Review* 30 (January 1830): 62–121.

Catlin, George. *Letters and Notes on the Manners, Customs, and Conditions of North American Indians.* 2 vols. 1844; rpt. New York: Dover, 1973.

Cawelti, John G. *Adventure, Mystery, and Romance: Formula Stories as Art and Popular Culture.* Chicago and London: University of Chicago Press, 1976.

——. *Apostles of the Self-Made Man.* Chicago and London: University of Chicago Press, 1965.

——. *The Six-Gun Mystique.* 2d ed. Bowling Green, Ohio: Bowling Green State University Popular Press, 1984.

Charvat, William. *Literary Publishing in America: 1790–1850.* Philadelphia: University of Pennsylvania Press, 1959.

——. *The Profession of Authorship in America: 1800–1870.* Ohio: Ohio State University Press, 1968.

Chittenden, Hiram Martin. *A History of the American Fur Trade of the Far West.* 2 vols. 1902; rpt. Stanford, Calif.: Academic Reprints, 1954.

Clark, William Bedford. "How the West Won: Irving's Comic Inversion of the Westering Myth in *A Tour on the Prairies.*" *American Literature* 50 (1978): 335–347.

Cleland, Robert Glass. *This Reckless Breed of Men: The Trappers and Fur Traders of the Southwest.* New York: Knopf, 1963.

Cochran, Thomas C. "An Analytical View of Early American Business and Industry." In Joseph R. Frese, S. J., and Jacob Judd, eds. *Business Enterprise in Early New York,* pp. 1–15. New York: Sleepy Hollow Press, 1979.

——. *Business in American Life: A History.* New York: McGraw-Hill, 1972.

——. *Frontiers of Change: Early Industrialism in America.* New York and Oxford: Oxford University Press, 1981.

Cochran, Thomas C. and William Miller. *The Age of Enterprise: A Social History of Industrial America.* New York: Macmillan, 1960.

Cohen, Abner. *Two-Dimensional Man: An Essay on the Anthropology of Power and Symbolism in Complex Society.* Berkeley and Los Angeles: University of Calif. Press, 1976.

Cooper, James Fenimore. *The American Democrat, or Hints on the Social and Civic Relations of the United States of America.* Cooperstown: H. & E. Phinney, 1838.

——. *The Letters and Journals of James Fenimore Cooper.* 6 vols. James Franklin Beard, ed. Cambridge: Harvard University Press, 1960–1968.

Crane, Stephen. *Prose and Poetry.* New York: Library of America, 1984.

Crockett, David. *A Narrative of the Life of David Crockett of the State of Tennessee.* 1834; rpt. Knoxville: University of Tennessee Press, 1973.

Cronon, William. *Changes in the Land: Indians, Colonists, and the Ecology of New England.* New York: Hill & Wang, 1983.

——. "Revisiting the Vanishing Frontier: The Legacy of Frederick Jackson Turner." *Western Historical Quarterly* 18 (1987): 157–176.

Dana, Richard Henry, Jr. *Two Years Before the Mast: A Personal Narrative.* Boston and New York: Houghton Mifflin, 1911.

DeVoto, Bernard. *Across the Wide Missouri.* New York: Bonanza, 1947.

———. *The Year of Decision: 1846.* Boston: Little, Brown, 1943.

Dick, Everett. *The Sod-House Frontier, 1854–1890.* Lincoln and London: University of Nebraska Press, 1954.

Douglas, Ann. "Art and Advertising in A Connecticut Yankee: The 'Robber Baron' Revisited." *The Canadian Review of American Studies* 6 (Fall 1975): 182–195.

Diggins, John P. *The Lost Soul of American Politics: Virtue, Self-Interest, and the Foundations of Liberalism.* New York: Basic Books, 1984.

Drinnon, Richard. *Facing West: The Metaphysics of Indian-Hating and Empire-Building.* Minneapolis: University of Minnesota Press, 1980.

Dula, Martha. "Audience Response to *A Tour on the Prairies in 1835.*" *Western American Literature* 8 (1973): 67–74.

Dunlop, M. H. "Curiosities Too Numerous to Mention: Early Regionalism and Cincinnati's Western Museum." *American Quarterly* 36 (Fall 1984): 524–548.

Ellis, David M., ed. *The Frontier in Development: Essays in Honor of Paul Wallace Gates.* Ithaca and London: Cornell University Press, 1969.

Ellsworth, Henry Leavitt. *Washington Irving on the Prairie, or A Narrative of a Tour of the Southwest in the Year 1832.* Stanley T. Williams and Barbara D. Simison, eds. New York: American Book Company, 1937.

Emerson, Everett. Review of *Astoria,* by Washington Irving. *North American Review* 44 (January 1837): 200–237.

———. Review of *A Tour on the Prairies,* by Washington Irving. *North American Review* 41 (July 1835): 1–28.

Emerson, Everett H. *Captain John Smith.* Twayne's United States Authors Series, 177. Boston: Twayne, 1971.

Emerson, Ralph Waldo. *Essays and Lectures.* New York: Library of America, 1983.

———. *The Journals and Miscellaneous Notebooks of Ralph Waldo Emerson.* 16 vols. William Gilman et al., eds. Cambridge: Harvard University Press, 1960–1982.

Fender, Stephen. *Plotting the Golden West: American Literature and the Rhetoric of the California Trail.* Cambridge: Cambridge University Press, 1981.

Filson, John. *The Discovery, Settlement and Present State of Kentucke.* 1784; rpt. Readex Microprint, 1966.

Fischer, Christiane, ed. *Let Them Speak for Themselves: Women in the American West, 1849–1900.* Hamden, Conn.: Archon, 1977.

Flanagan, John T. *James Hall: Literary Pioneer of the Ohio Valley.* Minneapolis: University of Minnesota Press, 1941.

Flint, Timothy. *The History and Geography of the Mississippi Valley: To Which is Appended a Condensed Physical Geography of the Atlantic United States, and the Whole American Continent.* Cincinnati: E. H. Fleet, 1832.

——. *Indian Wars of the West: Containing Biographical Sketches of Those Pioneers Who Headed the Western Settlers in Repelling Attacks of the Savages, Together with a View of the Character, Manners, Monuments, and Antiquities of the Western Indians.* Cincinnati: E. H. Fleet, 1833.

——. *The Life and Adventures of Daniel Boone, The First Settler of Kentucky, Interspersed with Incidents in the Early Annals of the Country.* Originally published 1833. Cincinnati: U. P. James, 1868.

——. *Recollections of the Last Ten Years Passed in Occasional Residences and Journeyings in the Valley of the Mississippi.* With introduction by Robert F. Berkhofer, Jr. 1826; rpt. New York and London: Johnson Reprint, 1968.

Folsom, James K., ed. *The Western: A Collection of Critical Essays.* Englewood Cliffs, N.J.: Prentice-Hall, 1979.

Frémont, Brevet Captain J. C. *Report of the Exploring Expedition to the Rocky Mountains in the Year 1842, and to Oregon and North California in the Years 1843–'44.* 1845; rpt. Readex Microprint, 1966.

Fussell, Edwin. *Frontier: American Literature and the American West.* Princeton: Princeton University Press, 1965.

Gallagher, Catherine. *The Industrial Reformation of English Fiction: Social Discourse and Narrative Form, 1832–1867.* Chicago and London: University of Chicago Press, 1985.

Garrard, Lewis. *Wah-to-yah and the Taos Trail; Or, Prairie Travel and Scalp Dances with a Look at Los Rancheros from Muleback and the Rocky Mountain Campfire.* Norman: University of Oklahoma Press, 1955.

Gates, Paul W. *Landlords and Tenants on the Prairie Frontier: Studies in American Land Policy.* Ithaca and London: Cornell University Press, 1973.

Gerber, John C. "Emerson and the Political Economists." *New England Quarterly* 22 (March 1949): 336–357.

Gilmore, Michael T. *American Romanticism and the Marketplace.* Chicago and London: University of Chicago Press, 1985.

Gilpin, William. *Mission of the North American People, Geographical, Social, and Political.* Rev. ed. Philadelphia: J. B. Lippincott, 1874.

Goetzmann, William H. *Exploration and Empire: The Explorer and the Scientist in the Winning of the American West.* New York: Vintage, 1966.

——. "The Mountain Man as Jacksonian Man." *American Quarterly* 15 (1963): 402–415.

——. *New Lands, New Men: America and the Second Age of Discovery.* New York: Viking, 1986.

Gregg, Josiah. *Commerce of the Prairies; or, The Journal of a Santa Fe Trader, during Eight Expeditions across the Great Western Prairies, and a Residence of*

Nearly Nine Years in Northern Mexico. 2 vols. 1844; rpt. Readex Microprint, 1966.

Grossman, James. *James Fenimore Cooper.* The American Men of Letters Series. New York: William Soane Associates, 1949.

Grund, Francis J. *The Americans in Their Moral, Social, and Political Relations.* 2 vols. London: Longman, 1837.

Hafen, LeRoy R., ed. *Mountain Men and Fur Traders of the Far West.* Lincoln and London: University of Nebraska Press, 1972.

Hall, James. "Flint on the Natural Sciences." Review of *Lectures upon Natural History, Geology, Chemistry, the Appoication of Steam, and Interesting Discoveries in the Arts,* by Timothy Flint. *Western Monthly Magazine* 1 (June 1833): 262–273.

——. *Legends of the West.* 2d ed. Philadelphia: Key & Biddle, 1833.

——. *Letters from the West.* 1828; rpt. Gainesville, Florida: Scholars' Facsimiles & Reprints, 1967.

——. Review of *A Tour on the Prairies,* by Washington Irving. *Western Monthly Magazine* 3 (June 1835): 329–337.

——. *Sketches of History, Life, and Manners in the West.* 2 vols. Philadelphia: Harrison Hall, 1835.

Hamilton, Cynthia S. *Western and Hard-Boiled Detective Fiction in America: From High Noon to Midnight.* Iowa City: University of Iowa Press, 1987.

Harriot, Thomas. *A Briefe and True Report of the New Found Land of Virginia.* 1590; rpt. New York: Dover, 1972.

Haskell, Thomas L., ed. *The Authority of Experts: Studies in History and Theory.* Bloomington: Indiana University Press, 1984.

Hazlett, John D. "Literary Nationalism and Ambivalence in Washington Irving's *The Life and Voyages of Christopher Columbus.*" *American Literature* 55 (December 1983): 560–575.

Hedges, William L. *Washington Irving: An American Study, 1802–1832.* The Goucher College Series. Baltimore: Johns Hopkins Press, 1965.

Heinzelman, Kurt. *The Economics of the Imagination.* Amherst: University of Massachusetts Press, 1980.

Hine, Robert V. and Edwin R. Bingham, eds. *The Frontier Experience: Readings in the Trans-Mississippi West.* Belmont, Calif.: Wadsworth, 1963.

Hoffman, Charles Fenno. *A Winter in the West.* 2 vols. 1835; rpt. Ann Arbor: University Microfilms, 1966.

Hoffman, Daniel. *Form and Fable in American Fiction.* New York: Oxford University Press, 1965.

Hofstadter, Richard. *The American Political Tradition and the Men Who Made It.* Twenty-fifth Anniversary Edition. New York: Knopf, 1977.

Hofstadter, Richard and Seymour Martin Lipset, eds. *Turner and the Sociology of the Frontier.* New York and London: Basic Books, 1968.

Hone, Philip. *The Diary of Philip Hone, 1828–1851*. Allan Nevins, ed. 2 vols. New York: Dodd, Mead, 1927.

Irving, John Treat. *Indian Sketches, Taken During an Expedition to the Pawnee Tribes*. John Francis McDermott, ed. Norman: University of Oklahoma Press, 1955.

Irving, Pierre Munro. *The Life and Letters of Washington Irving*. 4 vols. New York: Putnam, 1862.

Jefferson, Thomas. *The Writings of Thomas Jefferson*. 10 vols. Paul Leicester Ford, ed. New York and London: Putnam, 1892–1899.

Jehlen, Myra. *American Incarnation: The Individual, the Nation, and the Continent*. Cambridge and London: Harvard University Press, 1986.

Juricek. John T. "American Usage of the Word 'Frontier' from Colonial Times to Frederick Jackson Turner." *Proceedings of the American Philosophical Society* 110 (1966): 10–34.

Kime, Wayne. "The Completeness of Washington Irving's *A Tour on the Prairies*." *Western American Literature* 8 (1973): 55–66.

Kolodny, Annette. *The Land Before Her: Fantasy and Experience of the American Frontiers, 1630–1860*. Chapel Hill and London: University of North Carolina Press, 1984.

——. *The Lay of the Land: Metaphor as Experience and History in American Life and Letters*. Chapel Hill: University of North Carolina Press, 1975.

Lamar, Howard R., ed. *The Reader's Encyclopedia of the American West*. New York: Crowell, 1977.

Larson, Magali Sarfatti. *The Rise of Professionalism: A Sociological Analysis*. Berkeley and Los Angeles: University of California Press, 1977.

Latrobe, Charles Joseph. *The Rambler in Oklahoma: Latrobe's Tour with Washington Irving*. Muriel H. Wright and George H. Shirk, eds. Oklahoma City and Chattanooga: Harlow, 1955.

Lee, Robert Edson. *From West to East: Studies in the Literature of the American West*. Urbana and London: University of Illinois Press, 1966.

Leonard, Zenas. *Narrative of the Adventures of Zenas Leonard*. Milo Milton Quaife, ed. Chicago: Donnelley, 1934.

Levin, David. *History as Romantic Art: Bancroft, Prescott, Motley, and Parkman*. New York and Burlingame: Harcourt, Brace, 1959.

Limerick, Patricia Nelson. *The Legacy of Conquest: The Unbroken Past of the American West*. New York and London: Norton, 1987.

Lofaro, Michael A., ed. *Davy Crockett: The Man, the Legend, the Legacy, 1786–1986*. Knoxville: University of Tennessee Press, 1985.

——. ed. *The Tall Tales of Davy Crockett: The Second Nashville Series of Crockett Almanacs, 1839–1841*. Knoxville: University of Knoxville Press, 1987.

Lynn, Kenneth S. and the editors of *Deadalus*, eds. *The Professions in America*. Boston: Houghton Mifflin, 1965.

Macpherson, C. B. *The Political Theory of Possessive Individualism: Hobbes to Locke*. New York and London: Oxford University Press, 1962.

Martineau, Harriet. *Retrospect of Western Travel*. 3 vols. London: Saunders & Otley, 1838.

——. *Society in America*. 3 vols. 1837; rpt. New York: AMS Press, 1966.

Marx, Leo. *The Machine in the Garden: Technology and the Pastoral Ideal in America*. London and New York: Oxford University Press, 1964.

Mather, Cotton. *Selections from Cotton Mather*. Kenneth B. Murdock, ed. New York: Hafner Press, 1973.

McClary, Ben Harris, ed. *Washington Irving and the House of Murray: Geoffrey Crayon Charms the British, 1817–1856*. Knoxville: University of Tennessee Press, 1969.

McDermott, John Francis, ed. *The Frontier Re-examined*. Urbana, Chicago and London: University of Illinois Press, 1967.

——. ed. *A Tour on the Prairies*. By Washington Irving. Norman: University of Oklahoma Press, 1956.

——. ed. *The Western Journals of Washington Irving*. Norman: University of Oklahoma Press, 1944.

Melville, Herman. *The Confidence Man: His Masquerade*. Hershel Parker, ed. New York: Norton, 1971.

Merk, Frederick. *History of the Westward Movement*. New York: Knopf, 1978.

——. *Manifest Destiny and Mission in American History: A Reinterpretation*. New York: Knopf, 1963.

——. ed. *Fur Trade and Empire: George Simpson's Journal, 1824–25*. Rev. ed. Cambridge: Harvard University Press, 1968.

Meyers, Marvin. *The Jacksonian Persuasion: Politics and Belief*. Stanford: Stanford University Press, 1960.

Michaels, Walter Benn. *The Gold Standard and the Logic of Naturalism: American Literature at the Turn of the Century*. Berkeley: University of California Press, 1987.

Miller, Perry. "Afterword." In Washington Irving. *The Sketch Book*, pp. 371–378. New York: New American Library, 1961.

——. *The Raven and the Whale: The War of Words and Wits in the Era of Poe and Melville*. New York: Harcourt, Brace, 1956.

Milton, John. *The Novel of the American West*. Lincoln and London: University of Nebraska Press, 1980.

Mott, Frank Luther. *Golden Multitudes: The Story of the Best Sellers in the United States*. New York and London: R. R. Bowker, 1947.

Myers, Andrew B. "Washington Irving, Fur Trade Chronicler: An Analysis of 'Astoria' with Notes for a Corrected Edition." Ph.D. diss., Columbia University 1964.

——. ed. *A Century of Commentary on the Works of Washington Irving: 1860–1974*. Tarrytown, N.Y.: Sleepy Hollow Restorations, 1976.

——. ed. *Washington Irving: A Tribute*. Tarrytown, N.Y.: Sleepy Hollow Restorations, 1972.

Myres, Sandra L. *Ho for California!: Women's Overland Diaries from the Huntington Library*. San Marino, Calif.: Huntington Library, 1980.

Nerlich, Michael. *Ideology of Adventure: Studies in Modern Consciousness, 1100–1750*. Ruth Crowley, trans. 2 vols. Theory and History of Literature, 42. Minneapolis: University of Minnesota Press, 1987.

Neufeldt, Leonard N. "Thoreau's Enterprise of Self-Culture in a Culture of Enterprise." *American Quarterly* 39 (Summer 1987): 231–251.

Parker, Samuel. *Journal of an Exploring Tour Beyond the Rocky Mountains*. 1838; rpt. Minneapolis: Ross and Haines, 1967.

Parkman, Francis. *The Conspiracy of Pontiac and the Indian War After the Conquest of Canada*. 2 vols. Boston: Little, Brown, 1988.

——. *France and England in North America*. 2 vols. New York: Library of America, 1983.

——. *The Oregon Trail*. E. N. Feltskog, ed. Madison: University of Wisconsin Press, 1969.

Parrington, Vernon Louis. *Main Currents in American Thought*. 2 vols. New York: Harcourt, Brace, 1927.

Pattie, James O. *The Personal Narrative of James O. Pattie, of Kentucky*. Timothy Flint, ed. 1833; rpt. Readex Microprint, 1966.

Paulding, James. *The Backwoodsman: A Poem*. Philadelphia: M. Thomas, 1818.

——. *The Letters of James Kirke Paulding*. Ralph M. Aderman, ed. Madison: University of Wisconsin Press, 1962.

——. *Westward Ho!: A Tale*. 2 vols. New York: J. & J. Harper, 1832.

Pearce, Roy Harvey. *Savagism and Civilization: A Study of the Indian and the American Mind*. Rev. ed. Originally published as *The Savages of America: A Study of the Indian and the Idea of Civilization*. Baltimore: Johns Hopkins Press, 1967.

——. "The Significances of the Captivity Narrative." *American Literature* 19 (March 1949): 1–20.

Pessen, Edward, ed. *The Many-Faceted Jacksonian Era: New Interpretations*. Contributions in American History, 67. Westport and London: Greenwood Press, 1977.

Phillips, Paul Chrisler. *The Fur Trade*. 2 vols. Norman: University of Oklahoma Press, 1961.

Pike, Zebulon Montgomery. *An Account of Expeditions to the Sources of the Mississippi, and Through the Western Parts of Louisiana Territory*. 1810; rpt. Readex Microprint, 1966.

Pochmann, Henry A.. *Washington Irving: Representative Selections, with Introduction, Bibliography, and Notes.* New York: American Book Company, 1934.

Pocock, J. G. A. *The Machiavellian Moment: Florentine Republican Thought and the Atlantic Republican Tradition.* Princeton: Princeton University Press, 1975.

——. *Virtue, Commerce, and History: Essays on Political Thought and History, Chiefly in the Eighteenth Century.* Cambridge: Cambridge University Press, 1985.

Poe, Edgar Allan. *Edgar Allen Poe: The Imaginary Voyages.* Burton R. Pollin, ed. Boston: Twayne, 1981.

——. *Edgar Allan Poe: Poetry and Tales.* New York: Library of America, 1984.

——. Review of *Astoria* , by Washington Irving. *Southern Literary Messenger* 3 (1837): 59–68.

Porter, Carolyn. *Seeing and Being: The Plight of the Participant Observer in Emerson, James, Adams, and Faulkner.* Middletown: Wesleyan University Press, 1981.

Porter, Kenneth Wiggins. *John Jacob Astor, Businessman.* 2 vols. Cambridge: Harvard University Press, 1931.

Pourtalès, Count Alexandre de. *On the Western Tour with Washington Irving.* George Spaulding, ed. Norman: University of Oklahoma Press, 1968.

Randall, Randolph C. *James Hall: Spokesman of the New West.* Columbus: Ohio State University Press, 1964.

Rees, Robert A. and Alan Sandy. "Introduction." In Washington Irving. *The Adventures of Captain Bonneville,* pp. xix-xl. Boston: Twayne, 1977.

Ribault, Jean. *The Whole and True Discouerye of Terra Florida.* In John Winter Jones, ed. *Divers Voyages Touching the Discovery of America and the Islands Adjacent,* compiled by Richard Hakluyt, pp. 91–115. New York: Burt Franklin, [1965?].

Ridge, Martin and Ray A. Billington, eds. *America's Frontier Story: A Documentary History of Westward Espansion.* New York: Holt, Rinehart and Winston, 1969.

Riegel, Robert E. and Robert B. Athearn. *America Moves West.* 4th ed. New York: Holt, Rinehart and Winston, 1964.

Rogin, Michael Paul. *Fathers and Children: Andrew Jackson and the Subjugation of the American Indian.* New York: Random House, 1975.

Rosenthal, Bernard. *City of Nature: Journeys to Nature in the Age of American Romanticism.* Newark: University of Delaware Press, 1980.

Rourke, Constance. *American Humor: A Study of the National Character.* New York: Harcourt Brace Jovanovich, 1959.

Rozwenc, Edwin. "Captain John Smith's Image of America." In Michael Gilmore, ed. *Early American Literature: A Collection of Critical Essays,* pp. 11–21. Englewood Cliffs, N.J.: Prentice-Hall, 1980.

Rubin-Dorsky Jeffrey. *Adrift in the Old World: The Psychological Pilgrimage of Washington Irving*. Chicago and London: University of Chicago Press, 1988.

Ruland, Richard, ed. *The Native Muse: Theories of American Literature*. New York: Dutton, 1976.

Russell, Osborne. *Journal of a Trapper*. Aubrey L. Haines, ed. Lincoln and London: University of Nebraska Press, 1965.

Rusk, Ralph. *The Literature of the Middle Western Frontier*. 2 vols. New York: Columbia University Press, 1925.

Ruxton, George Frederick. *Life in the Far West*. LeRoy Hafen, ed. Norman: University of Oklahoma Press, 1951.

Schlesinger, Arthur, Jr. *The Age of Jackson*. Boston: Little, Brown, 1945.

Schlissel, Lillian, Vicki L. Ruiz, and Janice Monk, eds. *Western Women: Their Land, Their Lives*. Albuquerque: University of New Mexico Press, 1988.

Segal, Charles and David C. Stineback. *Puritans, Indians, and Manifest Destiny*. New York: Putnam, 1977.

Shell, Marc. *The Economy of Literature*. Baltimore and London: Johns Hopkins University Press, 1978.

Shenton, James P. *History of the United States to 1865*. New York: Doubleday, 1963.

Simmel, Georg. *On Individuality and Social Forms: Selected Writings*. Donald N. Levine, ed. Chicago and London: University of Chicago Press, 1971.

Slotkin, Richard. *The Fatal Environment: The Myth of the Frontier in the Age of Industrialization, 1800–1890*. New York: Atheneum, 1985.

——. *Regeneration through Violence: The Mythology of the American Frontier, 1600–1860*. Middletown, Conn.: Wesleyan University Press, 1973.

Slotkin, Richard and James K. Folsom, eds. *So Dreadfull a Judgment: Puritan Responses to King Philip's War, 1676–1677*. Middletown, Conn.: Wesleyan University Press, 1978.

Smith, Henry Nash. *Virgin Land: The American West as Symbol and Myth*. Twentieth Anniversary Reissue. Cambridge: Harvard University Press, 1970.

Smith, John. *The Complete Works of Captain John Smith (1580–1631)*. Philip L. Barbour, ed. 3 vols. Chapel Hill and London: University of North Carolina Press, 1986.

Sosin, Jack M., ed. *The Opening of the West*. New York: Harper & Row, 1969.

Spaulding, Kenneth A., ed. *On the Oregon Trail: Robert Stuart's Journey of Discovery, 1812–1813*. Norman: University of Oklahoma Press, 1953.

Spengemann, William C. *The Adventurous Muse: The Poetics of American Fiction, 1789–1900*. New Haven: Yale University Press, 1977.

Starr, Kevin. *Americans and the California Dream: 1850–1915*. New York: Oxford University Press, 1973.

——. *Inventing the Dream: California Through the Progressive Era*. New York: Oxford University Press, 1985.

Stegner, Wallace. *The Sound of Mountain Water*. New York: Dutton, 1980.

Stuart, Robert. *On the Oregon Trail: Robert Stuart's Journey of Discovery*. Kenneth A. Spaulding, ed. Norman: University of Oklahoma Press, 1953.

Takaki, Ronald T. *Iron Cages: Race and Culture in Nineteenth-Century America*. New York: Knopf, 1979.

Taylor, Bayard. *Eldorado, or, Adventures in the Path of Empire*. 2 vols. New York: Putnam, 1850.

Taylor, William R. *Cavalier and Yankee: The Old South and American National Character*. New York: George Braziller, 1961.

Thoreau, Henry David. *The Illustrated Walden*. Princeton: Princeton University Press, 1973.

Todd, Edgeley W., ed. *The Adventures of Captain Bonneville, U.S.A., in the Rocky Mountains and the Far West; Digested from His Journal by Washington Irving*. By Washington Irving. Norman: University of Oklahoma Press, 1961.

——. ed. *Astoria, or Anecdotes of an Enterprise Beyond the Rocky Mountains*. By Washington Irving. Norman: University of Oklahoma Press, 1965.

Todorov, Tzvetan. *The Conquest of America: The Question of the Other*. Richard Howard, trans. New York: Harper & Row, 1984.

Trachtenberg, Alan. *The Incorporation of America: Culture and Society in the Gilded Age*. New York: Hill and Wang, 1982.

Trollope, Frances. *Domestic Manners of the Americans*. Donald Smalley, ed. New York: Knopf, 1949.

Turner, Frederick Jackson. *The Frontier in American History*. New York: Henry Holt, 1921.

Unruh, John D., Jr. *The Plains Across: The Overland Emigrants and the Trans-Mississippi West, 1840–60*. Urbana: University of Illinois Press, 1979.

Veblen, Thorstein. *The Theory of Business Enterprise*. New York: Scribner's, 1935.

Vernon, John. *Money and Fiction: Literary Realism in the Nineteenth and Early Twentieth Centuries*. Ithaca and London: Cornell University Press, 1984.

Vitzthum, Richard C. *The American Compromise: Theme and Method in the Histories of Bancroft, Parkman, and Adams*. Norman: University of Oklahoma Press, 1974.

Vorpahl. Ben Merchant. *My Dear Wister: The Frederic Remington-Owen Wister Letters*. Palo Alto, Calif.: American West, 1972.

Webb, Walter Prescott. *The Great Plains*. New York: Grosset & Dunlap, 1931.

Welty, Eudora. *The Eye of the Story: Selected Essays and Reviews*. New York: Random House, 1977.

White, Hayden. *The Content of the Form: Narrative Discourse and Historical Representation*. Baltimore and London: Johns Hopkins University Press, 1987.

——. "The Fictions of Factual Representation." In *Tropics of Discourse: Essays in Cultural Criticism,* pp. 121–134. Baltimore and London: Johns Hopkins University Press, 1978.

Whitford, Kathryn. "Romantic Metamorphosis in Irving's Western Tour." *American Transcendental Quarterly* 5 (First Quarter 1970): 31–36.

Williams, Raymond. *Keywords: A Vocabulary of Culture and Society.* New York: Oxford University Press, 1976.

Williams, Stanley T. *The Life of Washington Irving.* 2 vols. New York: Oxford University Press, 1935.

Wister, Fanny Kemble, ed. *Owen Wister Out West: His Journals and Letters.* Chicago: University of Chicago Press, 1958.

Wister, Owen. *The Virginian.* New York and London: Macmillan, 1902.

Wright, Louis B. *Culture on the Moving Frontier.* Bloomington: Indiana University Press, 1955.

Wright, Will. *Sixguns and Society: A Structural Study of the Western.* Berkeley: University of California Press, 1975.

Zweig, Paul. *The Adventurer: The Fate of Adventure in the Western World.* Princeton: Princeton University Press, 1974.

Index